BlackBerry®
PlayBook™
FOR
DUMMIES®

BlackBerry® PlayBook™

FOR

DUMMIES®

by Corey Sandler

WILEY

John Wiley & Sons, Inc.

BlackBerry® PlayBook™ For Dummies®

Published by
John Wiley & Sons, Inc.
111 River Street
Hoboken, NJ 07030-5774

www.wiley.com

Copyright © 2011 by John Wiley & Sons, Inc., Hoboken, New Jersey

Published by John Wiley & Sons, Inc., Hoboken, New Jersey

Published simultaneously in Canada

For general information on our other products and services, please contact our Customer Care Department within the U.S. at 877-762-2974, outside the U.S. at 317-572-3993, or fax 317-572-4002.

For technical support, please visit www.wiley.com/techsupport.

Wiley also publishes its books in a variety of electronic formats and by print-on-demand. Not all content that is available in standard print versions of this book may appear or be packaged in all book formats. If you have purchased a version of this book that did not include media that is referenced by or accompanies a standard print version, you may request this media by visiting http://booksupport.wiley.com. For more information about Wiley products, visit us www.wiley.com.

Library of Congress Control Number is available from the publisher.

ISBN: 978-1-118-01698-5 (pbk); 978-1-118-16722-9 (ebk); 978-1-118-16723-6 (ebk); 978-1-118-16724-3 (ebk)

Manufactured in the United States of America

10 9 8 7 6 5 4 3 2 1

WILEY

About the Author

Corey Sandler is a voracious reader, an unstoppable traveler, and an indefatigable author of books. Also magazines, and ages ago, newspapers. At last count, he had written more than 160 books about computers and technology as well as history, sports, and business. Sandler travels all over the world conducting research and lecturing and consulting; he is within half a dozen of reaching the real century mark of countries visited: watch out Moldova, Kaliningrad, and Bolivia. You're up next.

Okay, so sometimes he is fatigable. That happens when you carry 150 pounds of luggage including a laptop, three cameras and lenses, a dozen books to read and consult, and a hogshead of lecture notes printed out and neatly bound to sit on a lectern. That's why he is also one of the world's most accomplished users of portable electronic communication devices: the latest, of course, being the BlackBerry PlayBook.

Sandler studied journalism (and also found time to take courses to program a gigantic mainframe computer) at Syracuse University. He began his career as a daily newspaper reporter in Ohio and then New York, moving on to a post as a correspondent for The Associated Press. From there he joined Ziff-Davis Publishing as the first executive editor of *PC Magazine*. He wrote his first book about computers in 1983 and hasn't come close to stopping. When he's not on the road and living on his smartphone and computer, he's at home on Nantucket island, thirty miles out to sea off the coast of Massachusetts. He shares his life with his wife Janice; their two grown children have their own careers elsewhere on the continent.

You can see Sandler's current list of books on his website at **www. sandlerbooks.com** and send an email to him at **PlayBookForDummies@ sandlerbooks.com**. He promises to respond to courteous inquiries as quickly as he can. Spam, on the other hand, will be electronically fried and given a proper burial.

Dedication

This book about the amazing BlackBerry PlayBook is dedicated to my truest and most accomplished traveling companion, my wife Janice. And to my children, William and Tessa, who are now engaged in journeys of their own.

—Corey Sandler

Author's Acknowledgments

This book bears just one name on the cover, but that's only part of the story.

Thanks to the smart and capable crew at Wiley, including Katie Mohr, Mary Bednarek, and the rest of the editorial and production staff who turned the taps of my keyboard into the book you hold in the electronic device in the palm of your hand.

Also, my appreciation to long-time publishing collaborator Tonya Cupp, who managed the process with grace and humor.

Special thanks to Research in Motion and Brodeur Partners for helping us get on the fast track for this project.

And most of all, thank you for buying this book. There is something magical about the bond between an author and a reader; all through the process I've thought about you and the sort of questions and problems you will expect me to answer. I hope I've exceeded your expectations.

Publisher's Acknowledgments

We're proud of this book; please send us your comments at http://dummies.custhelp.com. For other comments, please contact our Customer Care Department within the U.S. at 877-762-2974, outside the U.S. at 317-572-3993, or fax 317-572-4002.

Some of the people who helped bring this book to market include the following:

Acquisitions and Editorial

Project Editor: Tonya Maddox Cupp

Senior Acquisitions Editor: Katie Mohr

Editorial Manager: Jodi Jensen

Editorial Assistant: Amanda Graham

Sr. Editorial Assistant: Cherie Case

Cover Photos: ©istockphoto.com / Andrea Gingerich; image of BlackBerry PlayBook courtesy of BlackBerry (press image used with permission)

Cartoons: Rich Tennant (www.the5thwave.com)

Composition Services

Project Coordinator: Kristie Rees

Layout and Graphics: Samantha K. Cherolis, Noah Hart, Joyce Haughey, Corrie Socolovitch

Proofreader: Lisa Stiers

Indexer: BIM Indexing & Proofreading Services

Publishing and Editorial for Technology Dummies

Richard Swadley, Vice President and Executive Group Publisher

Andy Cummings, Vice President and Publisher

Mary Bednarek, Executive Acquisitions Director

Mary C. Corder, Editorial Director

Publishing for Consumer Dummies

Kathy Nebenhaus, Vice President and Executive Publisher

Composition Services

Debbie Stailey, Director of Composition Services

Contents at a Glance

Table of Contents

Introduction

I've been in the business of computer journalism a long, long time: all the
way back to when huge climate-controlled rooms held rows of clicking
and clacking mainframes and gigantic spinning hard disk drives that looked
(and sounded) like cement mixers. I remember the thrill when minicomput-
ers dropped to the size of a refrigerator. Next came suitcase-sized personal
computers, and then briefcase-shaped laptops. Just a few years ago we were
all enthralled at the arrival of textbook-sized netbooks. Along the way I paid
the price for lugging all of that equipment hither and yon: masseurs, physical
therapists, and orthopedic surgeons to soothe and repair shoulders, wrists,
and knees.

Ah, but that was so very yesterday.

Here's the latest in cure-alls for your technological needs: ***Take one tablet
and hit the road.*** Specifically: the super-powerful, brilliantly capable, and
slim BlackBerry PlayBook tablet.

About This Book

My mother and father did not raise any dimwits, and my wife and I have done
our best to give our children the best education possible. So why are we
gathered here in the pages of a *For Dummies* book? Here, let me quote one
of my favorite authors — myself, from some of the other *For Dummies* books
I've written:

> *BlackBerry PlayBook For Dummies is meant for people who are smart
> enough to know they could use a bit of extra explanation, tips, and hints to
> get the most out of their new device. And it's also for people who enjoy a
> bit of humor, or at least lighthearted writing, as they boldly go where they
> have never imagined they would have needed to go before.*

I'm going out on a limb here to say that most of you are reasonably technically savvy, even if this is your first experience with a full-featured, state-of-
the-art electronic tablet.

The BlackBerry PlayBook is very much a computer — it can perform word
processing, consult the Web, send and receive e-mail and instant messages,
and record and play back pictures, video, and music. (It is miles ahead of
the room-sized IBM mainframe I started with in the late 1960s.) In some
ways, the most difficult thing about using a tablet is dealing with its missing
parts: no keyboard, no mouse, no disk drive . . . and no instruction book.

That's why you're so smart to be reading *BlackBerry PlayBook For Dummies.* In these pages I'm your guide to setting up, using, and getting the very most out of one of the most exciting new types of electronic products available.

Conventions Used in This Book

Conventions? No, not the kind where you have to wear a name tag and go to parties with silly hats. I'm talking about the basic scaffolding that holds together this book: *BlackBerry PlayBook For Dummies* is more than just pages filled with pithy and clever explanations, tips, and tricks.

- **Numbered lists:** Start at number 1 and proceed to the last one in the list, in order, to accomplish a particular task.

- **Bulleted lists:** Bulleted lists (you're in the middle of one right now) represent things you should know about or do, but that don't demand being performed in a particular order.

- **Sidebars:** This book concentrates on *news you can use,* but there will be times I invite you to cast your eyes slightly away from the mainstream to read sidebars.

The BlackBerry PlayBook can connect to, exchange files with, and perform other feats of derring-do with both PC and Mac computers. There are no significant differences in use of the BlackBerry Desktop Manager software that, uh, manages the desktop on the computer side. For that reason I make no distinction between PCs and Macs; I refer to either and both as personal or laptop computers.

One other thing: the maker of the BlackBerry PlayBook, the BlackBerry smartphone, and the official suites of software and apps that run on one or the other of the devices is a Canadian company with the somewhat whimsical name of Research in Motion Limited. They often also refer to themselves by the acronym of RIM. And the company has become so inextricably tied up with its products that I make no distinction between RIM or BlackBerry when talking about any of the official products in the BlackBerry universe: the tablet, the smartphones, the operating system, or the apps.

How This Book Is Organized

Some people I know (my wife) will at times pick up a mystery novel and glance at the ending to assure that their investment of time will be satisfying once they get there. Speaking for myself, I prefer to start at the beginning, make my way through a well-written middle, and arrive at a beautifully constructed end.

The good news, and the solution to any possible minor marital discord, is that in a *For Dummies* book, you can have it both ways. You can start right here and read your way to the conclusion in a book that is logically organized and designed. Or you can jump directly to a section that interests you most or solves an immediate problem. Contents at a Glance is available, as well as a detailed Table of Contents, and the book's finished off with a comprehensive index. I'm quite proud of the effort that went into the organization of the book; here, let me show you the structure.

Part I: Getting Acquainted with the BlackBerry PlayBook

Take a tour of the BlackBerry PlayBook, examining its front and back and some of its side edges. There aren't that many parts to be seen: just a spectacular full-color high-definition touchscreen and a few ports for connecting to a computer, headphones, and a recharger for the tablet's long-life battery. All of the magic takes place on the touchscreen. And then I explain how to bridge the gap: wireless connections from a BlackBerry PlayBook to a BlackBerry smartphone. You want to *get connected.* The BlackBerry PlayBook includes a full-featured Internet browser that lets you explore the web with ease and speed. In this section, I show you how the BlackBerry PlayBook performs without wires: Wi-Fi, Bluetooth, and cellular communication.

Part II: Inspecting Apps and Programs

Explore the browser (including its sophisticated security features) and take a gander at web-based and native e-mail applications that let you take your office and your personal communication with you, and the BlackBerry Desktop Manager that helps keep things in order back at home base. In this section I also show you how to use the tools that allow reading, editing, or creating a file compatible with Microsoft Word or Microsoft Excel, and how to present a Microsoft PowerPoint show. From there I move on to the basic suite of utilities included with the PlayBook and the portal to the future: the BlackBerry App World store.

Part III: PlayBooking Around

Do you know how to get to Carnegie Hall? Yes, I know you need to practice: in this section I show you how to play music and podcasts on the PlayBook, enjoy astounding computer games, use the tablet as a digital still or video camera, and read a book.

Part IV: Keeping House

The beauty of a programmable computer — and that's what lies just beneath the PlayBook's surface — is that you can *change* much of the way it works and looks. Although some of my engineer friends might quibble, in the end the hardware exists to serve the software. In this part I show you how to customize your PlayBook in dozens of ways, and how to make it more secure.

Part V: The Part of Tens

Problems come to all things made by men and women. Here I show you ten smart things you can do to troubleshoot your way to happiness, then move on to ten nifty hints, tips, and shortcuts. And as an extra added bonus, you get an icon glossary, a visual guide to most of the important icons that serve as extra characters in the touch-and-slide vocabulary of the BlackBerry PlayBook.

Icons Used in This Book

Four icons are used in this book:

Here be dragons. Watch out. Be careful.

In case you missed something earlier on, here's a reminder of important stuff. And even if you didn't miss it, here's a brief refresh to your memory bank.

Let me tell you something you might not realize about how to use your BlackBerry PlayBook.

Not that you absolutely need to know this sort of information, but some of us like to understand a bit about how things work. Ask me how to get to the post office, and I'll tell you how a GPS system works. That's just the kind of guy I am.

In addition to seeing these graphic pointers in the margins, you will see icons from the PlayBook itself. They're there to help point you in the right direction.

Where to Go from Here

You might want to proceed from this very entertaining but rather general Introduction and dive right into Chapter 1. No one would blame you if you did. But actually, no rule says you have to read this book in the exact sequence in which it is presented. Even though *BlackBerry PlayBook For Dummies* has been meticulously planned and carefully edited so that it flows like a cool and refreshing mountain stream from beginning to end, you can also jump right into a particular section or chapter or page if you have an immediate need to know. That is, of course, why there is a contents at a glance, a more fulsome table of contents, and a professionally designed index. You're the master of your own domain; go forth and partake of the knowledge prepared for you here.

Ch-ch-changes

When RIM released the first model of the BlackBerry PlayBook in April of 2011, the hardware was firm, but the software was still in development. In fact, one of the first things new owners of a PlayBook are asked to do is connect to the Internet to download the latest version of the operating system. You can — and should — expect regular updates and improvements to the operating system in the first few years the PlayBook is on the market. Some of these changes will fix bugs and problems, while others will offer new functions and apps.

At the time this book was written and edited, the PlayBook and its operating system were in their infancy. We worked from final, released copies of both (not from incomplete beta versions) but the operating system in your tablet is almost certainly more recently updated and improved.

As this book goes to press, and in future years, RIM will be rolling out other versions of the BlackBerry PlayBook that add yet another means of communication: a link to the omnipresent cellphone network. There will be versions with specific hardware and operating system features for particular cellphone providers. Those editions of the PlayBook will work in a nearly identical fashion to the original Wi-Fi model (although some cellphone providers may add a few extra features particular to their networks and data plans. They'll almost certainly add a few bucks, or a few dozen bucks, to your monthly bill as well).

Occasionally, we have updates to our technology books. If this book does have technical updates, they will be posted at www.dummies.com/go/ blackberryplaybookfdupdates.

If you buy a model of the BlackBerry PlayBook with cellular communication, the book you're reading will provide you with nearly everything you need to know about using the tablet. All you need to know from your cellular provider is this: What have you added to the base Wi-Fi model, and why?

Similarly, the add-on marketplace was just getting up to speed to produce things that encase, attach to, or connect with the BlackBerry PlayBook. In addition to the obvious things like protective cases and desk stands, I expect to see innovative products like wireless keyboards, amplified stereo speakers, and the like.

And finally, as long as we're on the subject of comments and questions: I'd very much like to hear from you if you find a mistake (it's never happened before, but there's always a first time) or, even better, if you have a suggestion for improvements in future editions of this book. It's also nice to receive words of praise and gratitude. The author's life is a lonely one, locked away in a quiet office staring at a blank screen and trying to figure out a way to add 100,000 or so words to the document. (That last sentence boosted the total by 34 words.)

You can send e-mail to me at this special address: **PlayBookForDummies@ sandlerbooks.com**. I'll do my best to respond to polite queries quickly; impolite messages take much, much longer to get my attention. Most of all, thank you for buying this book.

Part I

Getting Acquainted with the BlackBerry PlayBook

The 5th Wave   By Rich Tennant

"Marketing said they'd make these things levitate off retailer's shelves. Apparently, someone in engineering heard them first."

In this part . . .

To use one of the current buzzwords of consumer electronics, when you "unbox" the BlackBerry PlayBook, you hold in your hand a lifeless, mute slab of plastic, glass, and electronics. There isn't much to see. In this first part of *BlackBerry PlayBook For Dummies,* I introduce you to the machine's soul, beginning in Chapter 1 with a tour and explanation of how to bring it to virtual life. In Chapter 2, you lay hands on the touchscreen (and the active frame that surrounds it), and I show how you can control the BlackBerry PlayBook with a touch, swipe, or slide of a finger or two. And I show you how to use a USB cable to exchange files with a personal or laptop computer. In Chapter 3, I introduce you to one of the PlayBook's distinguishing characteristics: its ability to connect wirelessly to a BlackBerry smartphone (and eventually to other devices) to share and synchronize data as you move about from home to office, office to office, and just about anywhere in the world. In Chapter 4, I explain how the device achieves wireless communication: Wi-Fi, Bluetooth, and (on some models) cellular radios.

Presenting the PlayBook

T he BlackBerry PlayBook, of course, is not the original tablet. Among the first were the pair carried down from Mount Sinai by a fellow named Moses several millennia ago. They were, I suppose, state-of-the art at the time: chiseled stone that held the Ten Commandments. And for the record, Moses immediately voided the warranty on his tablets by throwing them to the ground. He had to climb back up the hill and wait another 40 days and nights before he could receive the new model.

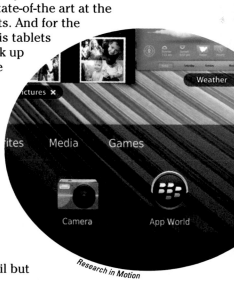

Research in Motion

Poking around the PlayBook

Research in Motion's BlackBerry PlayBook boldly goes where others have gone before. In the modern Era of the Tablet, we all pretty much know what to expect, at least when it comes to the basic components. And the BlackBerry PlayBook does not disappoint; this is a very solid piece of hardware.

This book explores its parts and parcels in great detail but here are the highlights:

- A 7-inch (measured on the diagonal) ultra-high–resolution bright and colorful display.

- A highly responsive touch-sensitive sensor system that allows you to point at, move around, and change items on the screen and permits a form of touch-typing on a virtual keyboard. Read Chapter 2 for more about your digits (not the phone type).

- A zippy main processor and dedicated graphics processor that allow for spectacular playback of video, photos, music, and (if you must) games. See Chapter 10 for this scoop.

- A very solid, purpose-built operating system for the tablet that allows you to customize and add all sorts of apps (what we used to call *software*) to teach your new gadget new tricks. See Chapters 6 and 9 for more.

- A means to connect to the Internet and to other devices (including your smartphone and personal computer) wirelessly or with a cable. Read Chapters 4 and 5 for this information.

When the BlackBerry PlayBook was first announced, Apple took multiple swipes at the upcoming tablet, saying its 7-inch touchscreen was just too darned small to be useable. Not so, said BlackBerry: the Apple iPad, they said, was too big to be portable. Eventually, the market will decide. But Research in Motion, the maker of the PlayBook, just may try to have it both ways; a 10-inch version of their tablet may arrive with the next wave of hardware from the company.

The evolution of the tablet

I don't think the ancient Egyptians had PowerPoint presentations in mind when they carved their first tablets around 3,200 BC. And the ancient Olmecs of southern Mexico and Guatemala of about 1,200 BC had a thing about birds, but they probably did not envision the game *Angry Birds*. But with a nod to Motorola in the promotion of their own tablet in 2011, here is a Reduced History of Tablets:

- **Egyptian hieroglyphic tablet:** about 3,200 BC. Nifty graphics, but not exactly a pocket-sized portable unit.

- **The Ten Commandments:** about 1,500 BC. Solid moral concepts with excellent durability (at least in version 2.0) but not very flexible; the contents could not be edited and though they needed no higher power source, moving them around was quite a schlep.

- **Rosetta Stone:** about 196 BC. One of the first multilingual tablets, but the screen was low resolution and the operating system was incomplete and rather difficult to decipher.

- **The Age of Modern Tablets:** about 2010 and beyond. Worth the wait. And the weight.

Being productive with it

Who here was surprised when RIM named their foray into the world of tablets the *PlayBook?* You don't "play" with corporate financial details or human resources records. But think about the meaning of the word *playbook,* as in a listing of the tactical plans for a sports team. A football quarterback (and the rest of his team) spends weeks obsessing over the playbook and adapting it to meet varying situations brought about by the opponent or by unexpected changes to the environment caused by weather or injuries or the personal wealth of the team owner. And if you've ever worked in an office or a store, you know that there is an overabundance of sports metaphors: scoring a big contract, going for the extra point, sales blitzes, and high-fives. So we have come to a reconciliation with the name. This professional grade tablet is meant to complement the corporate playbook.

The heart of the PlayBook is its ability to extend the reach of your smartphone and your desktop or laptop computer (and beyond that, onto the corporate intranet and the Internet). And yes, you can also play some games, and besides, who says success at work can't be fun?

The PlayBook, in its Bridge mode (see Chapter 3), allows you to tap into the contacts, calendar, and e-mail that is securely delivered to your BlackBerry smartphone. When you use the tablet in that way, it can be set up so that no critical information is stored on the PlayBook itself; instead, the tablet uses secure wireless communication as a *window* into the data held on the phone.

As an individual this may not matter to you; as an employee of a carefully managed company, institute, or government agency this may make all the difference in the world: Key to the concept of a "professional grade tablet" is the ability of a corporate or enterprise IT (information technology) department to set rules about exactly how the PlayBook can be used and what sort of information and applications can be installed on it.

But beyond that, you can also go directly to the Web to access e-mail, search engines, specific websites, and more. And then there is the rapidly growing library of apps that is available to be downloaded and installed on your PlayBook. As the great philosopher Yogi Berra may or may not have actually once said, it's tough to make predictions, especially about the future. But it is a lot of fun.

Playing it like a boombox

You can enjoy your music collection, watch videos and television shows, listen to podcasts, and otherwise own and operate your own cable television and radio station. BlackBerry has partnered with 7digital (a British firm headquartered in London) to offer its own version of the Apple iTunes or Amazon Music Store; see Figure 1-1 for one of its pages. Here you can purchase individual tracks or an entire album. I discuss music and video downloads in Chapter 10.

But back to the concept of the PlayBook as a serious productivity tool. All you have to do is take a look at some of the help screen videos (included in the operating system) to understand how the BlackBerry tablet could be used by a salesperson calling on a client or a corporate executive making a pitch to a board of directors: the PlayBook can deliver videos, PowerPoint presentations, spreadsheets, and all of the other tools of the modern road warrior. Come to think of it, a football coach could also use the BlackBerry tablet as a way to hold a playbook for the game, as well as videos of key matchups and game films.

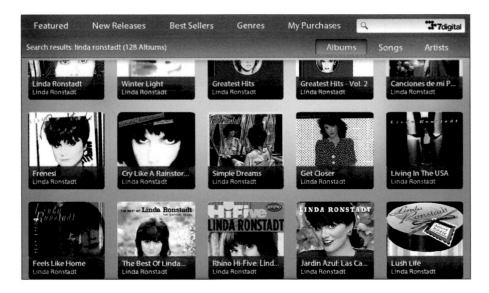

Figure 1-1: BlackBerry PlayBook offers a direct link to 7digital for buying music.

Chapter 6 discusses this in more detail, but I thought you'd like to keep this in mind: the BlackBerry desktop software, which runs on your personal or laptop computer, can synchronize your audio and video files so that you can travel with your collection as needed.

The PlayBook meets the Internet

The World Wide Web in the palm of your hand. That's been the case since the advent of smartphones, but — and let's be honest here — using the Internet on a tiny little screen connected to a relatively slow cellphone service isn't always the most satisfying experience. I have thought of it as kind of like trying to read *The New York Times* through a telescope: you get to see little pieces of the whole picture and going from page by page is very cumbersome.

But when RIM introduced the BlackBerry PlayBook with its new purpose-built operating system it included not only a reasonably sized, very high resolution screen, but also added a real Internet browser; see Figure 1-2. You can easily see most of a full page and you can move from section to section or adjust its size using a pinch of the fingers. I discuss browsing in Chapter 5.

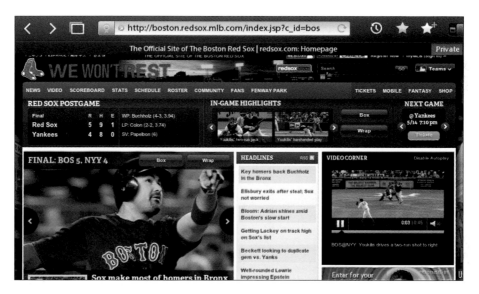

Figure 1-2: The full-featured browser of the BlackBerry PlayBook shows web pages with Flash and other advanced video, animation, and audio features.

Though the PlayBook didn't include its own e-mail program (a.k.a *client*) at first, you can easily retrieve your mail from a variety of web-based mail services. (RIM has promised to include an e-mail client as an update to the PlayBook operating system before the end of 2011.) And as an Internet-connected device, the PlayBook can use just about any service that's out there on the Web, including search engines, map programs, YouTube, and you name it.

Reading it like a book

As will become increasingly obvious if you make your way through this beautifully printed book, I am on the verge of becoming an old fogey. That is, an old fogey who is thoroughly modern when it comes to the latest electronic doodads. But I have been a professional journalist and author for more than four decades, and I can still remember the smell of ink as it was applied to paper by a thundering printing press. And I can remember the arrival of the Internet and the first bites it took out of printed literature. When the Web took off, it stole away much of the income that supported newspapers (remember classified ads?) and then came blogs and online publications that hastened the decline of newspapers and magazines. More recently came devices like the Amazon Kindle and a host of similar special-purpose electronic readers. On the one hand, any author's heart is gladdened at the sight of someone reading just about anything in just about any form. On the other hand, digital books present a challenge to traditional publishers and authors.

Enough of the sermonizing. If you're going to read a book on a digital device, the BlackBerry PlayBook offers one of the finest platforms for doing so. It has a screen slightly larger than that of the Kindle and its competitors, and that backlit screen is in full color and high resolution and linked to the Internet. You can store hundreds or thousands of titles in the internal memory of the tablet without adding an ounce to its already insubstantial weight.

The BlackBerry PlayBook comes with a link to the Kobo Books store, which offers a full range of titles; see Figure 1-3 for a listing of historical nonfiction. You can also download files from other sources, including free PDFs of classic public domain titles.

Things we haven't yet imagined

The folks over at Apple were jumping up and down seeking the attention of the world's media when RIM announced the BlackBerry PlayBook. "Look!," they said, "They're introducing a tablet without having any apps to run on it. It's doomed to fail!" Guess what? When the iPad was released to a hyperventilating crowd of Apple enthusiasts in April 2010, the endless assortment of apps it sees now weren't around. Several of those that could were merely enlarged versions of software designed for the much smaller and more limited iPod and iPhone.

Good for Apple. But let's remember that in the history of computing it has almost always been a process something like this: a nifty new piece of hardware comes out and then developers scramble to write software that takes advantage of its capabilities. The shelves at BlackBerry App World were rather thinly stocked when the PlayBook made its debut in April of 2011, but the pipeline is already getting filled and I expect to see thousands of nifty apps available well before the tablet reaches its first anniversary. Some of the programs will be BlackBerry versions of things we already see running on iPhone or Android devices; others will be new and amazing applications we don't yet know that we must absolutely have.

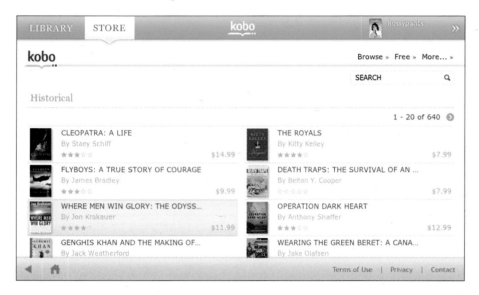

Figure 1-3: Kobo Books comes on the PlayBook as an ebook seller, but you can get files from other sources and use tools like Adobe Reader to enjoy them as you travel.

The PlayBook Has Needs Too, You Know

Well, obviously you need a PlayBook. But you won't be able to do anything with it, at least at first, until you connect to the Internet and configure it for the first time. Here's a list of everything you need:

🖝 **Access to a WiFi Internet point.** This is necessary to download updates to the operating system and obtain a BlackBerry ID. If you have a WiFi router in your home or office you can use that. Otherwise you can use an open connection at a library, a store, or an Internet café. View Figure 1-4 to see a successful link-up.

🖝 **If you own a cellphone version of the PlayBook, you need an account with a cellular provider.** Try as you might, you're not likely to be able to connect to your friendly neighborhood cell tower without some sort of a contract.

Figure 1-4: My BlackBerry PlayBook has connected to a secure WiFi system called Hudson, automatically negotiating login and password based on a previous visit.

That's all you absolutely *need*. With an updated PlayBook you can use its built-in apps. But you'll certainly want to expand on its capabilities by loading music, video, and data files from your computer and maintaining a WiFi or cellular link for Web browsing.

And so, here are some things you'll *want*:

- On-demand access by WiFi to the Internet. Once the device is set up, you don't *require* WiFi, but without it you will have to use slower (and sometimes costlier) methods like a Bluetooth link to a BlackBerry smartphone with a data plan, or (on a cellular model of the PlayBook) a direct link to a cellular data plan.

- A PC with an Intel or compatible processor running at 1GHz or faster, 512MB of RAM, a USB port (1.1 or higher), and the Windows XP SP3, Windows Vista, or Windows 7 operating system. On that system you'll want to install a copy of BlackBerry Desktop Manager for the PC; it's available for free from www.blackberry.com.

- An Apple Mac, a USB 2.0 port, Mac OS X version 10.5.8 or later. The version of BlackBerry Desktop Manager for Mac with support for the PlayBook wasn't available when the PlayBook was first released, but RIM was said to be feverishly at work on it. Visit www.blackberry.com and see if it's available now.

- A BlackBerry smartphone running OS 5.0 or later, including OS 6.0. Pairing a PlayBook with a compatible BlackBerry smartphone allows you access to all of the e-mail, contacts, calendar, and other information stored on the phone and also permits use of the phone as a modem to reach out to the Internet.

- An account with the 7digital music store, the Kobo Books store, BlackBerry App World, and perhaps some other third-party sites so you can download music, video, podcasts, books, and apps.

- Some sort of padded case for your BlackBerry to avoid scratches and damage but not so large as to make the package too big to carry in your coat pocket or purse. (You know what I mean: you don't want to make your PlayBook as large and cumbersome as something like an Apple iPad.)

Taking a PlayBook Tour

You could look at this relatively small black object with a screen, only four physical buttons, and just three connection ports, and ask, "Is that all there is?" Or you could revel in its simple elegance. Many users can go for days or weeks without ever touching the physical buttons. All of the interaction between humans and the machine takes place on the touchscreen and its surrounding frame (also called a bezel, which more-or-less rhymes with level). These users may exclaim, "That's all we need!"

You're going to devote almost all of your attention to just one face of your PlayBook: the part that has the screen. For our purposes (and according to the basic rules of geometry first defined by the ancient Greeks and not yet repealed) the three-dimensional rectangular object in front of us has six sides. Let us, for simplicity's sake, ignore the fact that its corners are rounded. It's almost a rectangle, okay?

Also for our purposes, assume that most of the time you will be using the PlayBook in what is called *landscape* mode. This is when you hold the tablet so that it is wider than it is tall. (The other way to hold the PlayBook is so that it is taller than it is wide, which is called *portrait* mode. That might be your preference when reading an electronic book or consulting a word document.) So, back to landscape mode. The tour's highlights appear in Figure 1-5, which shows the lay of the land.

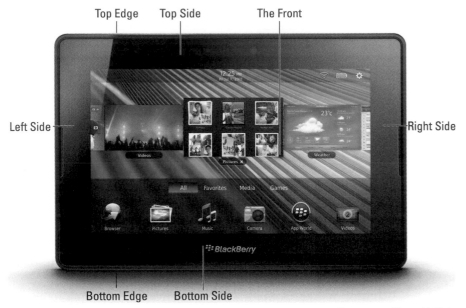

Photo courtesy of Research in Motion

Figure 1-5: All of the viewable parts of a BlackBerry PlayBook (except the back).

The left edge is handsome, isn't it? It's home to nothing of importance except a nicely tapered place to grab hold of your PlayBook. Amazingly, the right edge is just like the left, only on the other side. Move along, folks. There's nothing to see here.

The front

Here, of course, is the reason we are gathered together for this special occasion. The front is home to the single most important external piece of equipment: the high-resolution capacitive multitouch color screen. At the top side of the front are two components protected behind the glass screen. Left of center is a light that tells you whether the power is turned on or off, and just right of center along the top side is the front-facing camera (the one that looks you in the eye if you're using the tablet's screen). See Figure 1-6.

Along the left and right sides of the front you'll find a thin slot of about an inch in length; these are the speakers. (The speakers are automatically turned off when a plug is inserted in the headphone jack on the top edge. And one more very important element: the black frame (sometimes called a *bezel*) all around the touchscreen is an important part of the way you tell the PlayBook what to do. You can use your finger to swipe from the frame to minimize apps, show the menu, and make other commands.

Front-facing camera

Notification LED

Speaker—

—Speaker

Photo courtesy of Research in Motion

Figure 1-6: Components built into the front of the BlackBerry PlayBook include speakers, a power light, a regular camera, and a video camera.

It's easier to figure out the bottom. That's the part that has the word "BlackBerry" and seven little bullet-shaped marks; that's a graphic designer's representation of the delicious little drupelets that make up the fruit that we call a blackberry. Speaking for myself, I'd take a bowl of blackberries over a mushy apple any day of the week.

The top edge

Here you will find a powerful button. In fact, the button is so powerful and so important that it's all by itself, left of center. It is, in fact, the power button.

 When the unit is off, press and hold the silver button; release it to turn it on. It takes a few seconds to go through the mental gymnastics all computers need to boot themselves to life. See Figure 1-7 for its location.

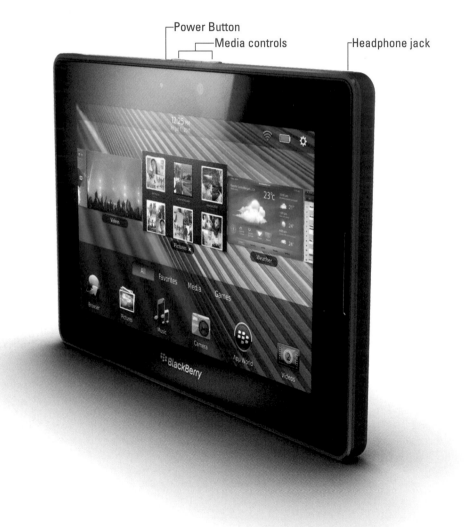

Photo courtesy of Research in Motion

Figure 1-7: The only way to turn on a completely powered-off tablet is to press and hold the power button.

I discuss this in more detail as a nifty tip in Chapter 16, but in short you don't have to turn off your PlayBook except perhaps when you're on an airplane; at other times you can just let it sleep.

In the top center, three small rocker switches make up the media controls:

–	Turn *down* the volume of any audio that's playing.
	Press once to play a track; press again to pause it, and so on.
+	Turn *up* the audio.
– and + buttons together	Take a snapshot of whatever is being displayed on the screen.*

The high-resolution image will be stored in the Camera folder on the tablet.

All the way to the right side of the top end is a small opening: Headphone jack. You can plug a 3.5mm connector into this small jack and enjoy high-quality stereo music and audio; use the same connector for future accessories such as standalone speaker systems and output to theater audio systems. Finally, two other small holes are at the left and right sides of the top end. These listening ports are for a pair of microphones within the PlayBook's case.

I use the words *headphones, earphones, and earbud,* interchangeably; they are each variations on the same idea: a plug attached to a wire which goes to a pair of tiny speakers that sit on your head or go in your ear. There's one other type of device: a *headset* includes a microphone that allows you to transmit or record your voice, as well as listen.

The bottom edge

There's not much to look at down here, but keep in mind three important bits of business. Looking at the BlackBerry icon on the front, the three tiny ports are, from left to right:

Micro HDMI

You can attach a cable (not included) to the port (shown in Figure 1-8) and its other end to a high-definition television screen or video projector. You need the proper cable — micro-HDMI at the PlayBook end and the appropriate connector for the device you want to use it with at the other. See Chapter 13 for more details.

Micro-USB

The port (refer to Figure 1-8) here has two purposes:

- ✔ Use the supplied AC adapter to recharge the internal battery of the PlayBook through this port.

- ✔ Use as the connecting point for a Micro-USB–to–USB cable (supplied as standard equipment) to attach the PlayBook to a computer so you can transfer files and synchronize. I describe this in more detail in Chapter 2. You can drag and drop any compatible files between folders on the two devices.

Charging contacts for accessory high-speed charger

Micro-USB port

HDMI port

64GB

Photo courtesy of Research in Motion

Figure 1-8: The Micro HDMI connector can send a high-definition signal to a TV or projector. The Micro USB connector can recharge the battery. Charging contacts are used with a BlackBerry cradle.

Using the USB cable to connect your PlayBook to a desktop or laptop computer allows what is sometimes called *sideways transfer* of documents and files. Your computer will treat the PlayBook's internal storage (its built-in 16, 32, or 64GB of flash memory) as if it were another disk drive.

Just speculating here, but the Micro-USB port is a perfect way to attach some sort of external storage device to the PlayBook. Perhaps an external hard disk drive or a flash memory device? How about accessory keyboards or controllers?

Charging contacts

An alternate (and speedier) way to recharge the PlayBook battery is to use a BlackBerry charging pod. This charger makes its connection magnetically, all but eliminating the possibility of damage to the tablet if it should fall out of the cradle. The contacts themselves can be seen in Figure 1-8.

Oh, and one other thing: the bottom also holds a set of small printed labels that help identify your model. At the left end is a marking that tells how much internal flash memory is installed (the initial release of the device offered models with 16, 32, or 64GB). At the right end is the model number and other identification.

The back

The blank slate on the underside of the PlayBook is mostly just a protective cover. There are no buttons or screens or plugs to be seen. If you don't believe me, take a look at Figure 1-9. There is, though, one little clear plastic opening: The rear-facing camera is at the top, above the silvery BlackBerry symbol.

Actually, if you consider the design of the PlayBook carefully, you will see that the forward-facing camera is nearly directly opposite the rearward-facing camera. Why is that important? If you set up your PlayBook as a broadcasting device for a video conference call, you can send images of yourself as well as other people you're facing around the table.

With the rear-facing camera you can achieve many things and possibly reach your full potential:

- Take still photos and video, which you can store on the PlayBook or send using a WiFi link.
- Sideways transfer the files to a personal or laptop computer using the USB cable and sent out from a computer.
- If you're using a version of the PlayBook that comes with a cellular phone transceiver, send images and videos that way. I discuss the cameras in detail in Chapter 11.

The great inside

Oh, and let me mention one other place, an area that few BlackBerry PlayBook users will ever see: the Inside. Here the clever engineers and designers have managed to squeeze all of the electronic parts that make this plastic case into a computer tablet. The following sections describe the most important of those pieces.

Rear-facing camera

Photo courtesy of Research in Motion

Figure 1-9: The back of the BlackBerry PlayBook has only one component worth noting: the high-resolution rear-facing camera.

Processor

The brain of the BlackBerry PlayBook is a specialized version of a computer microprocessor. It is made to be speedy yet cool (so you don't need a fan) and be powerful enough to run all sorts of amazing apps yet use wee bits of battery. It is assisted by a graphics processor and a few other special-purpose controllers.

Memory

The BlackBerry PlayBook has 1GB of memory dedicated to the processor and operating system. This fair amount of thinking room is twice as much as that bestowed on most of its competitors. Of that 1GB of memory, the PlayBook's operating system generally grabs about half to spread out its collection of 0s and 1s that instruct the device on how to respond to your touch and interact with other devices. On my unit, early in the life of the BlackBerry PlayBook, there was about 449.3MB of free or unused memory with all applications closed. Turning on the WiFi transceiver reduced free memory by just a tad, to 448.5. Later versions of the operating system may move those numbers up or down a bit.

Storage

This block of memory holds any files you create or download, as well as any apps you add. The initial models come with built-in memory of 16, 32, or 64 gigabytes (GB), and they *don't* let you add more storage by plugging in an extra block of memory; I wouldn't be surprised to see that sort of feature offered by third-party manufacturers.

I have two observations about storage:

- Even 16GB is a lot of space, but more is almost always better than less. If you can afford the extra few hundred dollars to buy a unit with 32 or 64GB of storage, I recommend you do so.

- On the other hand, if you end up with a 16GB base model, you should conduct regular housekeeping sessions to remove unnecessary files; store them elsewhere — on your BlackBerry smartphone or on a computer — and leave your PlayBook with as much available space as you can.

One other important point: this storage is a form of *non-volatile memory;* that means once data is recorded to it, that information stays in place even when the power is turned off.

Radios

Your little tablet is a power broadcasting station, capable of using two or three different modes of wireless communication.

- The basic PlayBook model includes WiFi and Bluetooth transmitters and receivers. Use these to link to a wireless network or directly to another device.

- Cellular models add a cellular radio capable of communicating with one of the various data systems spread around the world. Various cellular providers offer adaptations of the BlackBerry PlayBook that work with their particular frequencies and transmission methods.

Battery

The engine for the entire enterprise — a high-tech Lithium-ion device that provides enough electrical power for the processor, screen, memory, storage, and radios for hours and hours — is rechargeable.

Places on the screen

Consider some metaphorical places on the front touchscreen *when you are looking at the home page.* Although the entire screen can display a single image or document page, the operating system divides it into three areas (labeled in Figure 1-10):

✓ **Status bar.** The top portion of the screen is where you get notifications about your tablet when in use. Typically you'll see info like the number of messages in the e-mail inbox, the time and date, the connection status for Bluetooth or WiFi communication, and the battery charge. All the way to the right is the option button, which opens up pages of controls for the device.

✓ **Open apps.** The central portion of the screen is the home of any apps currently running on the device.

✓ **App list.** The bottom third of the screen displays a scrollable list of available apps. You can tap these options:

- **All** to see all (how unlikely)
- **Favorites** to see just those apps you love
- **Media** for audio and video apps
- **Games** for entertainment
- **BlackBerry Bridge** to jump electronically from your tablet to your linked BlackBerry smartphone to use some of its data or facilities; see Chapter 3

Status Bar

Open Apps

App List

Photo courtesy of Research in Motion

Figure 1-10: The three regions of the BlackBerry PlayBook touchscreen are marked here; use the surrounding frame (a.k.a bezel) to initiate commands.

Putting on a charge

One of the greatest charms of the BlackBerry PlayBook is its wirelessness. You can browse the Internet, read e-mail, consult the calendar on your BlackBerry phone, and do anything else you want without connecting by a power cord. That is, of course, until the battery runs out of juice. How long will that take? In a word, it *depends*. You should be able to get a total of four to eight hours of use from a fully charged battery. For more details, see Chapter 14.

2

Getting Companionable

In This Chapter

▶ Upgrading the OS

▶ Pairing to a smartphone

▶ Making the USB Connection

▶ Taking a swipe at PlayBook gestures

▶ Customizing your PlayBook

▶ Understanding Internet tethering

▶ Preparing for cellular communication

*T*he BlackBerry PlayBook is an amazing piece of hardware, but in truth it is more impressive for what it lacks rather than what it has. How can things that are missing be so wonderful? It comes down to the magic of downsizing. The PlayBook tablet has no physical keyboard or mouse, no CD or DVD, and it fits into a (large) pocket. It depends upon a device that most of us carry with us at all times: our fingers. The key to a tablet's usability is its touchscreen: a double-duty device that not only displays text and images but also responds to taps, slides, swipes, and pinches.

Starting It Up, Mick Jagger Style

You should be able to fire up your Playbook immediately upon getting it. That's the good news. The not-quite-so-good news is that you won't be able to do much with the PlayBook until you go through about half an hour's worth of setup.

If you have been issued a PlayBook by your corporate or enterprise IT department, they may well have done the setup work for you. They would do this not just because they like you, but also because they want to set some security parameters on the PlayBook that protect secrets or other important data. If that's the case for you, just say "Thanks," and move on to later in this chapter.

Step 1: Connect the tablet to an outside power source (the AC adapter or a computer USB port).

Step 2: Turn on the PlayBook by pressing and holding the little silver button on the top edge for a few seconds.

Let the little guy know you mean to start making beautiful music (or business) together. After coming to life, just follow the onscreen instructions. It all comes pretty naturally. It starts with a "Welcome!" Just swipe across the screen to move past the page and into the setup wizard.

WiFi or cell connection

Who am I? Where am I? And what's the latest scoop? Well, yes I know that the BlackBerry PlayBook isn't alive. But it does have certain needs that must be dealt with before it can do that thing that it does so well. You can mostly just sit back and respond to questions as they appear; the PlayBook will look around for an active WiFi network (or with cellular data versions, an active cell tower). See Figure 2-1.

Step 3: Turn the WiFi Connectivity option to On.

Step 4: Choose Open Networks from the Select a Network menu.

You need an active WiFi connection to the Internet to set up the basic PlayBook model. Versions of the tablet that use a cellular data link can most likely do this using the data stream.

This book deals here with the WiFi configuration. (If you have the BlackBerry PlayBook with a cellular radio and subscription, your cellular provider will most likely preconfigure the device or customize the startup screens to meet its particular needs.)

WiFi systems come in two basic types:

✔ An **unsecured** system is wide open, just waiting for any passersby to latch on to its radio waves and go surfing. You may find unsecured WiFi at libraries and cafés; some individual users don't bother to lock their front door or their WiFi network. An unsecured WiFi network may or may not be a bad thing for the owner; as long as any individual computers in the home or office don't allow file sharing — access to the contents of hard drives — then all that's likely to happen is free hitchhiking by friends and strangers.

✓ A **secured** WiFi network, on the other hand, requires that any would-be user get permission — usually in the form of a username and password — in order to get on the system. Some public systems may freely hand out the passwords (sometimes called *keys*), while other places restrict use: buy a coffee and get 15 minutes of time on the Internet.

Figure 2-1: Connect to a WiFi signal to complete the initial setup.

In the simplest of systems, all you see is a sign-in screen that asks for a username and password. On more complex and managed systems, you may have to enter additional details, such as departmental or billing codes. One of the great appeals of the BlackBerry for system managers of large enterprises is the ability to add customized layers of security.

The BlackBerry PlayBook supports all three of the most commonly used systems for securing access to a WiFi service:

✓ **WEP.** Wired Equivalent Privacy is an older security algorithm that has been mostly superseded by WiFi Protected Access.

✓ **WPA Personal.** WiFi Protected Access adds some levels of security to protect against things like the capture and alteration of data by an outside attacker.

✓ **WPA2 Personal.** WiFi Protected Access II, also known as WPA2, is the most secure of the three systems.

As a user, you don't get to choose which system to use. That determination is made by the WiFi system owner; your assignment — mostly handled automatically by the operating system of the BlackBerry PlayBook — is to configure the tablet properly and to enter a valid password. If you've already established a WiFi connection, the PlayBook will automatically reconnect if it detects that same service. If the PlayBook finds more than one familiar network, it offers you a choice.

When a new wireless network is detected, the tablet will display a standard login screen (user name and password) if the system is set up that way. Some systems may have non-standard login requirements; in that situation, choose Connect Manually and fill in the fields you see.

Step 5: Once connected to a WiFi system, swipe on the screen to continue the process.

Date and time

The next assignment is to set the date and time, as shown in Figure 2-2. You can have the PlayBook figure out the actual time based on Internet clocks in combination with the local time zone, or you can enter the information by rolling through the days and the hours using your fingers. You can also choose between a.m. and p.m. 12-hour clocks or use military or International 24-hour notation.

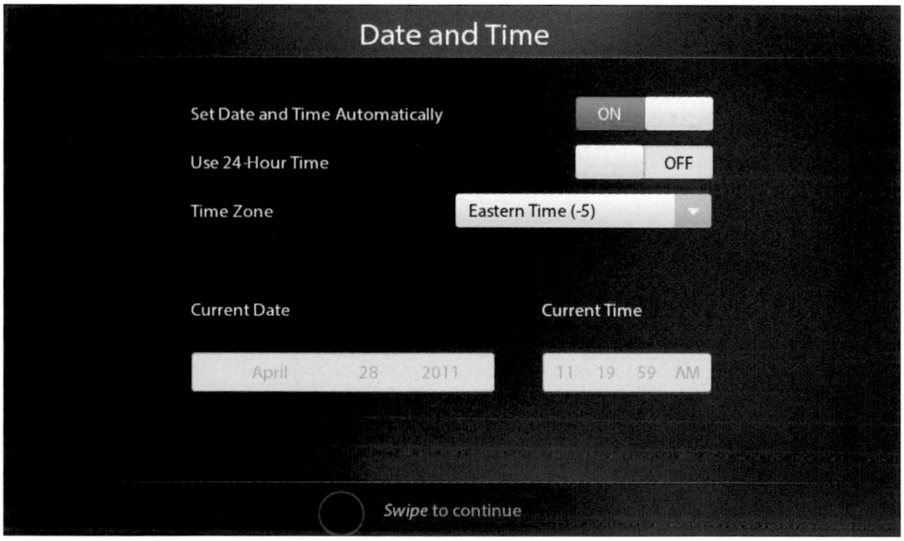

Date and Time		
Set Date and Time Automatically	ON	
Use 24-Hour Time		OFF
Time Zone	Eastern Time (-5)	

Current Date: April 28 2011

Current Time: 11 19 59 AM

Swipe to continue

Figure 2-2: PlayBook requires an accurate date and time.

Whatever you do, make sure the date and time are accurate. If not, you run the risk of problems with updates and download versions.

IDing yourself

Next you need to apply for a BlackBerry ID or apply an existing one to your new PlayBook.

Step 6: Identify your home country and agree to all of the legalese.

You don't have a choice. If you don't tap I Agree, you're not going to be able to set up the tablet. The BlackBerry ID is the single thing you use to sign in for all related sites, services, and applications, including the BlackBerry App World store.

Step 7: Get that user ID!

You get to choose your own user ID, and it's usually an e-mail address associated with your PlayBook. (If IT manages your PlayBook, they may handle all communication with RIM on your behalf with a master ID or make other arrangements.)

For most users, it makes sense to use the same ID for your tablet and your principal BlackBerry smartphone.

Upgrading the OS

It takes a long time to design a piece of hardware (in Canada and many other places around the world), have it manufactured (in Taiwan), shipped to stores, and then delivered into the waiting hands of customers. But usually, once the hardware is finished it doesn't change for the life of a particular model. Not so the operating system and software. They also require a lot of effort, but they can be easily updated and upgraded. In fact, the first wave of BlackBerry PlayBook tablets arrived in stores in April of 2011 with an already-outdated operating system. And the team at Research in Motion and its operating system subsidiary QNX continue to work on new features and improvements.

And so, once you register a BlackBerry ID, the system contacts the mother ship — RIM's computers — and installs a new version of the OS. You can't skip this step, and you wouldn't want to: you're going to want the latest version of the operating system on your tablet.

Step 8: Wait for updates.

The recommended method for downloading the OS to your BlackBerry PlayBook is to connect the tablet to an outside power source (such as the AC adapter or a computer USB port). *Don't* rely on the tablet's not-yet-fully-charged battery during this initial update. Generally it's smart to use external power during any update.

Pairing to a smartphone

At any time you can pair a BlackBerry smartphone to your BlackBerry PlayBook. (This is one of the key differences between this tablet and the others.) See Figure 2-3 for the start of the pairing process.

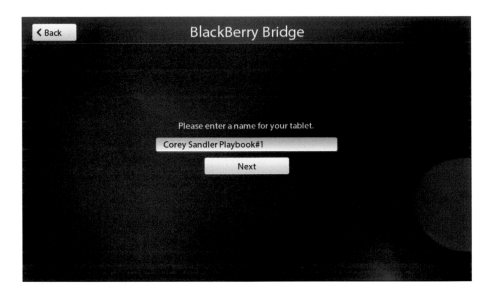

Figure 2-3: The Bridge allows you to use the cellular facilities and some of the data on your BlackBerry smartphone to extend the PlayBook tablet.

The process of pairing uses a utility called BlackBerry Bridge. You can think of this as using your PlayBook as a window into the contents of your BlackBerry smartphone: contacts, phone numbers, calendar, and other information. We cross the BlackBerry Bridge in great detail in Chapter 3.

Step 9: Configure other (important but optional) items, including the BlackBerry Desktop Software.

Feel free to configure your system right now, but if you're like most people you'd like to start (pardon me) *playing* with your PlayBook right now. That's fine; once the system has been updated with the latest operating system you can start putting it through its paces. You can deal with each of the configuration steps — including the BlackBerry Bridge, the BlackBerry Desktop Software, the browser, and other apps — when you need to use them.

The initial setup includes some basic lessons you can go through onscreen; see Figure 2-4 for the start of the tutorial session.

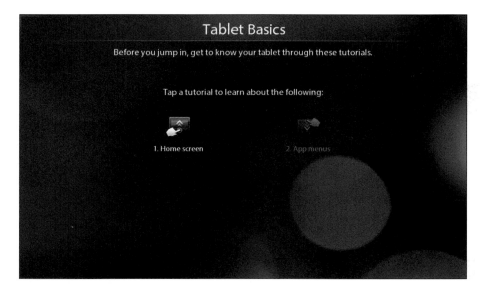

Figure 2-4: The setup process includes a brief tutorial on how to use touchscreen gestures and some configuration option details.

Attaching to a PC or Mac by USB

With all the BlackBerry PlayBook's wireless capabilities, it is still necessary (and sometimes easier) to connect to a personal or laptop computer with a wire (so you can transfer and synchronize certain files). When a BlackBerry PlayBook is attached to a personal computer it essentially is treated as if it were an external hard drive. You can copy files to or from it, and a special BlackBerry software program can *synchronize* files so that both devices hold the same copy of the latest versions of those files.

The tablet comes with its very own cable, with a Micro-USB connector at the end that attaches to the PlayBook (the same port used by the battery charger), and a full-size USB connector that plugs into a port on any current PC or Mac computer.

The PC Connection

The setup for the two types of computer is slightly different, but once the proper instructions are made, they are essentially the same in operation.

Installing BlackBerry Desktop Manager on a PC

To share files between a Windows-based PC and the BlackBerry PlayBook, the best practice is to install (on the PC) a copy of the BlackBerry Desktop Manager program; that software is offered free by Research in Motion. Here are the necessary steps:

1. **Turn on your BlackBerry PlayBook and connect it to a powered-on computer using the supplied USB cable.**

   The PlayBook informs you that it's installing drivers on the PC.

2. **On the PC, double-click the BlackBerry PlayBook CD drive icon.**

3. **Open the Drivers folder and double-click Setup.exe.**

   The installation program runs.

4. **Indicate your geographical region and accept the license agreement.**

5. **Click Install.**

6. **When the PC asks, disconnect the BlackBerry PlayBook and then reconnect it.**

The alternate method to installing BlackBerry Desktop Manager on your PC is to use a browser on that computer to visit www.blackberry.com/desktop and initiate a download from that website.

File sharing with a Windows PC via USB connection

With BlackBerry Desktop Manager installed, anytime you connect your BlackBerry PlayBook to the PC, it is treated as an external connected hard drive. In the notification area of the computer's screen you will see a message that the PlayBook is being installed as a drive, and you will see its drive letter. (On my test machines, it was consistently labeled as Drive Z.) You will also see a notice on your BlackBerry PlayBook that it is connected to a computer; see Figure 2-5. Tap Dismiss to clear the notice and use the BlackBerry Desktop Manager features.

Figure 2-5: The BlackBerry PlayBook will tell you when it detects its connection by USB cable to a PC.

1. **Go to Windows Explorer on your PC.**

   (One route is to click My PC.) When you get there, you'll see a drive identified as PlayBook [PIN: 500xxxxxx].

2. **Double-click the network drive icon to access the PlayBook folders.**

3. **Open any of the folders to see their contents.**

   You can also open a second folder on your PC using Windows Explorer and navigate to any location on your computer.

4. **Drag and drop files in either direction — to or from the PlayBook.**

   You can also highlight a file, right-click to copy it, and then click in another folder and right-click to paste it there.

The Mac connection

Begin by installing the Mac version of BlackBerry Desktop Manager on the Apple computer. Here's how to install BlackBerry Desktop Manager on a Mac:

1. **Turn on your BlackBerry PlayBook and connect it to a powered-on Mac computer using the supplied USB cable.**

2. **On the desktop or within Finder, double-click BlackBerry PlayBook CD.**

3. **Double-click the BlackBerry Desktop Manager Installer.**

   The installation starts.

4. **Accept the License Agreement and click Continue Installation.**

   When the installation is completed, you're prompted to reboot your Mac. Stop! Follow Step 5 first!

5. **Remove your BlackBerry PlayBook from the USB port.**

6. *Now* **reboot your Mac.**

7. **After the reboot is complete, reattach a powered-on PlayBook.**

   You may see a message on the Mac announcing that a new network interface has been detected; if you do, click Network Preferences and click Apply. If not, you can proceed.

   After the PlayBook has been set up in Network Preferences, the tablet share appears on the desktop whenever the PlayBook is connected to the computer.

8. **Click the Playbook icon on the desktop.**

   The PlayBook share appears.

9. **Move files between the computer and the PlayBook.**

Using the BlackBerry Desktop Manager

The BlackBerry Desktop Manager can help you synchronize files (including data, contacts, calendar items, to-do lists, and more) between the two devices. BlackBerry Desktop Manager can also create backups of your BlackBerry PlayBook or BlackBerry smartphone file or restore those files to either device. I discuss advanced use of the BlackBerry Desktop Manager in Chapter 6.

Taking a Swipe at PlayBook Gestures

You can accomplish just about anything you want on the tablet using one or sometimes two fingers. They're called gestures.

The active area for the touchscreen of the BlackBerry PlayBook extends beyond the visible screen to include the black frame (or bezel) that surrounds it. Some PlayBook gestures start or end on the bezel while others are confined to the screen. The tutorial screens show you how to use the frame to initiate or end gestures; see Figure 2-6 for an example.

The frame around the screen is touch-sensitive.

Figure 2-6: The active area of the BlackBerry PlayBook extends beyond the touchscreen to include the bezel that surrounds it.

Mastering basics

Feel free to follow these basic gestures on your BlackBerry PlayBook if you've got one sitting next to this book.

 ✔ **Drag.** What, a drag? To move an item from one place to another touch it and keep your finger in place on the item. Then slide your finger to where you want the item to reside. You can drag on the diagonal or you can move something up or down, left or right. When the item is where you want it to be, simply lift your finger from the screen.

✔ **Swipe.** Touch the screen and keep contact with it as you slide your finger up or down, left or right. This swipe can be used to scroll through a list on the screen, move a web page one direction or another within the browser, spin through a stack of apps or icons, control a game, and do anything else a programmer assigns to that particular touch.

✔ **Pinch.** To zoom in or out of a web page, or to enlarge or reduce the size of a picture or other content, touch the screen with the pointing finger and thumb of one hand and pinch together or apart. No rule says you have to use your pointing finger and thumb, or that they have to be from the same hand. If you're able to do this sort of digital gymnastics with other fingers, or perhaps your toes, more power to you.

Here's a pinch in: And here's a pinch out:

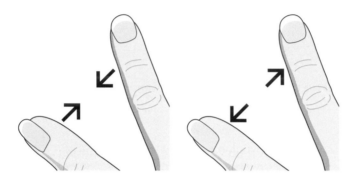

Moving around within the PlayBook

These more-advanced gestures get into the innards of the operating system and the exteriority of the apps and utilities of the BlackBerry PlayBook.

Showing the home screen

To show the home screen and minimize any app that may be running, swipe up from the bottom of the bezel onto the screen. See Figure 2-7 for a tutorial lesson.

Showing the menu

Would you like fries with that? Or perhaps additional features, options, and help for the app you're currently using? To show the menu, swipe down from the top of the bezel onto the screen. To close the menu, tap anywhere on the screen *other* than in the menu.

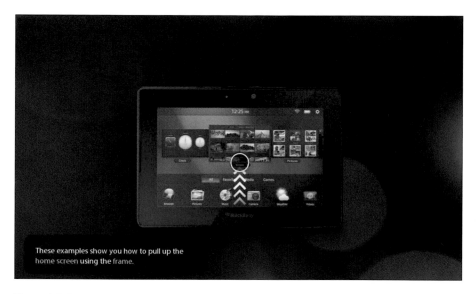

These examples show you how to pull up the
home screen using the frame.

Figure 2-7: Read the tutorial and then try out your swipes (in this case, raising the home screen).

Switching between home screen views

To change the view of installed apps and utilities, swipe left or right in the
lower part of the home screen. The views change between All, Favorites,
Media, Games, or BlackBerry Bridge.

Gesturing within an app

Once an app's up and running, you're going to issue commands and enter
information from the screen. It's all taps and swipes, but there may be some
slight differences in design from one product to another.

Following are the basics of making gestures within an app. Feel free to try
any and all combinations of taps, swipes, and pinches with each new app
you open or add to your PlayBook: you won't break the hardware with your
experimentation, assuming you use your fingers and not a claw or fork.

  ✔ **Switching between apps:** To quickly jump between any open apps with-
     out having to return to the home screen, do the following from within
     one of the apps: Swipe left or right from either side of the frame or bezel
     onto the screen. An app has to be open — that is, loaded — to jump
     between apps with swipes.

✔ **Showing the status bar:** From within an app you can quickly show the status bar, which tells you the time and date, whether the tablet is communicating by WiFi or Bluetooth (or both), and battery-charge level. Make a diagonal swipe from the upper-left side of the bezel onto the screen or a similar swipe from the upper-right side of the bezel onto the screen.

Depending on the app, you may also see certain other controls such as a pause button to stop video or audio; it becomes a play button once tapped. One other important control available from the status bar is the ability to lock the image orientation. That way it doesn't change from landscape to portrait (or the other way around) if the tablet's position changes.

✔ **Closing an app:** To close an app, go to the home screen by swiping up from the bezel onto the touchscreen. The app gets smaller. To shut down the app, either touch the minimized app and keep your finger on it as you swipe up toward the top of the screen, or tap the small X below the app.

✔ **Showing options in an app:** In most apps, you swipe down from the top bezel to show basic options. For example, within the Pictures app this move reveals the trash can (which you can tap to dispose of an unwanted image) or the camera icon (which allows you to jump from pictures you've taken to the app that controls the PlayBook cameras).

✔ **Tapping into a command or menu:** One other gesture you may find in many apps is the tap-and-hold. This gesture lets you open a new set of commands in a pull-down menu, or in the browser to open links in a new tab. In the Word To Go text editor, tapping and holding a block of text selects those characters and lets you use other commands to cut, copy, or delete that material. Similarly, once a block of text is in the tablet's memory, the tap-and-hold gesture can identify where you want to paste that material. I discuss the specifics of Word To Go, Sheet To Go, and Slideshow To Go in Chapter 7.

Changing the Keyboard

The basic keyboard for the BlackBerry PlayBook is a recognizable version of the familiar QWERTY device that most of us have learned to master to some degree or another. That keyboard can be seen in Figure 2-8.

The PlayBook variant is nicely designed and actually pretty easy to use. It has only lowercase letters. When you start a new sentence, the tablet automatically capitalizes the first letter.

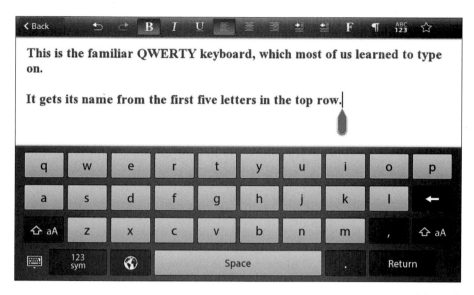

Figure 2-8: Most users will choose the familiar QWERTY keyboard, in its easy-to-use virtual onscreen version.

Table 2-1	Keyboard Tricks
To Do This...	*Do This*
Make an uppercase letter (somewhere other than first thing in a sentence).	Tap the ↑ pad of the virtual keyboard.
Insert a number or a common symbol (such as $ or @).	Tap the 123SYM button. The common symbols are the ones you would expect for ordinary text including grammatical indicators like parentheses, the question mark, exclamation symbol, and the like.
Insert mathematical operators or symbols for the Euro, the Yen, the Pound, and some other international characters.	Tap the 123SYM button and then tap the blue circle.
Insert Danish-y letters or trademark symbols.	Press and hold some of the characters on the top-level keyboard. In the window that pops up above the letter, tap the symbol you want to insert.

There's no reason why Research in Motion, or another company, might not offer more keyboard variations in the future. Almost certainly the BlackBerry PlayBook will roll out in other parts of the world with keyboards that support other needs such as Cyrillic or Asian characters.

But you also have the choice of two other keyboards if you prefer to use them (or if you want to goof on someone and change their preference before they sit down to compose a memo; forget I said that, please).

The QWERTZ keyboard is used in some parts of Central and Eastern Europe, taking into account the relative disuse of the letter Y and the more common usage of Z. It also adds *umlauted* vowels, like ä, ö, and ü. AZERTY is adopted by French speakers in France and Belgium and some other parts of the world. One keyboard that was missing, at least in the initial release of the BlackBerry PlayBook: the DVORAK layout, a supposed improvement on the QWERTY design that was put forth in 1936.

Whichever keyboard you choose, you can adapt its onscreen display slightly by choosing amongst U.S. or U.K. English, French, Spanish, German, or Italian. You make your selection by tapping the symbol of a globe. As you can see in Figure 2-9, this changes, for example, the word Return on the keyboard to, respectively: Return, Retour, Intro, Zurück, or Invio.

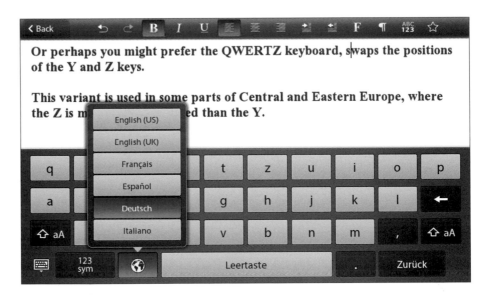

Figure 2-9: Choosing a keyboard language changes the labels of some commands; this is a separate step from choosing a different character layout.

Customizing a Configured PlayBook

Don't worry too much about decisions you make in the initial setup of your brand-spanking-new BlackBerry PlayBook. With the exception of downloading the most current OS and agreeing to the user agreement, everything else can be adjusted as you proceed to use the tablet and as your work habits change.

To adjust settings on the PlayBook, you need to display the status bar and then tap the gear symbol in the upper-right corner.

If you're not already at your home screen, you can quickly get to the status bar, which contains the gear icon, by swiping diagonally from the upper-left side of the bezel onto the screen like this or a similar swipe from the upper-right side of the bezel onto the screen.

When you tap the gear, you'll see a display of more than a dozen controls and reports generated by the tablet. I say more than a dozen because this is an area where Research in Motion is likely to add features. The original version of the BlackBerry PlayBook had 14 choices here; the cellular versions of the tablet are likely to add one or more sets of controls or reports.

The following sections go through the available information and customization screens in an order that is not the same as the one presented by RIM. Why? Because my sense of logic demands a reshuffling. I have divided the basic options into three groups: maintenance and security, operations, and communication. Let us proceed.

Maintenance and security

Here are five categories: About, Software Updates, Storage & Sharing, Security, and General.

About

This is your PlayBook's information panel. It actually has five pages; you can get to more data by tapping the ↓ down arrow.

✔ On the **General** tab, shown in Figure 2-10, you see the BlackBerry ID associated with the tablet, along with its serial number. Also listed here is the OS version installed; these three bits of information are very important for any calls for support you make to the manufacturer. You can also see the number of applications, music tracks, and videos installed in the tablet's memory.

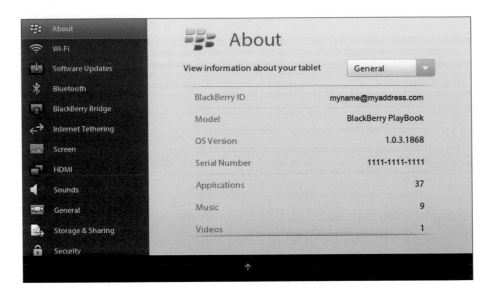

Figure 2-10: The General tab of the About panel tells you essential information about the model, OS version, and serial number, along with the ID.

✔ The **Hardware** tab has one other important bit of information: the PIN associated with your PlayBook. You may need to locate this number to register some applications and for some communications tasks. On this tab you get a report of the total amount of storage and memory in the device. You'll also see the amount of free storage and free memory.

If the level of free storage or memory is very low, the tablet is likely to slow down or even freeze. You can't increase the amount of total memory within the BlackBerry PlayBook (at least in its initial version); all models come with 1GB of RAM. Similarly, the included storage can't be expanded: you can buy models with 16, 32, or 64GB. If your tablet is slow to respond or begins to act flaky (that's a highly technical term), shut down unneeded apps to expand the amount of free memory. Similarly, clear out unneeded stored files to open up some electronic breathing room.

The last bit of information on the Hardware tab tells you the boot time, which is the last time your PlayBook was turned on. This time is different from the last time your PlayBook was brought back to life from a deep sleep. Most users don't need to turn off their tablet very often and they only reboot to install an update to the operating system or certain apps.

- ✔ The **OS** tab gives you more details on the specific build of the operating system in your tablet. Included is information about Flash player and AIR. You can't adjust any settings here, but you may be asked to consult this page if you call Research in Motion for assistance with a support issue.

- ✔ When you tap the **Network** tab you see some of the specifics of the wireless transceiver. IPv4 and the more current IPv6 are essential elements to identify your tablet to the Internet. The MAC address is used by a WiFi router to conduct local communication.

- ✔ The **Legal** tab: the lawyers made them do it. If you read this page once, that is probably one more time than most others will bother. Oh, go ahead and make a lawyer happy.

Software Updates

You will likely receive e-mail or other notifications from RIM when a major OS update is available. If you want to be proactive about it, tap the Software Updates tab and then tap Check for Updates. You'll see the tab in Figure 2-11.

You need a WiFi connection or Internet tethering to a BlackBerry smartphone in order for the PlayBook to check whether the OS is current; the process is very quick, usually reporting back in seconds. If an update needs to be installed, you get instructions. The software is first downloaded to your device and then installed; in most cases you have to allow the tablet to shut down and reboot to complete the process.

Figure 2-11: You can wait for notification of available updates, or check for them from this page from time to time.

Storage & Sharing

If you're looking for some of the reasons the BlackBerry PlayBook is attractive to corporate and enterprise IT managers — the keepers of company secrets — you'll find some of the answers here. See Figure 2-12 for the principal controls.

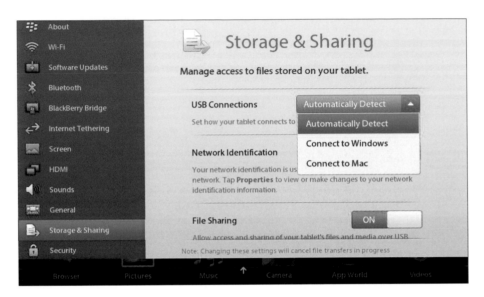

Figure 2-12: You're the master of your own data, which is one of the appeals of the professional-grade PlayBook tablet.

- ✔ **USB Connections** instructs the tablet how to react when it detects a wired connection over a USB cable. The default setting is Automatically Detect. If, however, you have both a Microsoft Windows and Apple Mac system, you can tell the PlayBook to recognize only one or the other.

- ✔ **Network Identification** allows you to personalize the tablet network name, workgroup, and username. If you don't enter identification of your own, the PlayBook will cleverly call itself PLAYBOOK-XXXX, with the last four digits coming from the PIN that's assigned at the factory.

I would only consider this a mandatory assignment if you have multiple PlayBooks on the same workgroup, in which case you would want to make sure each one had a distinct name.

✔ **File Sharing** is one of the important security features of the systems. Turned on, you are permitting access to and sharing of files and media stored in your PlayBook anytime it is connected by USB cable to your computer.

✔ **WiFi Sharing** permits movement of files over a wireless network.

✔ **Password Protect** lets you require a password before files can be moved to or from the tablet, shown in Figure 2-13. If you decide you want to change the password, there is a button for that; you have to enter the original password before you can change anything. If you forget the password, the only solution is to reset the system to factory defaults, a process I describe in Chapter 15.

Figure 2-13: Applying a password before sharing files over a WiFi link is an extra level of security that may be quite important to some corporate and individual users.

Security

Here you can make a number of decisions about security-related behavior, including security permissions (for applications) and the public and private keys for certain networks. Here you can also set a general password for your PlayBook; if you choose to do so you will need to enter the code every time you boot the tablet. In addition, you can lock the PlayBook and require a password after a specified period of inactivity. This is a great protection against the pain of leaving your PlayBook in the backseat of a taxicab.

General

Most users won't want to change the Application Behavior setting from Default; leaving it as is means an application stays active in the background until another application is maximized. However, if you're running on battery power, leaving an application running in the background can quickly run down the charge.

- ✔ **Paused.** No applications in the background will use the tablet's processor until you tap to activate them.

- ✔ **Showcase.** This makes all open applications active, whether they're in the foreground or background. That's really nifty: you could listen to music while you play a game and your browser downloads a huge file. In a perfect world, everything will work properly and there will be no slowdown of any of the applications. We generally do not live in a perfect world.

- ✔ **Demo Mode.** This runs short movies anytime the PlayBook is idle and plugged into a charger; otherwise, the demo mode would just run down the battery anytime the tablet wasn't doing something else. When it comes down to it, this feature may appeal to a retail store that wants its BlackBerry PlayBook tablets display to put on a pretty face at all times. For those of us who are already enamored, it serves no real purpose.

Should you change application behavior? It doesn't hurt to experiment with the various settings, but I suggest that you'll get more enjoyment and productivity by leaving it at its default setting.

Some software developer may ask (or require) changing Application Behavior settings to allow some nifty new program to wash the dishes and dance the mazurka at the same time. Remember that you can always change the setting back to Default if you notice lowered performance.

Operations

Here are five categories related to the way you interact with or receive information from your tablet: Keyboard, Screen, Sounds, Date & Time, and HDMI.

Keyboard

Earlier in this chapter I discuss the three types of onscreen keyboards for the BlackBerry PlayBook: QWERTY, QWERTZ, and AZERTY. In Figure 2-14 you can see the panel where you specify your choice. (For those in the United States and Canada as well as much of the rest of the world, the QWERTY keyboard is standard.)

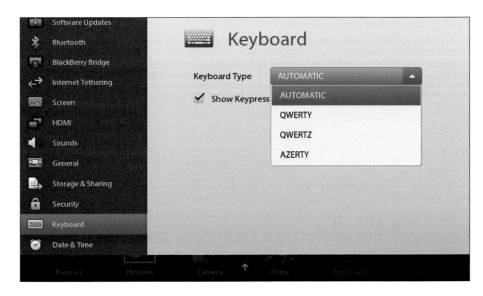

Figure 2-14: You can choose a specific character layout at the Keyboard panel and turn on or off keypress popup, which confirms your onscreen taps.

You can also turn on or off keypress popup. When this is on (the default setting) every time you tap on a character in the keyboard you are rewarded with a brief enlarged and colorful version of the character just below your fingertip. It's a good way to make sure you have hit the right character. If this bothers you, turn it off.

Screen

Here you can customize settings for the screen when it runs from the battery, as well as when it's plugged into a power source.

1. **Tap Battery.**
2. **Make adjustments.**
3. **Tap Plugged In to set your choices for that condition.**

   You can adjust the brightness of the screen using a slider. In the same panel you can also set the amount of time before the screen goes black when the system is idle (called backlight time-out), and the amount of time before the entire system goes into standby. See Figure 2-15.

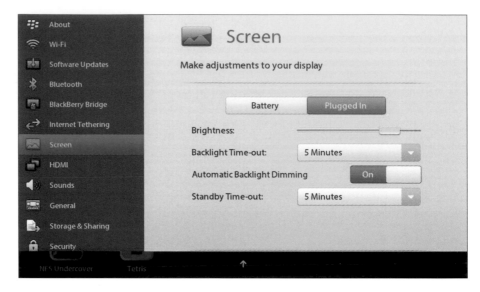

Figure 2-15: The Screen panel allows you to adjust the power usage and turn off automatic backlight dimming.

Sounds

Three sliders allow you to adjust the volume for different type of sounds:

- ✓ **Master Volume** sets an overall level.
- ✓ **Keyboard Feedback** adjusts the volume of the reassuring little clicks you hear as you use the virtual onscreen keyboard.
- ✓ **Notifications** sets the level for tones generated by messages, calendar events, and tasks.

Date & Time

If you choose your local time zone and turn on Set Date and Time Automatically, the tablet keeps things up to the moment for you. You can also choose to use 24-hour time display (2330 means 11:30 p.m.). If you turn off the automatic setting, you can manually adjust the date and time.

HDMI

The High-Definition Multimedia Interface, shown in Figure 2-16, is a digital signal that can extract a stunning wall-sized image from your little BlackBerry PlayBook. This is a truly gee-whiz feature: you can connect to an HD flatscreen television, certain computers, and some LCD projectors. The signal can also carry audio.

To use this feature, you need to buy a special cable that has a micro-HDMI connector at one end and a full-size HDMI connector at the other. You can get the cable from RIM or from most electronics stores.

Once the cable is in place, the PlayBook detects the HD device and you can choose a display mode; choose the one that looks best on the system you're using. The same goes for aspect ratio, which determines whether the image is stretched to fill the frame or adjusted with a zoom or fill; again, choose the one that looks best. One other choice, Default to Mirror Mode, determines whether the HD device shows exactly the same image as is seen on the PlayBook or whether you want to show one image on the tablet and another on the big screen. One example: displaying speaking notes on the PlayBook while using Slideshow To Go to project a PowerPoint presentation on the big screen.

The HDMI output of the BlackBerry PlayBook is truly astounding, but it isn't always perfectly compatible with every device; that's probably not the fault of RIM, because high-definition displays have gone through many changes in their relatively brief existence. Some images generated by the PlayBook may not perfectly fill an HD display, and I have also seen occasional jitteriness in the image, which may be caused by some minor incompatibility between the devices. Make sure you use a good quality HDMI cable, and keep your PlayBook updated to take advantage of adjustments.

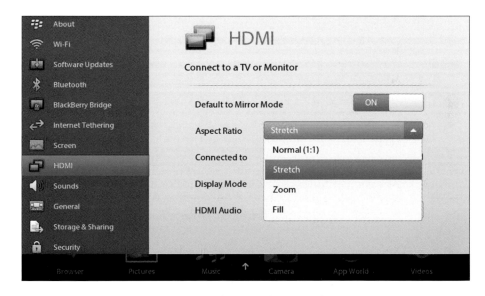

Figure 2-16: The HDMI panel includes settings to adjust that video output.

Communication

As Cool Hand Luke never said, "What we cannot have here is a failure to communicate." The BlackBerry PlayBook is all about communication; it really doesn't serve much purpose without a link of some sort.

WiFi

The basic mode of communication for the PlayBook, in many situations, is a WiFi connection to a hotspot; it may be a router in your home or office that is under your control or supervision, or it may be to a public hotspot at a hotel, airport, Internet café, or other location.

On this page, shown in Figure 2-17, you can turn off the WiFi transceiver. After that you can select a network. The pull-down menu offers choices:

- **Available Networks.** A listing of all signals the PlayBook detects.
- **Open Networks.** Unsecured networks that you can use without a password or security key.
- **Saved Networks.** Networks you've used before that you want to be able to quickly reconnect to.

Your BlackBerry PlayBook will import information about WiFi networks saved on your BlackBerry smartphone when you connect the two devices using BlackBerry Bridge. I discuss WiFi connectivity in more detail in Chapter 4.

Bluetooth

BlueTooth is a short-range data network between various electronics (for example, between your PlayBook and your smartphone, or between your PlayBook and a wireless headset or other peripheral). Bluetooth communication is essential for the BlackBerry Bridge function, a system that permits you to use your tablet to access e-mail, calendar items, and other data on your phone. I discuss Bluetooth connectivity in more detail in Chapter 4.

Believe it or not, not every technological advancement in computing and communications is Made in America. They're not even all Made in China or Taiwan. The Bluetooth wireless standard was put forth by Ericsson in Sweden as a means for devices to communicate with each other locally. A technician and amateur historian dubbed the standard in honor of Harald Bluetooth, a Scandinavian king who brought together the two warring communities of Denmark and Norway in the tenth century. Bluetooth operates in the same 2.4 GHz band used by WiFi radio but at a much lower power level.

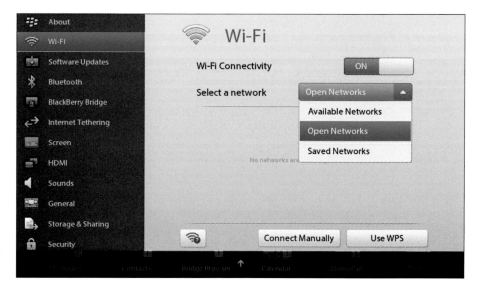

Figure 2-17: The WiFi panel allows you to turn that radio on or off (as well as automatically connect to any networks within range).

BlackBerry Bridge

The Bridge is one of the keys to using your PlayBook in conjunction with a BlackBerry smartphone. Communication takes place using BlueTooth. The control page, shown in Figure 2-18, allows you to connect quickly to a phone you've already configured, or to set up a new connection. The BlackBerry PlayBook comes with BlackBerry Bridge software as part of its operating system; you have to download and install the other half of the link on your BlackBerry smartphone. I discuss BlackBerry Bridge connectivity in more detail in Chapter 3.

Internet tethering

The basic model of the BlackBerry PlayBook also allows for an alternate means of communication with the Web. Internet tethering is a sophisticated system that uses a Bluetooth radio link to connect your PlayBook to a BlackBerry smartphone, and then to use that smartphone as your connection to Web. The control panel is shown in Figure 2-19. When you do this, you will be using the cellular data link of your phone.

Figure 2-18: The master control for BlackBerry Bridge lets you set up a link to a BlackBerry smartphone or disconnect an existing wireless connection.

Figure 2-19: Internet tethering is a direct means to use a smartphone to share a connection to the Internet.

You're prompted to select a wireless service profile to connect to the Internet using tethering. Many major cellular service providers are listed, but you can also tap Add Profile to enter connection details.

A few important words of caution here:

- ✔ The cellular data link may be considerably slower than a WiFi connection.

- ✔ Be sure you understand the costs associated with using your BlackBerry smartphone, especially if you're roaming internationally or otherwise away from your home location.

- ✔ Some cellular providers may block tethering or limit the amount of data that can be exchanged using this method.

If you intend to use Internet tethering, take the time to call your cellular provider and discuss all of the associated charges for data plans as well as any restrictions.

Cellular

Research in Motion sells a number of BlackBerry PlayBook models that add a cellular transceiver in the tablet. Cell providers usually sell these units, and usually with a data plan. Various models use 3G, 4G, and other gee-whiz technologies. As a user, you're limited to the technologies used by the cellular provider you choose. In other words, if the provider offers 4G service, the version of the PlayBook they will sell will have that facility. Cellular providers will likely add their own control or reporting panel so you can monitor your connection.

As with Internet tethering, be sure you understand the costs associated with data plans, especially if you're roaming internationally.

3

Bridging the Gap: Connecting the PlayBook to a BlackBerry Phone

In This Chapter

▶ Linking a BlackBerry PlayBook to a BlackBerry smartphone

▶ Attaching proper file types

▶ Setting up the BlackBerry Bridge

▶ Opening the Bridge for business

*D*espite the fact that a tablet with a cellular radio could make phone calls, even the svelte PlayBook is a bit oversized for the task. And although a BlackBerry Bold and BlackBerry Storm are truly impressive pieces of engineering (with reliability, connectivity, and security surpassing all of its competitors), they don't make the grade as a comfortable, satisfying way to read a page of text or view a screen of video.

What is there to do? Why, build a bridge. A BlackBerry Bridge.

The BlackBerry Bridge consists of two pieces of software — one is part of the BlackBerry PlayBook's OS and the other is a *free* app that can be installed in most current BlackBerry smartphones.

In between the smartphone and the BlackBerry PlayBook, communication takes place using short-range wireless communication: Bluetooth to be precise. And so, you can keep your BlackBerry smartphone in your pocket, in a case hooked to your belt, or in your purse and work away on your PlayBook without an intervening wire.

The bottom line? Once you have the two devices linked, or *bridged,* you will see a number of special apps appear on the BlackBerry PlayBook; think of these as electronic pipelines from the phone to the tablet. When, for example, you tap the BlackBerry Bridge version of the calendar, your PlayBook displays your datebook with information it has temporarily loaded from your phone. In Chapter 6 I explain more about how to use these apps, as well as the Bridge-less equivalent that RIM added to the BlackBerry PlayBook as a standalone suite of apps.

Not all BlackBerry smartphones are capable of running the BlackBerry Bridge app. You need a model that uses BlackBerry Device Software 5.0 or later, including operating systems 6.0 and 7.0. Phones that should work with BlackBerry Bridge include Bold, Storm, Torch, and certain models of Curve and Pearl devices. Be sure to confirm with RIM if you have any doubt about an older phone.

Buying into a Bridge

If you own both a BlackBerry PlayBook and an up-to-date BlackBerry smartphone, using the BlackBerry Bridge adds a separate level of apps: e-mail, calendar, contacts, Messenger, and more, each enhanced for display on the larger, more colorful, PlayBook touchscreen (shown in Figure 3-1). You could think of your BlackBerry PlayBook as an external monitor for your BlackBerry smartphone, also adding a touchscreen and a virtual onscreen keyboard. You can keep your BlackBerry PlayBook on your desk or in your hands, and your BlackBerry smartphone can stay in your pocket or on your belt or in your purse.

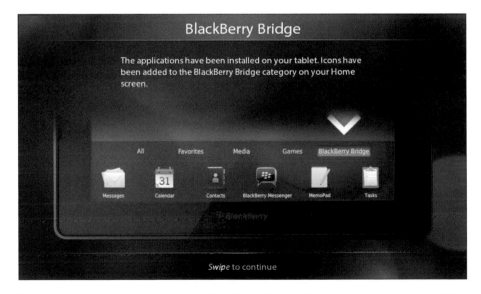

Figure 3-1: Bridge apps appear on your BlackBerry PlayBook's home page after successfully connecting to a BlackBerry smartphone.

And the BlackBerry Bridge can go one step further, setting up Internet tethering between the PlayBook and current BlackBerry smartphones and certain models of third-party smartphones with Bluetooth communication.

Why might using the Bridge be important?

- ✔ Most people keep a cellphone with them nearly all the time. The svelte BlackBerry PlayBook might not be with you at all times.

- ✔ Because the way the BlackBerry Bridge works, the data for the phone's calendar, contacts, messages, and memo pad aren't stored on the PlayBook.

- ✔ For some users the BlackBerry Bridge allows Internet access using the phone's data plan rather than a separate account — at additional cost — for the BlackBerry PlayBook. This access would be valuable when WiFi was not available.

TECHNICAL STUFF

Taking the Bridge to somewhere

An update to the BlackBerry PlayBook operating system a few months after the initial release of the tablet brought a *native* set of calendar, contact, and memo apps to the device, and the information can be synchronized with your smartphone. And a cellular-equipped version of the PlayBook was also in the pipeline to follow the original WiFi model. So why was the BlackBerry PlayBook launched with a Bridge in place? The short answer is that it was all a matter of time. RIM didn't have a secure enough version of its e-mail client, BlackBerry Instant Messenger, calendar, and other core applications when it launched the PlayBook. The other matter of time (and cost) was that the first fleet of PlayBooks out the door offered WiFi and Bluetooth wireless communication but not a cellular radio. The PlayBook was designed to run the BlackBerry Tablet OS, an operating system based on the QNX operating system; this is a different OS than the one used in BlackBerry smartphones. (QNX is a variant of Unix, a well-proven and very stable operating

system that's used in all sorts of equipment including automotive and medical products.)

Research in Motion built its reputation and much of its business success upon its dedication to the security of its e-mail and instant messaging (IM) services. BlackBerry-to-BlackBerry IMs, called PINs, travel on a separate communication system and unlike most e-mail and other messaging services, intermediate copies of the data aren't kept along the way; the only devices that hold a PIN message are in the hands of the sender and the recipient. (This design pleases legal compliance officers at corporations and even at the highest level of the federal government, where President Barack Obama became the first commander-in-chief to carry a personal smartphone: a customized BlackBerry with extra added security features.)

RIM could have come up with a less-than-optimized e-mail and calendar client for the BlackBerry PlayBook when it was released in April 2011, but doing so would have put at risk

(continued)

their claim of selling the first "professional grade tablet." In the accompanying figure you can see RIM's explanation of the process from the BlackBerry PlayBook help system. It's a bit clunky, with a few extra steps here and there, but it does work. So with the initial release of the BlackBerry PlayBook we were sold a Bridge to Somewhere: the somewhere being the internals of the already-proven BlackBerry smartphone, a device that already connects securely to RIM's servers and a device that can already be actively managed and controlled by a corporate or enterprise IT department.

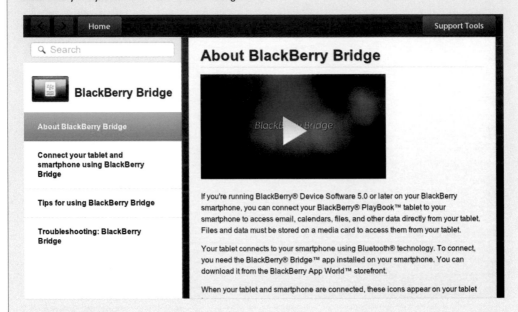

The fact that the tablet does not store the data it accesses across the BlackBerry Bridge makes the PlayBook as secure as the phone with which it communicates. And the ability of the BlackBerry PlayBook to tether to the data services of the phone it reaches on the other side of the Bridge is (for some users) the icing on the cake. Finally, even though native apps are here doesn't reduce the value of the Bridge for users who prefer to use the smartphone as their primary device and use a tablet as a peripheral.

Using the BlackBerry Bridge to gain access to a smartphone's Web connection is a form of Internet Tethering, but they are not identical services. When you link your BlackBerry PlayBook to a current model BlackBerry smartphone you will have access to something called the Bridge Browser; this is a BlackBerry-to-BlackBerry solution. If you instead use Internet Tethering, you can connect your tablet (in theory) to *any* smartphone from any maker and with any cellular provider. The devil, alas, is in the details; some cellular providers will block this sort of access or at least demand payment of extra fees. And some non-BlackBerry smartphones may not play well with the PlayBook. This is a situation where you should make use of the free (and excellent) 90-day support that comes with your BlackBerry PlayBook.

Why might using the Bridge not be important?

✏ You prefer to store your data on your BlackBerry PlayBook and your corporate IT department doesn't object (or if you're an individual user and manage your own systems and grant yourself permission to carry your data in the tablet).

✏ You buy a BlackBerry PlayBook with built-in cellular communication and pay a provider for a separate (or add-on) data plan to gain Internet access.

To use the Bridge browser within BlackBerry Bridge, the BlackBerry smartphone must be set up with Bluetooth DUN (Dial-up Networking) enabled. Some IT managers may block this feature for security reasons. And some cellular providers may block Bluetooth DUN for BlackBerry smartphones or for smartphones from other manufacturers because it doesn't fit into their definition of a data service plan; in other words, because the provider wants to sell you a different, almost certainly more costly way to access the Internet.

Linking the Tablet to the Phone

As we have already explored, Research in Motion has a business plan that emphasizes security and reliability above bells and whistles. Not that its devices don't eventually reach the point where they will ring your chimes or toot your horn: it's just that they reach that point after having built a very solid foundation.

Here was the problem (or opportunity) presented to the RIM designers:

✏ Find a way to allow the owner of a nifty new BlackBerry PlayBook tablet access to all the important information stored on their BlackBerry smartphone. This would include things like:

• **Contacts.** Names, addresses, phone numbers, and notes about people with whom you deal. You can quickly initiate an e-mail or a message based on the information you find in a contacts list.

• **Calendar.** On the BlackBerry smartphone, the calendar can exist as a standalone database or can be synchronized with a corporate calendar or the contents held in a computer-based program like Microsoft Outlook. You can look at your calendar on a daily or monthly view. For example, see Figure 3-2.

• **MemoPad.** Notes or clippings you've stored for your own purposes. I keep the current ferry schedule from the mainland to my island home and office, a hardware store shopping list, and random jottings of *bon mots,* marvelous inventions I need to produce, and encrypted records of credit card numbers in case I lose my wallet but keep my phone.

Figure 3-2: The BlackBerry smartphone calendar is displayed in its larger and easier-to-use Bridge form on a BlackBerry PlayBook.

- **Tasks.** An electronic form of a To-Do note, somewhere between a calendar item and a MemoPad jotting. You can enter a reminder on your phone, assign it to a date and time, categorize it by type, and then give it a priority. All that needs to be done . . . is to complete the task.

- **Messages.** A look-see from your PlayBook into the built-in e-mail and IM service maintained on your smartphone. Take advantage of the reading pane and larger screen to go through you stack of messages. You can reply to the sender using the larger onscreen keyboard; other features include Reply All and Forward. You can attach files from your tablet or smartphone. And you can flag a message to indicate its urgency.

- **Bridge files.** Browse and open files stored on the smartphone's media card, a plug-in block of flash memory available on most BlackBerry phone models. Later in this chapter you can see the file types that are supported for viewing using the Bridge files utility.

✓ Design the system in a way that maintains the vaunted security of the BlackBerry smartphone while exploiting the advantages of the BlackBerry PlayBook. The solution here: keep the information on the BlackBerry smartphone and avoid storing it in the BlackBerry PlayBook. When you disconnect the BlackBerry Bridge the data remains where it was — on the phone.

✔ Allow the BlackBerry PlayBook owner another way to access the Internet (by connecting to the cellular data link already in place on the BlackBerry smartphone). It's called the Bridge Browser, and it lets you use your tablet, its larger screen, and advanced Web browser on the data plan of your BlackBerry phone. See Figure 3-3 for a session on the tablet in connection to the phone.

If you're using a BlackBerry PlayBook that's managed by an IT administrator, and if that well-meaning security-obsessed manager permits it, you can use BlackBerry Bridge to connect through your BlackBerry smartphone to browse your organization's intranet.

Figure 3-3: Strictly coincidental: using the Bridge Browser to connect to the Internet through the data plan of my BlackBerry smartphone, I found a front page ad on *The New York Times* marketing the BlackBerry PlayBook.

Now this is a classic high-tech good-news, possibly bad-news case study. Let me break it down:

✔ As a BlackBerry smartphone user, you're already paying for a cellular contract for voice calls. Nothing changes here.

✔ Most BlackBerry smartphone owners pay an additional monthly fee for Web access and data services such as e-mail and instant messaging. That won't change either.

✔ Here comes the possibly less-than-good news. In theory, if you have one of the original model BlackBerry PlayBook tablets, you can use BlackBerry Bridge to connect to your BlackBerry smartphone and use the phone's cellular data connection to surf, check e-mail, and do all the wonderful things we all do in our modern electronic lives. And the beautiful thing, at least for the moment: you'd be using your existing smartphone data plan and pay nothing extra for using the PlayBook over the cellular connection.

So what is the possible bad news? Some cellular providers may choose to limit or disable the use of the cellular data link in the phone across BlackBerry Bridge. Or they may charge an additional fee. But back to the good news: if you stay on the WiFi link (*not* the Bluetooth-powered BlackBerry Bridge) you should be able to find free or low-cost connections to the Internet that don't involve the sometimes-greedy fingers of cellular providers.

Setting Up BlackBerry Bridge

To build a bridge between a BlackBerry PlayBook and a BlackBerry smartphone you need the BlackBerry Bridge software on both devices, a Bluetooth wireless connection running on both devices, and just a small amount of time to set up and manage the connection.

The PlayBook comes with the BlackBerry Bridge functionality built into its operating system. You must add an app (supplied free by RIM) to current model BlackBerry smartphones; you can get it from the BlackBerry App Store. (*Note:* It wouldn't be an unreasonable expectation to see BlackBerry Bridge made part of the standard offerings included on BlackBerry smartphones released in coming years.)

Adding Bridge on a BlackBerry phone

There are two ways to add BlackBerry Bridge to a BlackBerry smartphone; neither requires heavy lifting and both are free. And there are two times when it can be done: during the initial configuration of your BlackBerry PlayBook or after it is up and running. In Figure 3-4, I show part of the process for installing the utility during initial setup of the device.

The process is similar in either situation, with slightly different onscreen guidance. My recommendation: skip the BlackBerry Bridge configuration when you first set up your tablet and come back to it later once the BlackBerry PlayBook is up and running. It's just a little bit simpler to do it on an already-configured tablet.

Figure 3-4: When you first turn on the power to a new BlackBerry PlayBook you will be offered the chance to configure Bridge on a BlackBerry smartphone; you can do it at that time or later once you have the tablet up and running.

Scanning for a Bridge

If you have a current BlackBerry smartphone that includes a camera, you can add the app with help from the BlackBerry PlayBook tablet. I'll call that process Scanning for a Bridge. Do the following:

1. **From the PlayBook's home screen tap the gear icon to display the panel of controls.**

2. **Tap BlackBerry Bridge.**

3. **Give your PlayBook a name.**

   Don't call it PlayBook, because sooner or later you're going to be in a room with more than one BlackBerry tablet. I call mine "Corey Sandler PlayBook#1" which leaves room for additions to the fleet.

4. **Tap Install Now.**

   A copy of the BlackBerry Bridge app to your BlackBerry smartphone starts downloading. See Figure 3-5 for the onscreen instructions.

5. **Put down your PlayBook and pick up your BlackBerry smartphone.**

Figure 3-5: On a current BlackBerry smartphone with a camera, you can scan the barcode displayed on the screen of the BlackBerry PlayBook to initiate download of the Bridge software.

6. **Go to the BlackBerry App World icon on the phone and connect to RIM's store.**

   You need a data plan with your cellular provider in order to connect your BlackBerry smartphone to BlackBerry App World for downloading. Make sure you understand data charges associated with that plan and be aware that costs can be very high if you're roaming away from your provider — especially if you're in a foreign country.

7. **With the BlackBerry App World open on your phone, press the menu key and click Scan a Barcode.**

   The built-in camera comes to life.

8. **Point the camera lens (on the side away from the keypad) at the barcode that appears on the PlayBook's screen.**

   Hold the phone a few inches away and keep it steady for a couple seconds to allow the phone to autofocus on the barcode and recognize it. In Figure 3-6, you can see the author's very own hands holding his very own BlackBerry smartphone, preparing for a scanning operation.

The phone will now understand that you want to download BlackBerry Bridge and do so, as seen in Figure 3-7.

Figure 3-6: A current BlackBerry smartphone can use its built-in camera to scan a barcode.

Applying for a Bridge permit

You can add BlackBerry Bridge to your smartphone another way: do it yourself, without using the phone camera as a scanner. I call this method Applying for a Bridge Permit. It's not quite as nifty, but it works:

1. **Go to BlackBerry App World on your BlackBerry smartphone.**
2. **Search for** BlackBerry Bridge.
3. **Download BlackBerry Bridge to your phone.**

Figure 3-7: Over the airwaves, the BlackBerry Bridge app arrives for installation within my BlackBerry Bold 9700 smartphone.

Opening the Bridge

After BlackBerry Bridge is installed on your phone, you can open a link between the two devices. The simplest way to begin is this way:

1. **Go the home screen and click the Manage Connections icon.**

   The icon looks like a small radio antenna.

2. **Click in the Bluetooth check box.**

   That turns on that form of radio communication.

3. **Make sure your BlackBerry is set to be Discoverable by other devices.**

4. **Turn on Bluetooth connectivity on the BlackBerry PlayBook.**

5. **Make Bluetooth discoverable.**

   See Figure 3-8.

Figure 3-8: Bluetooth communication is essential to link a BlackBerry PlayBook to a BlackBerry smartphone across the Bridge. Both devices must be discoverable.

6. **Now go to the BlackBerry PlayBook and click the gear icon.**

   The controls appear.

7. **Tap BlackBerry Bridge.**

8. **Follow the instructions to pair your tablet to your phone.**

   See Figure 3-9 for a successful electronic marriage. Once the process has been successfully accomplished, future attempts at connection should be quick and seamless.

   One fast shortcut to a BlackBerry connection is to tap one of the BlackBerry Bridge app icons on the tablet's home page: Bridge Browser, Calendar, MemoPad, Tasks, or Bridge Files.

   If a link doesn't exist, the PlayBook will tell you what needs to be done. The connection can be done with a manual pairing or, once again, you can ask the tablet to display a barcode for you to scan with your phone.

9. **Acknowledge a message displayed on your tablet or phone that asks you to permit the other device to open the Bridge.**

   • The **automated process** displays a numerical code on each device; see Figure 3-10 for an example. You need to verify that the same code appears on each.

Figure 3-9: When your BlackBerry PlayBook has successfully paired to a BlackBerry smartphone, the device name and arrows appear in the control panel.

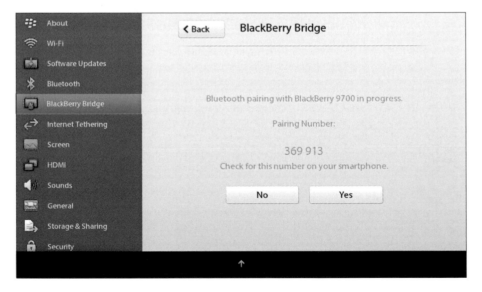

Figure 3-10: In automatic pairing, numbers appear on the tablet and smartphone.

● If you chose a **manual process** (which walks you through the steps on each device), the final approval comes when the BlackBerry PlayBook displays a setup code that you must enter into a corresponding permission panel on your smartphone; see Figure 3-11.

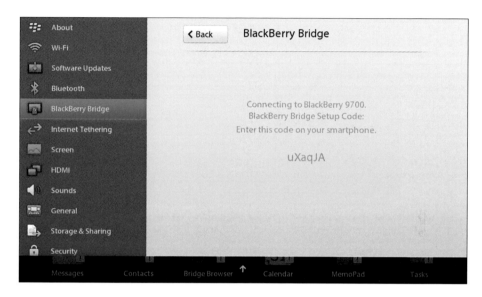

Figure 3-11: In a manual pairing process, the BlackBerry PlayBook generates characters that you will have to enter (including capping) on the smartphone.

Either way — automatic or manual — these protections guard against an attempt by an outsider to hack into your BlackBerry fortress. After two devices have been granted permission to interact with each other, you don't have to go through the verification process; instead, they recognize each other anytime they're both powered on and within communication range.

When all is ready to go, you see a report of successful pairing. One version of the message is shown in Figure 3-12, part of the initial setup. If the devices have been previously paired, a notification appears on each device when they're electronically reacquainted.

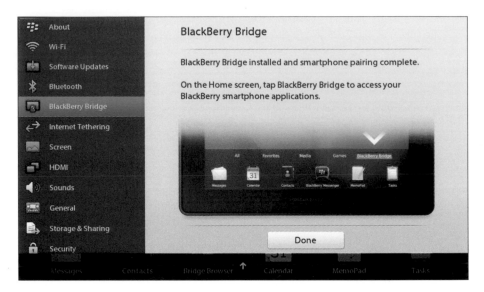

Figure 3-12: Success! The devices are paired, and you can get to the BlackBerry Bridge apps from the BlackBerry PlayBook's home page.

In my experience using BlackBerry Bridge in the early days and weeks after the release of the BlackBerry PlayBook, the system occasionally seemed to lose its mind and I had to uninstall the Bridge app from my smartphone, remove recognition of the phone from the PlayBook, and repeat the process. This may have been caused by the flurry of OS updates that were pushed out when the tablet was first released to the public. In theory, the Blackberry Bridge will work with a BlackBerry smartphone running OS 5 or later; I can attest to the fact that my personal BlackBerry Bold 9700 was able to cross the Bridge using that operating system; I can also tell you that it was more reliable and perhaps a bit quicker after I upgraded the phone to OS 6. Consult your cellular provider for help getting and installing updates to your phone.

Advanced training for Bridge users

Anyone who has used a BlackBerry smartphone will be quickly at ease when working on a BlackBerry PlayBook linked by the Bridge. All of the basic functions — the calendar, contact book, e-mail, MemoPad, and tasks — are there. The difference is that they show up on a much larger screen in a much more usable design.

Among the biggest beneficiaries of the Bridge is the calendar, which you can now easily use in monthly view — something that was tough on the small screen of a BlackBerry smartphone. And the Bridge Browser substitutes the advanced BlackBerry PlayBook browser for the somewhat hobbled BlackBerry smartphones.

Here are some advanced tips for using BlackBerry Bridge.

Locking the Bridge

You can lock the Bridge to prevent unauthorized access to the data on your phone, which isn't a bad idea for anyone — and especially if you store sensitive information. Remember that the information stays on the phone but doesn't move over to the PlayBook in ordinary use; the password actually locks access to the phone.

The lock will use whatever password has been put in place on the phone; if you haven't established one and you want to lock the phone, you have to close the Bridge and add a password on the smartphone. To enable the lock, follow these steps:

1. **Connect the PlayBook to the smartphone by BlackBerry Bridge.**

2. **Go to the tablet's home screen and tap the Bridge icon.**

   It shows you the connection status and the name of the phone to which the tablet is linked.

3. **Tap the Lock button to lock the link.**

   Tap Unlock to remove the need for a passcode.

Sorting the mail

The PlayBook's mail app lets you sort mail according to which incoming address was used. (BlackBerry smartphone users are allowed to link to as many as ten accounts using the BIS service; if your phone is managed by a corporate IT department under BlackBerry Enterprise Services there may be other rules in effect, allowing more or less incoming accounts.)

At the top of the message inbox, depending on the current view, tap either

- All Messages
- The name of the currently displayed address; choose the one you want to see

Viewing mail by folders

To view a specific folder of your mail, follow these steps:

1. **Tap the down arrow at the top of the message pane.**

2. **Choose View Folders.**

   You see all registered e-mail accounts and the subfolders within.

3. **Choose one to view.**

   To return to the general display, tap the down arrow again, and choose All Messages.

Moving mail to a folder

You can move a message from its existing folder to another that already exists on the account by tapping the mail folder icon at the bottom of the screen; it sits just to the left of the red flag icon.

Attaching the Proper File Types

Security! The designers of the BlackBerry PlayBook must have that stenciled on the front of their computer screens, which is actually a pretty good watchword in these sometimes threatening times. Many of the decisions they made about the type of file that can be attached, transferred, or stored on the BlackBerry PlayBook are related to finding the most secure way to protect business or personal information. (This is very much unlike the thought process of some other computer companies that seem to view all decisions through a marketing lens: what will earn the most profit?)

Corporate Bridge tenders

Enterprise IT departments that actively manage their BlackBerry smartphone or BlackBerry PlayBook devices may set rules that exclude certain types of files. If a company or institution uses the BlackBerry Enterprise Server, the BlackBerry Bridge won't allow attachments to be saved to the BlackBerry PlayBook's internal memory. Instead, you can save the attachment only to the Micro SD card of the BlackBerry smartphone. BlackBerry Bridge doesn't allow you to send attachments via e-mail or BlackBerry Messenger. However, the BlackBerry PlayBook tablet is subject to the same IT policy restrictions as the BlackBerry smartphone that is active on the BlackBerry Enterprise Server.

On the BlackBerry PlayBook, the following types of files are supported for viewing using the Bridge files utility:

- ✔ PDF files, for display using Adobe Reader
- ✔ DOC or DOCX text files for use with Word To Go
- ✔ XLS or XLSX spreadsheet files for use with Sheet To Go
- ✔ PPT PowerPoint files for use with Slideshow To Go

In ordinary use of the BlackBerry PlayBook, these types of files — from specific locations — can be opened and used:

- ✔ PDF files stored to the internal memory of the tablet or sent as attachments to e-mail
- ✔ XLS, XLSX, DOC, DOCX, or PPT files sent as an e-mail attachment or saved to the internal memory of the tablet
- ✔ Pictures, videos, and music files

Communicating sans Wires: WiFi, Bluetooth, and Cell

In This Chapter

▶ Why WiFi?

▶ Knowing Bluetooth's beauty

▶ Hearing me out on cellular links

*B*ack at the dawn of the age of the personal computer there were lots of jokes about how we were still decades behind the old cartoon detective Dick Tracy. As long ago as 1946, Tracy used to walk around town with a 2-Way Wrist Radio that kept him in constant communication. By the time Tracy arrived on television in 1964, it was a 2-Way Wrist TV. We didn't know it then — and I'll be darned if I can figure out how he managed it — but he had a smartphone (or a tiny BlackBerry PlayBook).

Here are the ways a BlackBerry smartphone or a BlackBerry PlayBook can communicate:

Wi-Fi

Wi-Fi Connectivity

Select a network

Hudson
Saved Network

✔ **WiFi.** Using an open or secured wireless link in a home, office, or other location using a device called a *router* that connects to a computer or directly to the Internet. WiFi typically works up to a few hundred feet.

✔ **Bluetooth.** A low-power version of WiFi that directly links devices. For example, the BlackBerry PlayBook and most BlackBerry smartphone models can speak to each other across a room. When a PlayBook uses Bluetooth to work with a smartphone, it can use that device as its entrance ramp onto the global information highway.

✔ **Cellular connection.** As this book goes to press, the first cellular-capable versions of the BlackBerry PlayBook were arriving.

✔ **USB cable.** A Micro-USB cable (from the PlayBook or a BlackBerry smartphone) can connect to a computer for directly transferring files, data, and setting. That same cable can also be used to go through the computer and out onto a network or the Internet.

In this chapter you explore all three available forms of wireless communication. Chapter 2 explores the USB connection using BlackBerry Desktop Manager.

Connecting Your PlayBook to WiFi

Using WiFi on your PlayBook begins with setting up the tablet, which I discuss in Chapters 1 and 2. With the PlayBook configured to work with WiFi, turn on the PlayBook's WiFi transceiver. You have two ways to do that.

Here's one way to do this:

1. **Go to the home screen and tap the Gear button.**

   The list of options appears.

2. **Tap WiFi.**

   You see the screen shown in Figure 4-1.

3. **Next to WiFi Connectivity, make sure the word On appears.**

   If not, touch the switch and slide it to the left.

4. **For Select a Network, choose one of these options:**

   • **Available Networks** to see a list of all possible connections.

   • **Open Networks** to see only those that do not require a security code or other sign-in.

   • **Saved Networks** to go to a list of networks you have previously configured.

5. **If more than one network is listed on the page, choose one to work with.**

   In general, choose the one that you know to be secure and that has the strongest signal, indicated by the most number of green bars.

Turn up your radio

Consider the most important distinction between WiFi and cellular communication: WiFi is basically a form of point-to-point radio communication. Your BlackBerry PlayBook (or other device) picks up a radio signal and establishes an electronic account that allows bidirectional communication within the umbrella of the WiFi signal. The closer you are to the transmitter/receiver, the stronger the signal is likely to be and as you move away from that source the signal grows weaker until it eventually cannot be used any more. Put another way, when you move outside the range of a WiFi site you must re-establish a new connection with a new transmitter and receiver. By contrast, a cellular system is designed specifically to work with moving objects. The best example is chatting (as a passenger, please) in a moving car on a superhighway.

Figure 4-1: The WiFi control panel shows the radio is on, a good signal is found (two out of four bars), and allows you to select a network.

Here's the other way. If the system is already configured to search for networks, follow these steps:

1. **Go to the home screen and tap the WiFi icon.**

   The icon is in the status bar at the top.

2. **Next to WiFi Connectivity, make sure the word On appears.**

   If not, touch the switch and slide it to the left.

3. **If more than one network is listed, choose one to work with.**

   In general, choose the one that you know to be secure and that has the strongest signal, indicated by the most number of green bars.

4. **Proceed based on the type of access granted:**

   - **Open Network.** Connect and proceed to use the WiFi.

   - **Secured WiFi.** Type in the network password and tap Connect. Some systems may also require a username.

   - **WiFi Protected Setup (WPS).** This requires physical access to the router hardware with these steps:

   1. Choose Use WPS.

   2. On the router, press the WPS button.

   3. On your PlayBook, tap Start to initiate communication; the process is shown in Figure 4-2.

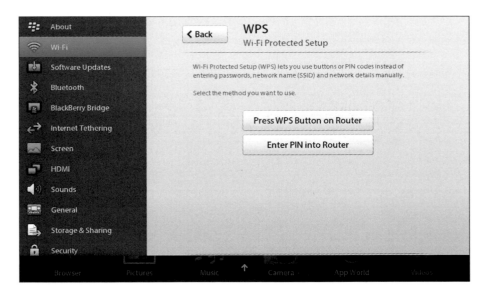

Figure 4-2: The WiFi Protected Setup works with certain types of routers that have built-in self-identification processes.

- **WiFi Protected Setup PIN Code.**

1. Choose Use WPS.

2. On the administration screen for the WiFi router, type in the PIN that is displayed.

- **Manual Connection.**

1. Choose Connect Manually.

2. Type in the name of the network.

3. If the network is hidden, select Hidden SSID.

4. Choose the security type and specify any additional information.

5. Tap Connect or tap Save (to save without connecting); See Figure 4-3.

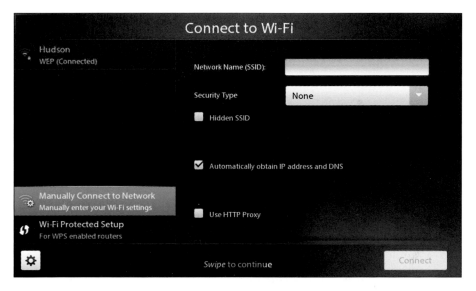

Figure 4-3: This screen shows manual configuration from the initial BlackBerry PlayBook setup.

Advanced options for secure networks

Remember: the BlackBerry PlayBook may look like an ordinary consumer grade tablet, but it has a wide range of professional-grade security features. The idea is that you can have the convenience of your BlackBerry but the security of a government spy agency or a bank. I'm speaking, of course, of the agencies and the banks that have their acts together, not the ones that end up in the headlines for losing laptops with the personal information of tens of thousands of clients.

Various secure networks have different security requirements. Consult the owner of the network or a system administrator for assistance if necessary. Shown in Figure 4-4 are some of the common bits of information you may need in order to manually configure a network that isn't fully open, as shown in the control panel of the WiFi network, reachable from the home screen:

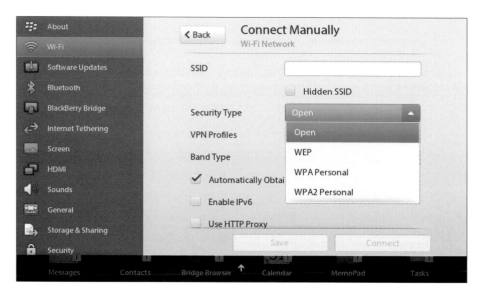

Figure 4-4: If you need to manually configure a WiFi connection, the process can involve several pages of choices and details.

- ✔ **Network Name.** Enter the name that you want to see in your list of saved WiFi networks.

- ✔ **SSID (Service Set Identifier).** If the WiFi network is hidden, type the SSID (the name the network uses to identify itself). On the PlayBook, select the Hidden SSID check box; the PlayBook will look for a network using that name.

- ✔ **Security Type.** Set the security type that the WiFi network uses. The basic options are Open, WEP, WPA Personal, WPA2 Personal, WPA Enterprise, or WPA2 Enterprise.

- ✔ **Security Subtype.** Enterprise versions of secure WiFi systems often use a secondary security form. You don't get to choose the one that sounds most interesting; you have to use the one specified by the network administrator.

✒ **Username and Password.** If required by the administrator, you will need to enter this information.

✒ **VPN Profiles.** If required, choose the VPN (Virtual Private Network) profile for the network. Get this information from the network administrator.

✒ **CA Certificate.** If necessary, set the root certificate that your tablet should use to verify that it's connecting to the correct WiFi network. If the network requires a certificate, you need to transfer it to your tablet before you can connect. Certificate authority information is generally provided to BlackBerry users in a secure corporate environment; this information is supplied by a system administrator.

✒ **Enable IPv6.** Decide whether the network uses the advanced IPv6 protocol; this information would be supplied by an administrator.

✒ **Automatically Obtain IP Address.** When the box is checked — the default — you don't need to enter an Internet protocol address to identify your tablet; that would be taken care of automatically by the operating system. If your system administrator sets up your system differently, clear this check box if you need to manually specify an IP address for your tablet, and enter the information provided by the manager of your corporate or enterprise system.

✒ **Use HTTP Proxy.** Tap and enable this check box if you want to connect to a proxy server, a function that a system administrator might put in place; you will be instructed which options to use.

✒ **Allow Inter-Access Point Handover.** If the network spans multiple access points, this box allows you to instruct your tablet whether it should remain connected when you move from one access point to another.

Changing or reordering saved networks

Once you've connected to a network, the PlayBook makes it easy to reconnect when you're in the same electronic neighborhood. If more than one of the saved networks is within reach, the PlayBook will choose the one closest to the top of the list.

You can reorder the list or delete networks. To do so, tap the gear icon and then choose WiFi. In the drop-down list, tap Saved Networks.

To change options for a saved network, tap the network. Then do any of the following actions:

Move a saved network up or down in the list

Follow these steps:

1. **Turn off WiFi connectivity.**

2. **Tap Saved Networks.**

3. **Touch and hold the network and drag it where you want it.**

Delete a saved network

Follow these steps:

1. **Turn off the WiFi connectivity.**

2. **Tap Saved Networks.**

3. **Tap the pencil icon.**

4. **Tap the trashcan icon that's beside the network you want to delete.**

Stop the PlayBook from automatically connecting to a saved network

Follow these steps:

1. **Tap the name of a saved network.**

2. **Clear the Enable Profile check box.**

3. **Tap Save.**

File sharing using WiFi

You can share files back and forth between your BlackBerry PlayBook and a WiFi equipped personal or laptop computer. It's not one of my favorite ways of using the PlayBook; in fact, although it can be made to work, it is a rather complex process, (This may be an area where RIM will make improvements to the operating system.)

Very few desktop machines have WiFi transceivers; on the other hand, nearly all current laptop computers have them.

Here's how to share files by WiFi:

1. **From the BlackBerry PlayBook home screen, tap the gear icon.**

2. **Tap the Storage & Sharing panel.**

3. **Press and hold on the screen; then move it up so that WiFi Sharing appears; see Figure 4-5.**

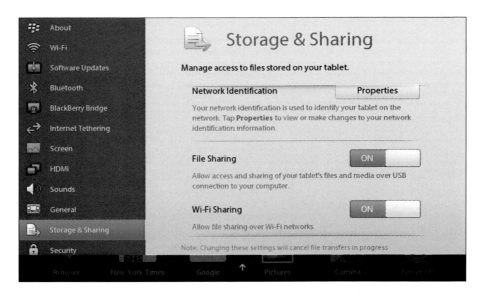

Figure 4-5: You can turn on or off WiFi sharing from the Storage & Sharing panel.

4. **Make sure the WiFi Sharing toggle is On.**

   If not, touch and hold the switch and slide it to the right so that the On indicator is blue.

5. **Tap the About panel on the left side of the screen.**

6. **Tap the View Information arrow and select Network.**

7. **From the Network screen, determine the wireless IP address (IPv4) for your PlayBook.**

   The screen is shown in Figure 4-6.

8. **Switch over to your WiFi–equipped laptop or other device, and go to the IP address of the PlayBook.**

9. **On a Windows computer, open the Run dialog box.**

10. **Enter** *xxx.xxx.x.x.*

    Replace *x* with the actual IP address of the BlackBerry PlayBook you got from the Network screen. And don't include that last period.

    On a Mac computer, select Go⟿Connect to Server and enter **smb:// xxx.xxx.x.x.** Replace *x* with the actual IP address of the BlackBerry PlayBook.

If you've done it right, you're connected to the Media folder on the BlackBerry PlayBook, which contains subfolders for documents, music, photos, videos, books, and more. You can then move files between the computer and the folders.

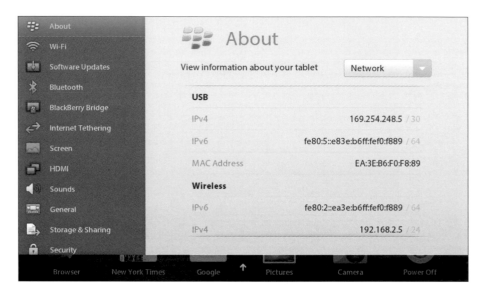

Figure 4-6: The wireless IP address is necessary to enable WiFi file sharing to a laptop or other device.

If you have problems setting up this WiFi connection, I have two suggestions:

- ✔ Call BlackBerry PlayBook support during your 90 days of free assistance and ask them to help.
- ✔ Rely on the USB cable for transfer of files. It is quicker, easily set up, and reliable.

Communicating until You're Blue in the Tooth

Once you give permission for a particular pairing between devices, your PlayBook tracks that agreement and, usually, automatically connect to that device anytime it is within range.

Automatic reconnection of devices that have previously paired in a Bluetooth link will only happen if the Bluetooth radio is on in both pieces of equipment and no changes have been made to the settings. For example, both devices have to be set as discoverable.

Managing a Bluetooth session

To initiate a Bluetooth communication session, follow along:

1. **Go to the PlayBook home screen.**

2. **Tap the gear icon.**

3. **Tap the Bluetooth control.**

   The control is along the left side of the screen, as shown in Figure 4-7.

4. **Choose settings:**

   • **Bluetooth Connectivity.** Move the slider to the right to turn on the Bluetooth radio.

Figure 4-7: The Bluetooth control panel shows whether wireless radio is on and whether your device is discoverable.

• **Discoverable.** When you first pair up two devices, they each must be listed as *discoverable.* (Think of this as wearing a sign to a high school mixer reading, "I'm available." It would have made things so much less awkward in life, but I digress.) You can set Discoverable to On, Off, or On for 2 minutes (which is a form of speed dating: your device can be seen but only for enough time to quickly make an assignation).

• **Paired Devices.** Once a pairing has been made, that device name is listed on the PlayBook screen. If the connection is currently active, a green two-way arrow appears alongside the device.

• **Delete a Saved Device.** When a device has been saved, the pen-like edit button appears at the right side of the Paired Devices line. Turn the Bluetooth Connectivity slider off, and then on, and then tap the pen icon; the trashcan icon appears alongside saved devices. Tap the trashcan to delete a saved device.

• **Add New Device.** Tap the button that offers to add a device, and then choose either Search (actively look for other devices to which it might connect) or Listen (send out a Bluetooth "Hello").

• **Device Properties.** You can learn a bit about the properties of a paired device, including its assigned name and its electronic address, by tapping the Properties button. An example is shown in Figure 4-8.

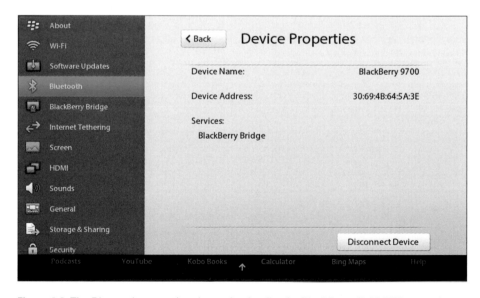

Figure 4-8: The Bluetooth properties shows the details of a BlackBerry Bold 9700 smartphone communicating with my PlayBook through the BlackBerry Bridge.

Supported Bluetooth profiles

The BlackBerry PlayBook works with most of the common profiles employed by Bluetooth devices. To find out if your tablet supports a specific Bluetooth enabled device, find out what profiles it uses. The PlayBook, as initially delivered by RIM, supports the following profiles:

- **Dial-up Networking (DUN).** This profile allows you to tether your PlayBook to a cellphone (any current model BlackBerry as well as many other smartphones or other Internet-connected devices) to link to the Internet. The beauty here: you don't need a separate data plan for your BlackBerry PlayBook. But all is not perfect in this world of ours: some providers block tethering or limit the amount of data.

- **Human Interface Device (HID).** The PlayBook uses this profile to connect to a wireless keyboard or similar device. Some headsets may also use HID.

- **Serial Port Profile (SPP).** The PlayBook uses SSP to connect to a BlackBerry smartphone through the BlackBerry Bridge application.

The Bluetooth process generally works quite seamlessly; the most common problem is a device not set as Discoverable for the initial pairing.

You may need to take some special steps:

- **Enter a passkey pairing number.** Some connections may generate a passcode and display it locally. For example, a BlackBerry smartphone may show a code on its screen; move over to your PlayBook and enter the code in the screen shown there. In certain arrangements, the other device may have a set code not displayed onscreen. You may need to consult that device's manual or a system administrator. If you don't know the code, try this super-secret, impossible-to-guess code: 0000. It just may work.

- **Reconnect to a paired device.** In the list of paired devices, tap the name of the device and then tap Connect.

- **Change options for a paired device.** In the list of paired devices, tap the name of the device and make adjustments as available.

- **Delete a paired device.** In the list of paired devices, tap the name of the device and then tap Delete.

- **Make your tablet discoverable.** To allow other Bluetooth-enabled devices to search for and attempt to connect to your tablet, set Discoverable to On.

- **Limit the chances of an unwanted attempt at access.** Set the Discoverable switch to 2 Minutes Only. Tap Add New Device and then tap Listen.

Linking Up Via Cell

The advantage of a cellular radio is that signals can be found just about anywhere; the disadvantage is that you will need a contract with a provider, which means additional cost.

As this book goes to press, RIM has announced its intention to sell the PlayBook through cellular providers. It will customize the tablet to offer 3G, the faster 4G specification, and perhaps other forms of cellular communication. The cellular version of the PlayBook will likely include all (or nearly) the features of the WiFi device (including Bluetooth for local communication).

The presence of a direct link to the Internet through a cellular data connection will make Internet tethering less useful on those models; in fact, cell providers may disable that function in the devices they sell, preferring that users pay for a cellular plan or add-on feature for the PlayBook rather than piggybacking on a data plan for a BlackBerry smartphone.

Phoning Home with Comwave's App

One of the first significant communications tools offered by a third-party company for the BlackBerry PlayBook extends the intriguing world of Voice Over Internet (VOIP) to the tablet.

Comwave's ePhone app, available through BlackBerry App World, lets you make and receive calls through the PlayBook from nearly anywhere in the world; all you need is a WiFi signal. If this sounds like the highly successful Skype utility, that's because it's similar.

Comwave's ePhone connects to about 60 countries around the world; see Figure 4-9. You can get a virtual phone number in Canada, the United States, and a number of other countries for your device, making it inexpensive or free for people to call you — if your PlayBook is connected to a WiFi signal. It also allows video chats between the PlayBook and another tablet or computer with a camera.

VOIP has been around for a while; I've used it in my office for more than a decade. The technology takes voice (and sometimes video and texting) and sends it as a digital signal across the Internet; at the receiving end it can be heard or seen without further conversion on a computer or other digital device or it's converted into an analog signal that can be used with a standard telephone.

Figure 4-9: Comwave's ePhone, offered at BlackBerry App World, allows phone calls to and from about 60 countries.

On the plus side:

- ✔ VOIP is almost always significantly less expensive than a traditional phone call and certainly less costly than using a cell phone to call from out of your home area. In some plans, communication between clients of the same VOIP provider are free or deeply discounted.

- ✔ Some services allow you to send video as well as text messages using the same connection.

On the not-so-plus side:

- ✔ Voice communication can sometimes be tinny or scratchy, and often lags between your words into the PlayBook (or other device) and their arrival in a receiver somewhere else in the world.

- ✔ You're dependent upon a reliable WiFi signal to call.

- ✔ As this book goes to press, RIM hasn't fully enabled the PlayBook to accept a plug-in or Bluetooth microphone, so you must use the PlayBook's built-in microphone. You can hear the other party through the speakers or through earphones plugged into the PlayBook.

Part II
Inspecting Apps and Programs

The 5th Wave   By Rich Tennant

"I can be reached at home on my cell phone, I can be reached on the road with my pager and PDA. Soon I'll be reachable on a plane with email. I'm beginning to think identity theft wouldn't be such a bad idea for a while."

In this part . . .

The BlackBerry PlayBook has amazing capabilities on the Internet. Chapter 5 explores Web surfing using the full-featured browser, and Chapter 6 shows you how to keep in touch wherever you are with e-mail and instant messaging and explains how the BlackBerry Desktop Manager can sync you right up to your personal or laptop computer. Chapter 7 helps you create or edit word processing or spreadsheet files and present PowerPoint shows from the tiny machine that is the BlackBerry PlayBook. Chapter 8 moves to the suite of built-in utilities that are ready, willing, and able to pitch in at the swipe of a finger. Go shopping in Chapter 9 to browse the shelves of BlackBerry App World.

Surfing the Web

*T*he Web browser that is part of the operating system of the BlackBerry PlayBook was, as the British like to say, purpose-built. It was not adapted from a version made for a large-screen computer or for a tiny-screen smartphone. This version feels and works very much like the browsers you're already familiar with: Internet Explorer, Firefox, and Chrome, for example. And unlike some other browsers, including the one trumpeted by Apple, it supports most of the bells and whistles we have come to expect, if not love, on the Web. In a word, it supports the flashy Adobe Flash standard, which brings animation, bidirectional streaming of audio and video, and other features.

In the original version of the operating system, the BlackBerry PlayBook included full support for Adobe Flash 10.1 as well as the advanced HTML 5 Web programming language. The OS is likely to be upgraded over time to keep pace with future improvements to those standards and others.

Exploring the Wowser of a Browser

Figure 5-1 offers a view of a web page in landscape mode. Only about 15 percent of the screen displays the address bar and a simple set of browsing tools, and if you don't want to give even that much, tap the screen. You can also rotate your BlackBerry PlayBook 90 degrees and look at a web page in portrait mode, as seen in Figure 5-2.

Previous page

Next page   Address bar   Reload or cancel   Add to bookmarks

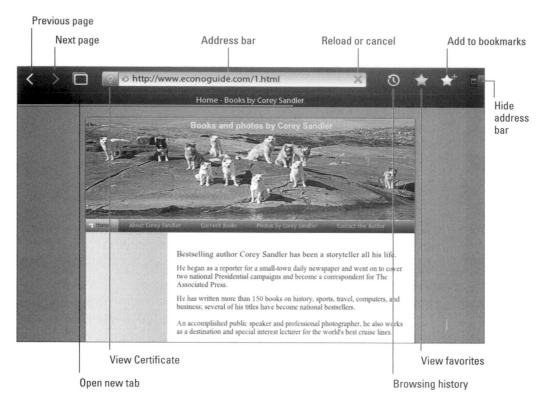

Hide
address
bar

View Certificate   View favorites

Open new tab   Browsing history

Figure 5-1: In landscape mode, you generally see the entire width, but have to scroll down to see the bottom.

Here are the elements of the screen, starting in the upper-left corner.

✔ **Previous page.**

✔ **Next page.** If you've backtracked a bit in your recent browsing, you can go through subsequent pages by tapping here.

✔ **Open a new tab.** Just as you'd expect from a full-featured browser, you can have open several web pages at a time. If you open multiple tabs, your browser and the PlayBook may slow down if one or more of the pages has active content (such as video).

    • **Open a tab:** Click the icon, and then tap the New Tab command in the status bar. Once you have multiple tabs in use, the tabs icon shows the number open.

    • **Switch between tabs:** Swipe down from the top frame to show the thumbnails. Tap the thumbnail you want to view.

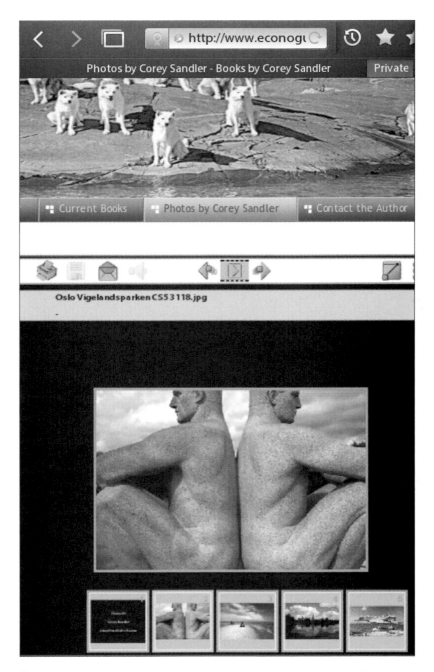

Figure 5-2: Portrait mode shows more vertical elements but may crop width.

✔ **View certificate.** If you're visiting an encrypted page, tapping here lets you look at the security certificate (one way to assure that you've reached the actual page you desire and that the communication is secure).

✔ **Address bar.** Here is the address for the web page you're visiting.

- To enter a new address, tap in the bar to bring up the virtual onscreen keyboard.

- To go to a web page, enter its address and then tap Go.

- To search for a web page, type in what you're looking for and tap Go.

The onscreen keyboard has a .com key, but if the address you want has a different suffix, press and hold down the .com key. You can then choose from .net, .org, .edu, .gov, .ca, or .biz. Also, the default search engine is Microsoft's Bing. You can change your preference by going to the General screen of Options and choosing one of the offerings.

✔ **Loopy arrow or X.** Tap Reload or Cancel.

✔ **Browsing history.** The tablet keeps track of the pages you've visited recently, *unless you have enabled private browsing,* which helps protect your privacy. Chapter 13 tells how to enable private browsing.

✔ **View favorites.** Tap here to display small versions of the web pages you have chosen to save as favorites.

✔ **Add to bookmarks.** Tap here to add the currently displayed page to your favorites, or to add the current web page as an icon on your PlayBook's home screen. This means you don't have to wait for the browser to load before you pick from the bookmarks. A page of bookmarks is shown in Figure 5-3. To delete a bookmark, tap the pen icon to bring up X marks alongside all the favorites. Tap any you want to remove. Close the favorites listing to end your edit.

✔ **Hide address bar.** Tap the box in the right-upper corner of the browser to hide the address bar and the other commands. This gives you a nice, clean view but you'll have to re-enable the address bar to go somewhere else. The fastest way to re-enable the address bar is to close the browser and then reload it.

Physics in focus

There are so many gee-whiz features in the BlackBerry PlayBook, but for many users the niftiest of them all is this: holding the World Wide Web in your hand. Response is quick, the image is sharp and colorful, and the size feels just right. And I say this with full knowledge of the snarky putdowns of the PlayBook by Apple CEO Steve Jobs, who tried to dismiss the product's seven-inch screen as too small. Apple's iPad is larger, to be sure, and heavier and bulkier and inconvenient in almost any setting except sitting at your desk or in an armchair at home. For road warriors who need to surf the Web or check their e-mail or do productive work, the PlayBook feels just right. This chapter explores the highly capable Web browser that is part and parcel of the BlackBerry PlayBook.

In full disclosure, the images and text on a PlayBook version of a Web page are certainly going to be smaller than you would see on a 30-inch desktop LCD. The laws of physics haven't been repealed. But there are some important compensating factors: the screen is extremely sharp and bright. You're going to be holding the PlayBook much closer to your eyes than you would view a monitor on your desk. During the time I spent writing this book I regularly switched back and forth between the image on the PlayBook and the corresponding image on my desktop monitor; most of the time I found reading easier on the handheld device.

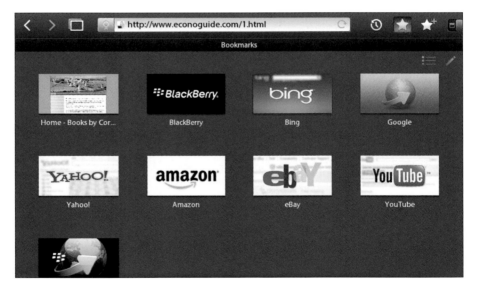

Figure 5-3: The browser comes with several browser bookmarks already in place; you can add your own or edit the set.

The Microsoft connection

Soon after releasing the PlayBook, RIM announced it would strengthen (or tighten, depending on your point of view) its connection to Microsoft. The partnership means that Microsoft will invest resources in the BlackBerry platform as well as in its own Windows phone devices. As a first step, Microsoft's Bing became the preferred search engine and maps application for BlackBerry devices. Future PlayBook OS updates are expected to bring further integration of Microsoft products, including cloud services such as Office 365, which will link RIM's BlackBerry servers to Microsoft data centers. That would allow easy access to stored data for smartphone and tablet users. Office 365 wasn't quite ready for prime time when the BlackBerry PlayBook was introduced.

Moving through a browser page

Few web pages fully fit on the PlayBook screen, but the information is all there to be seen. To move up or down on the page, simply touch the screen and, with your finger still touching the screen, move the display up or down.

To enlarge the view of the page, you have two options.

Enlarging the screen: Way 1

Double-tap a column of text to expand it to fill the full width of the screen. This works very well in reading multi-column newspaper and blog pages. Double-tap a second time to return the display to its original view.

Enlarging the screen: Way 2

Use the pinch-out gesture: Put your thumb and pointer finger anywhere on the page and move them apart to enlarge the view. To return to the original view, use the pinch-in gesture, bringing the fingers toward each other.

Opening a downloaded file

If you've downloaded a file to your PlayBook, you can get to it quickly within the browser by swiping down from the top bezel and then tapping Downloads.

Changing browser options

As any user of the World Wide Web can attest, it's sometimes a bit of the Wild Wild West out there. Again, RIM has come to the rescue with some useful security and privacy features for the PlayBook browser.

To display the browser options, swipe down from the top frame. Then tap the gear icon. Here are the available options:

- **Turn on private browsing.** Tap Privacy & Security and then set the Private Browsing switch to On. When on, the browser only stores your history, *cached* files (temporary copies of pages you have visited), cookies, and certain other technical information. When you close the browser, this information is deleted. See Figure 5-4 for an example of settings.

- **Delete saved data.** Tap Privacy & Security and then tap Clear All.

- **Share your location with websites.** If you don't mind allowing websites to know where you're located, tap Permissions and then set the Allow Websites to Access My Location switch to On. Sometimes this is a nice feature; for example, your local news page may display the forecast for your current location. Sometimes, though, I prefer to keep my identity to myself.

Figure 5-4: The Privacy & Security page offers many sophisticated adjustments for the browser.

✓ **Choosing a home page.** Not all that surprisingly, the PlayBook browser comes to you with its home page as www.blackberry.com. To change it, open the browser and swipe down from the top bezel to display the status screen. Tap the gear icon and then choose General. You're presented with a page full of customizations; tap in the open section alongside Home Page and type in the Web address you want to use.

Choosing a Communication Link

The BlackBerry PlayBook can connect to the Internet four different ways. The makers of the tablet didn't do this to confuse you; they did it to offer options for different working conditions.

Here are the possible links.

The BlackBerry PlayBook Browser

The tablet can connect directly to the Internet using its own WiFi transceiver and an available WiFi network. The PlayBook can work with any of the current specifications for WiFi (in technical terms, these are called 802.11a, 802.11b, 802.11g, or 802.11n) and can also communicate at either of the standard radio frequencies of 2.4 GHz or 5 GHz.

In many situations, using a WiFi connection is free (or relatively inexpensive; you might have to pay an hourly fee or buy a cuppa coffee). On the downside, there is a slight possibility of a security threat using a WiFi system that you don't manage.

The BlackBerry Bridge Browser

When you pair your PlayBook to a BlackBerry smartphone using the BlackBerry Bridge, your tablet will use the cellular data facilities of the phone to connect. No WiFi connection is involved. This form of connection is considered very secure (especially if the BlackBerry smartphone connects to a BlackBerry Enterprise Server at a corporate intranet).

On the downside, cellular data communication may be slower than WiFi, and there may be extra charges or restrictions placed on the amount of data used by a smartphone. Contact your cellular provider for details about your data plan.

Bluetooth tethering to Dial-Up Networking (DUN)

This lets you scoot around the data charges some cellular providers try to charge, although it probably isn't the most satisfying browsing experience. Using a Bluetooth connection, you can link your BlackBerry PlayBook to a BlackBerry (or other cellphone) and then use a dial-up Internet connection. If you've been involved with computers for more than a few years, you remember telephones and modems and slow, slow connections. The PlayBook automatically uses its built-in browser in a dial-up connection.

If you choose to use DUN, you shouldn't have to pay data charges, although you may have to pay for cellphone call minutes. Confirm the details of your phone agreement with your cellular provider.

Data link from a cellular-enabled PlayBook

If you own a BlackBerry PlayBook with a 3G, 4G, or other cellular radio, you can link directly to the Internet from the tablet without involving a BlackBerry or other smartphone. You will, though, have to agree to a contract with a cellular provider. Be sure you understand all of the details of that plan. In this sort of connection, your PlayBook will use its own browser.

Extending the Browser's Reach

At the risk of repeating myself, let me tell you once again that the browser included in the svelte little BlackBerry PlayBook is a heavy-duty full-featured utility. I was impressed to find that it includes many of the advanced features recently introduced into browsers for personal computers. The following features are worth noting and mastering.

No Beowulf

In Woody Allen's classic film *Annie Hall,* there's a moment that almost anyone would have been happy to pull off at least once. Allen is in line waiting to get into a movie theater, and the guy in front of him is spouting some pretentious nonsense about the critic and philosopher Marshall McLuhan. Allen challenges the man, and as an argument seems ready to begin, Woody turns around and says, "That's funny, because I happen to have Mr. McLuhan right here." End of argument.

True story: as I was writing this book, I took exactly one day off to see my son take his latest star turn in an Off-Broadway musical; in the lobby a spirited but friendly discussion broke out about the name of a former Broadway actor whom no one could bring to mind. I reached for my BlackBerry PlayBook, jumped to the web and found the name. The medium truly is the message.

Capture a web link

Capture a web link for a story or item you find online. Simply press and hold your finger against the item. A pop-up appears, like the one in Figure 5-5, offering the following choices:

- **Open Link.** Opens the link for the item you have selected.

- **Open Link in New Tab.** Isolates the item and opens it in a new tab within the browser.

- **Copy Link.** Puts the link into the tablet's memory; you can paste it into an e-mail or a document.

- **Save Link As.** Saves the details of the link on your PlayBook or on a BlackBerry smartphone (attached through the BlackBerry Bridge).

Figure 5-5: Capture a link to paste into a word processing document or send it in an e-mail.

As an author, and speaking on behalf of the publisher, we take matters of copyright seriously. Take care not to appropriate someone else's copyrighted photos or art without permission. In general, you can make copies for your own use but not for republication or resale unless you have permission.

Capture an image

Capture an image you find online this way: Press and hold your finger against the item. A pop-up appears on the screen, like the one in Figure 5-6, offering the following choices:

- ✔ **Save Image.** The PlayBook will save a copy of the file in its own memory or on a BlackBerry smartphone (connected via BlackBerry Bridge). You can change the filename, but the file type will be set as a compressed JPEG with a .jpg extension.

- ✔ **Copy Image Link.** Record the details of the image location to the PlayBook's memory. You can paste that link into an e-mail, a word processing document, or other file.

- ✔ **View Image.** Displays the image by itself without surrounding text and other items.

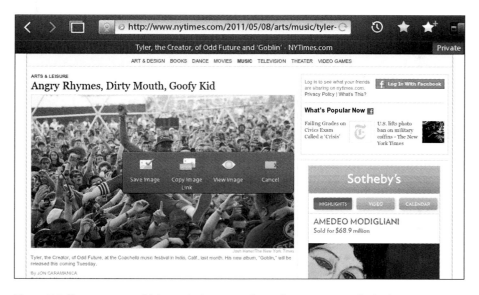

Figure 5-6: You can save a high-resolution copy of most images you see in the browser, or you can copy the link to that image for future reference.

Send an e-mail

Send an e-mail to an address you find in the browser by pressing and holding your finger on a web address. (It will look like *someone@somewhere.com* or similar.) The PlayBook will automatically open the e-mail client on a BlackBerry smartphone that's linked through BlackBerry Bridge.

Research in Motion is expected to introduce its own native e-mail client to run on the BlackBerry PlayBook. When that occurs, some of the functions (including sending e-mails and links from the browser) won't need BlackBerry Bridge if a WiFi or cellular signal can be used instead.

Tap into built-in web links

The PlayBook comes with a set of predefined apps, complete with a pretty icon, that take you directly from the home page (or your favorites section) to one of several popular Internet sites: social networks, web-based e-mail, and a hugely popular video collection. In the initial release, the companies with this sort of arrangement include YouTube, Gmail (from Google), Hotmail (part of the Windows Live package from Microsoft), Twitter, AOL Mail, and Yahoo Mail. For examples, see Figures 5-7 and 5-8.

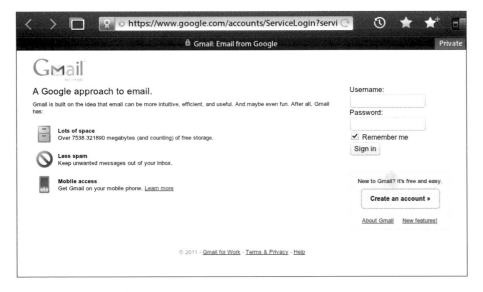

Figure 5-7: Sign on for Gmail.

Tapping any of the predefined icons will take you directly to a site's front page or its sign-in page, without having to first load the browser.

The direct YouTube link takes you to a mobile version. Your first visit shows the featured selection, which often includes paid advertising; tap Top Rated, Most Viewed, or Recent Videos to see (usually) amateur videos that have gone viral. You can tap the magnifying glass icon in the lower-left corner of the YouTube page to search for videos on a topic of your choice. I chose Sardinia in Figure 5-9.

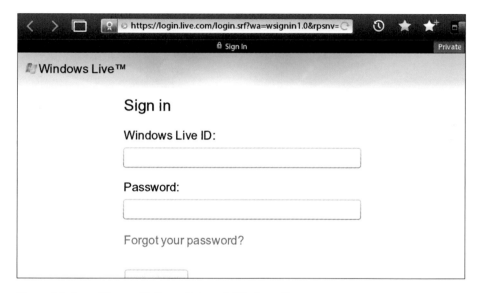

Figure 5-8: Enter Microsoft's Hotmail through Windows Live.

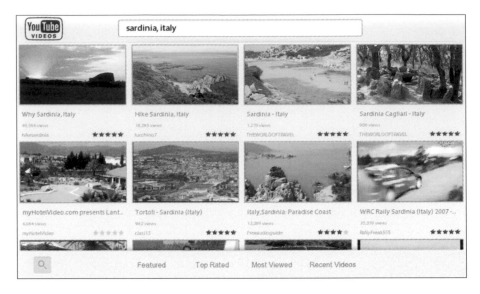

Figure 5-9: I've asked YouTube to show me a collection of videos about Sardinia, a Mediterranean island of Italy.

Once you find a YouTube video you want to explore, either tap it to see it in a small window on your BlackBerry PlayBook, or double-tap it to have it fill the screen.

6

Managing Tasks: E-mail, Messaging, Contacts, and Calendar

Call it a BlackBerry PlayBook, or call it a tablet, or call it Lovely Rita. The bottom line is that what you've got here is a small computer. And although browsing the web, viewing a video, or shooting pictures are all very nice, for many users, the true beauty of the PlayBook lies in its ability to manage one's virtual life.

I travel the world and there are now very few places on the planet I *can't* keep in touch with business clients, family, and friends by cellphone, e-mail, text messages, instant messaging, video chat, and other modes of communication. I have my up-to-date lifetime collection of contacts (with phone numbers, e-mail addresses, messaging IDs, and more) with me all the time. And I carry my increasingly complex calendar with me.

In this chapter, you explore the BlackBerry PlayBook as an e-mail, calendar, contact, and task manager. I also take a poke at explaining why the high security built into BlackBerry devices made it a difficult row to hoe for RIM.

For updates, and there will be plenty for this chapter, visit www.dummies. com/go/blackberryplaybookfdupdates.

A BIS of This, A BES of That

We live in an alphabet soup of acronyms, and RIM (Research in Motion) is no exception; you've got to know some of your ABCs in order to properly configure your BlackBerry PlayBook. And when it comes to communication you must start with one important distinction: BIS versus BES.

If you're on your own, with a BlackBerry PlayBook or BlackBerry smartphone that you set up and manage by yourself, you almost certainly are a user of BIS. On the other hand, if your BlackBerry tablet or smartphone comes with corporate, governmental, or institutional strings attached, you just might be a user of BES.

Allow me to explain:

- **BIS is the BlackBerry Internet Service.** Think of it as very similar to the ISP (the Internet service provider) that brings the web to your personal computer, except that BIS is specific to the BlackBerry world.

- **BES is the BlackBerry Enterprise Server.** This server is usually an extension of a corporate intranet (the private network maintained within a company or institution). The manager of a closed intranet can set all sorts of security, privacy, and productivity restrictions on the user's access to e-mail and the outside world of the Internet.

BIS is for the masses

For individual users, BIS works just fine. You get unrestricted (more or less) access to the Internet and great e-mail service right to your BlackBerry device. The actual mechanism is this: your smartphone communicates with your cellular carrier (AT&T, Sprint, T-Mobile, or Verizon, as examples of major United States carriers) and the carrier operates a server that goes out to the Internet for web pages and e-mail.

Horse, meet cart

Research in Motion has built its reputation and its market share on the strength of its data communication features. Until the launch of the BlackBerry PlayBook in mid-2011, everything revolved around that smartphone device. With the arrival of the PlayBook, things became even more exciting — and more than a little bit complicated. The BlackBerry PlayBook hit the market without a *native* (core) set of *personal information manager (PIM)* tools. You know: email, calendar, and so on.

Why? The bottom line is that RIM has been so devoted to maintaining its nearly ironclad security for data communication that its hardware got ahead of the software. According to insiders at the company, the security design for its BlackBerry smartphones and the accompanying proprietary mail and message servers that RIM maintains for its users were so tightly tied together that it took untold months of work by entire squadrons of programmers to figure out a way to allow multiple devices (as in a PlayBook and a BlackBerry smartphone) to share the same identity. The other part of the equation was a firm decision by the deep thinkers at RIM to please corporate, institutional, and governmental users (as well as individuals who

are concerned about privacy and security) by keeping sensitive data out of the BlackBerry tablet's memory. In the standard configuration, all of the data is held either in the memory of a BlackBerry smartphone or even further away, in a secure storage site.

By this way of thinking, if a PlayBook is lost or stolen, there will be nothing of value in its memory banks *unless the user has put data in a word processing, spreadsheet, PDF, or other file and made a conscious decision to store it on the tablet.*

Why was it considered better to keep data on a BlackBerry smartphone and reach into that device from a BlackBerry PlayBook? The thinking was along these lines: we tend to keep our phones closer to us, they can be protected with a pretty strong password, and we can also load them with security apps that can wipe away all data and disconnect them from the cellular network by sending a special command from another device.

By the time you read these words, though, RIM is scheduled to have the core apps ready. They've promised PIM tools for the PlayBook, and I've seen it in pre-release form.

Communication between your BlackBerry device and the carrier is *encrypted,* meaning it would be very tough for someone to eavesdrop on that part of the exchange. Using a BlackBerry smartphone or a BlackBerry Playbook that connects to the BIS cellular stream is, in general, much more secure than connecting to an open Internet through WiFi or Bluetooth or a basic cable modem or DSL system. See Figure 6-1.

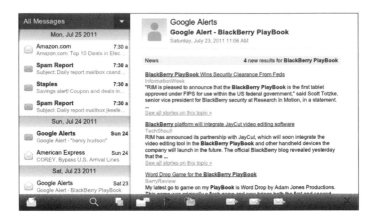

Figure 6-1: Peek into the Messages app on a PlayBook using the BlackBerry Bridge.

What isn't protected? Any information you provide to a website, like your name and credit card number, is only as secure as the web operator allows it to be. If someone hacks into the records of a major online site (cough — Sony PlayStation — cough) and steals the information, well — you're as vulnerable as the next person, and it has happened more than a few times.

Check your credit card, banking, and financial institution reports regularly and don't hesitate to contact these companies if you see a transaction you don't recognize.

Sneaky business

Earlier in this chapter I say that BIS users get "unrestricted (more or less) access to the Internet . . ." Here's what I mean: like it or not, an ISP can and sometimes does get involved in determining what websites you can access, what types of attachments you can send or receive, and how much data you can download or upload (or how fast the data moves). As an example, many cellphone carriers charge by the megabyte for data; others may offer "unlimited" plans, but these sometimes include fine print that says the carrier can either slow down or stop the transmission of data once you reach a certain level in a particular month.

Other carriers may charge you when you use features like the BlackBerry Bridge browser, which in theory allows a BlackBerry PlayBook owner to access the Internet by connecting to a BlackBerry (and perhaps another brand) smartphone and using the theoretically unlimited data plan on the phone for the purposes of the tablet. See Figures 6-2 and 6-3.

Figure 6-2: The Message app lets you search for an e-mail, text message, or instant message.

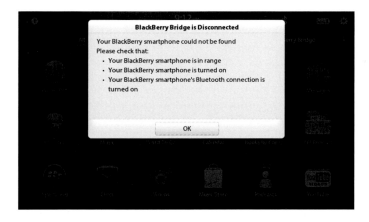

Figure 6-3: Enabling the Bridge on the PlayBook and phone is a must for communication between the two.

One more thing: although you might think you're buying a BlackBerry smartphone with all of the features intended to be offered by its maker RIM, when you contract with a cellular provider, they take control of what standard features and apps are included on the device.

The same would apply if you buy a BlackBerry PlayBook from a cellular provider; if you purchase a WiFi-only PlayBook from a source other than a cellular provider, the tablet will come with the full suite of programs and apps (at least on the WiFi side of the equation). The cellular provider can still limit how a BlackBerry smartphone communicates and interacts with a BlackBerry PlayBook. Indeed, AT&T and several other smaller providers were very slow in supporting the BlackBerry Bridge feature when the PlayBook first came on the market, and the ultimate resolution included some extra charges for functions other companies were allowing for free. And you thought the cell phone companies were always thinking of you as a friend and partner.

I would consider making a recommendation about the best cellular provider to use with the BlackBerry PlayBook, except that anything I say today probably would change tomorrow and then again next week. Your best bet is to carefully examine the fine print of any cellular contract before agreeing to it, and not to hesitate to switch carriers if one is better suited to your needs than another.

BES means business

Consider BlackBerry Enterprise Server (BES). The first (or last) stretch of communication is, once again, the link between your BlackBerry device and the cellular provider, and that data is encrypted in the same way BIS is. However, with BES the cellular provider *doesn't* connect your PlayBook or your smartphone to the public Internet; instead, it routes the data to the company or institution that operates its own BES.

In a BES system, an IT (more alphabet soup, anyone? information technology) manager sets the controls and limits on the server. Your data travels in an encrypted form as a cellular signal, and then continues in a virtual closed tunnel to the intranet and the dedicated server. There's more to the BES system, too: an IT manager can install customized or specialized software on the server or push those apps out to run on BlackBerry phones or the BlackBerry PlayBook.

Without any James Bond–like interception, the only way for someone to read your mail or the data stream is to get inside your corporation or institution — or to steal your BlackBerry device. (And in a managed system, that purloined phone or tablet usually requires a password to operate. And the phone can be remotely wiped of its data, or be shut out of the BES stream once its absence is noted.)

And just as is the case with a cellular provider, a managed BES system can be set up to block access to certain websites. That's right: your employer might insist that you use your BlackBerry device only for work-related purposes and make it impossible to watch sitcoms, play Angry Birds, or shop for shoes.

The Feds are on the case

The folks at Research in Motion are so devoted to their reputation for high security that they sought — and received — Federal Information Processing Standard certification for the Black-Berry PlayBook. This made it the first, and thus far only, tablet with this particular stamp of approval from an agency of the federal government.

The FIPS rating from the National Institute of Standards and Technology is a requirement for any data communication device to be used by U.S. government agencies. It attests to the strength of cryptography and other security methods used in the making of the hardware and software. FIPS certification arrived four months after the BlackBerry PlayBook was on the market and nearly a year after the device was first announced. Was this one of the reasons native PIM apps were so late to be released? The answer, apparently, is classified.

And so here, in a nutshell, is the reason RIM's BlackBerry devices became so popular in corporations and institutions and even in the White House. More so than nearly any other portable cellular or data device, a BlackBerry can be locked down, buttoned up, and protected like a high-tech tank.

Apps Core on a BlackBerry Smartphone

In RIM's world, e-mail, contacts, and calendar are integrated with each other. For example, if someone sends me an invitation to an event, I can accept it and all of the details — including reminders — insinuate themselves into my calendar. Or I can start with my calendar and add contacts to an event and then send that contact an invitation by e-mail, text message, or instant message. For want of another name, I'm calling the package a personal information manager (PIM).

Why am I describing the PIMs on a smartphone when this book is about the BlackBerry PlayBook? Because the promised native apps for the PlayBook are based on the same structure and commands as those on the smartphone, and because the BlackBerry Bridge, which you can set up between the tablet and most BlackBerry phones, allows the PlayBook to reach into the phone and bring the data onto its larger screen.

The basic built-in personal information and productivity apps on a BlackBerry smartphone are called, with elegant simplicity:

✔ **Messages.** This is a catch-all phrase for a catch-all app. A BlackBerry device can receive e-mails, text messages, video messages, and instant messages, and they all end up here, in a nicely presented and neatly organized display. This is also the place from which you can send any of the aforementioned to someone else.

✔ **Contacts.** The people you know and work with are here, gathered nicely in an alphabetized and searchable directory. You can include e-mail addresses, BlackBerry PIN information, instant messaging IDs, voice phone numbers, snail mail addresses, and notes.

✔ **Calendar.** This holds a few days', a few months', or years' worth of appointments, reminders, and other information. I'm a real old-timer; I've kept my calendar on my computer for decades, and the calendar app in my BlackBerry is synchronized to a desktop database that reaches back to the Twentieth Century.

✔ **Tasks.** You can set up a specialized to-do list for nearly any purpose. You can tie it to the calendar to set up alarms and e-mail reminders.

✔ **MemoPad.** This catch-all utility stores notes, reminders, recipes, formulas, plot twists for your next bestseller, or any other snippet of information. A search function allows you to hunt for words in the title of any stored memo. See Figure 6-4.

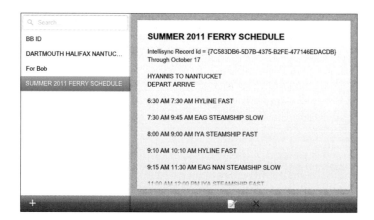

Figure 6-4: The BlackBerry MemoPad is a quick way to jot notes.

Getting the Goodies onto Your PlayBook

Once more, the BlackBerry PlayBook can communicate the following ways: the basic model includes a WiFi transmitter and receiver that can connect to the web through a public or private router. That basic model also includes a Bluetooth radio system that can communicate with most current models of BlackBerry smartphones. The third version of the PlayBook adds various cellular data radios (GSM, CDMA, or other specifications).

How do you get your e-mail, calendar, contacts, tasks, and other personal information onto your PlayBook?

You have three choices:

- ✔ Use the secure native suite of tools on the PlayBook itself, as promised for delivery by RIM. (When they arrive, you can read all about it at www. dummies.com/go/blackberryplaybookfdupdates.) Depending on the final details and decisions you make yourself, the data may live somewhere in the cloud (on servers far, far away) or on a private server locked away at a company or institution. The means of communication will be WiFi and the Internet, or a cellular data link.

- ✔ With the BlackBerry Bridge, connect from your PlayBook to your BlackBerry smartphone and access the data from there. The Bridge uses Bluetooth communication.

- ✔ Use a set of third-party e-mail and calendar apps, connecting to them by WiFi or by USB cable to a desktop or laptop computer. Tools from Google, Yahoo, or your Internet service provider are examples of third-party providers. These programs are generally capable and easy to use, although they lack the promise of security that's at the heart of official RIM apps. Data for these apps can live on your PlayBook, at the provider's site, or a combination of both.

This chapter looks at the first two solutions. As I note, they're related: The BlackBerry PlayBook apps act very much like their cousins on a BlackBerry smartphone. The only significant difference lies in the way the data gets moved around, and RIM has pulled out the stops to keep that element as secure as possible.

All Hail BlackBerry E-mail

In addition to its relatively high level of security, another strong point of both BES and BIS is the fact that they push mail to your device. A *push* system, surprisingly enough, acts just as its name suggests: it pushes mail to your device as soon as the server receives it. By contrast, other designs only get the mail when you issue a command to go out on the Internet and look for it; these are sometimes called *polled* or *polling* systems.

RIM's design for its e-mail service is extremely flexible. It can send along messages that are sent using:

- ✓ A BlackBerry e-mail address
- ✓ An address provided for you by your cellular provider
- ✓ An address within a corporate intranet (if the IT administrator allows)
- ✓ An address at nearly any other online location

For example, my personal BlackBerry account is set up to poll the e-mail sent to several domains that I own through a third-party ISP, as well as to receive the occasional official communication from RIM. Many users also instruct RIM's servers to poll their accounts on services like Gmail, Hotmail, and Yahoo, and then push the results to their phone over the cellular network.

Many computer users are familiar with, or at least recognize, popular e-mail stands like POP and IMAP, which the vast majority of systems use. But as part of the enhanced security built into the BlackBerry world, RIM uses its own protocols. It's all done behind the scenes, with no muss or fuss.

Don't Kill the BlackBerry Messenger

BBM is RIM's very own version of an instant messaging service. BBM allows any two BlackBerry users who have a data plan on their phone to communicate with each other anywhere in the world; under most circumstances there are no per-message charges.

With the BlackBerry PlayBook, BBM is available as a component of the BlackBerry Bridge; when you wirelessly connect your tablet to a BlackBerry smartphone, you can send and receive instant messages from the PlayBook. See Figure 6-5. You'll benefit from the larger onscreen virtual keyboard and the larger display.

If your BlackBerry smartphone or BlackBerry PlayBook somehow arrives without BBM or BlackBerry Bridge BBM installed, simply visit the BlackBerry App World and download it to the device; the program is free for all registered owners of either device.

Figure 6-5: A BBM session is under way on BlackBerry PlayBook, connected by Bluetooth to a BlackBerry smartphone.

BBM essentials are as follows:

- ✔ *To start a conversation,* tap a contact. Then type a message. Tap Return to send the message.

- ✔ *To access advanced features,* tap one of these in the lower-right corner: Ping, Multi-person Chat, and Attach Files.

- ✔ *To add a contact,* tap the + sign in the lower-left corner. Enter the contact's PIN or e-mail address, and then tap Send Invite.

- ✔ *To select Multi-person Chat,* tap the icon and select multiple contacts for your party-line chat.

- ✔ *To add an emoticon* to your message, tap the smiley face.

BBM over the Bridge

If you connect your PlayBook to your BlackBerry smartphone using BlackBerry Bridge (see Chapter 3 for how to do that), your BBM contacts and all of your messages show up on the tablet. (In the Bridge world they still live on the phone, not the tablet; the PlayBook reaches into the phone for the data.) Any changes, deletions, or additions you make on your tablet will show up and be stored on your phone.

The promised native version of BBM will work with contacts stored on the BlackBerry PlayBook itself or accessible from a remote site using WiFi (or, on some models, a cellular data link).

Are you PINned for the prom?

Every BlackBerry device, smartphone and PlayBook alike, has its very own electronic identification issued by the mothership back at RIM. This personal identification number (PIN) is part of the security and authentication fortification that makes a BlackBerry a BlackBerry. The PIN ensures that the correct mail is delivered to the proper device. It is also an element of the communication used for updates to the operating system and the management (and payment) for apps downloaded from BlackBerry App World. And if you use BlackBerry Messenger for instant messaging or Video Chat for visual conferencing, the PIN is an essential part of the process for establishing a link.

A BlackBerry PIN is an eight character hexadecimal (base 16) identification number. I'm going to make one up right here on the spot: 500Z9999. That isn't a real hexadecimal number, since the only allowable alphanumerical characters are 0 through 9 and A through F. But you didn't expect me to give a real PIN, right? In any case, a hex number of eight characters reaches up to a number in single-digit billions, which should be enough to last for a while.

How do you find the PIN for your BlackBerry PlayBook? It's listed in many places. When you first register your PlayBook with RIM, you'll see it listed. If you connect your tablet to the BlackBerry Desktop Manager on a computer, you'll see the PIN displayed. And then there is this way:

1. **Tap the options icon.**

2. **On the left panel, tap About.**

3. **If it isn't already selected, tap the pull-down menu and choose the Hardware tab.**

   Your PlayBook's PIN is listed here.

Having a good BBM

To start a BBM session, you must follow these general steps:

1. **Add a contact to your BlackBerry device.**

2. **Get that person's permission to communicate.**

   See Figure 6-6. You must know one of the following to use BBM:

   • The person's PIN

   • The e-mail address that's associated with the person's device

3. **Send either a Request by PIN or Request by Email message.**

   If they accept your invitation to chat, the service is permitted between those two PINs.

Figure 6-6: To invite someone to a BBM session, you can send an invitation using an e-mail address or PIN found in your Contacts.

General smooth BBM moves are as follows:

 ✔ *To send a message using BlackBerry Messenger,* click a name in the contacts list; then select and click Start Conversation. Type a message and press Enter.

 ✔ *During a BBM session, choose Send a File or Send a Voice Note.* The Voice Note feature is an interesting function that allows you to conduct a one-side-at-a-time conversation from almost anywhere in the world. Record a message and send it as a note, and then wait for the other party to do the same. It's not quite the same as calling someone using the telephone function of a smartphone, but in international locations it's considerably less expensive or sometimes completely free of charge (within the terms of your data plan).

 ✔ *To exit a conversation* (this doesn't mean to end it), press the Escape key. This allows you to conduct more than one BBM session, with different contacts, at the same time.

 ✔ *To end a conversation,* select and click End Conversation.

Getting in Touch via Contacts

The Contacts database helps tie together all of the elements of the personal information apps. From a contact, you can

 ✔ Initiate an e-mail
 ✔ Start a BlackBerry Messenger session

- ✔ Add someone to a meeting from the listing about them
- ✔ Start a video chat
- ✔ Place a phone call (on a BlackBerry smartphone)

 To help organize your contacts, you can assign them to one or more groups. For example, you can have a group for your own business, or for clients, prospects, and suppliers. You can have groups of friends or members of the family. You assign groups on the Contacts screen.

Contacts essentials

Contacts essentials are as follows:

- ✔ *To add a contact,* tap the + sign at the lower left. Enter the details and tap Save.

- ✔ *To find a contact,* swipe through the list on your phone, or tap one of the letters on the left side of the screen (a sort of electronic simulation of a Rolodex).

- ✔ *To search contacts,* tap the magnifying glass. Then start entering a name and the tablet will display a list of possible matches.

- ✔ *To edit a contact,* tap the edit symbol, to the left of the red X delete button.

- ✔ *To delete chats or contacts,* tap the red X. You'll enter into an edit mode, and then you can tap X next to any chat or contact you want to delete.

- ✔ *To fill in contact details* (including name, title, company, e-mail, phone numbers, and notes), tap the contact icon.

- ✔ *To assign an icon for a contact* (that little bit of art will appear on your phone or tablet when a phone call or e-mail from that contact arrives), tap the existing photo or the placeholder for the picture. Without a picture, you'll see a gray icon of a human head, like a clothing store dummy.

- ✔ *To change your screen name,* pick the name that is displayed when you appear on the screen with someone in a BBM session. Click Edit My Info to exercise your creativity.

- ✔ *To update your own profile,* tap your own name (and picture if you've already added one) at the upper left. My Profile opens and you can change:

    - *Display Name.* The name that appears on other user's screens when you're BBMing.

- *Personal Message.* Go ahead, give yourself a motto. Or put the title of your company below your name. (A word of warning: everyone who communicates with you by BBM is going to see this. That means employers, potential employers, family, and friends. Think twice before putting in something that might embarrass you in certain circumstances.)

- *Status.* You can indicate that you're Available or Busy. It may not be appropriate for your BlackBerry PlayBook or other device to automatically respond to a request for an instant message session at all times and in all places; in fact, I'm *sure* it's not appropriate. (Some consumer versions of BBM, and some customized by an IT department, may have options listed other than Available or Busy.)

- *PIN.* Your device's PIN is automatically filled in here. Every BlackBerry device, PlayBook and smartphone included, has a unique identifier.

- *Time Zone.* It helps other participants to see in which time zone you reside. This might help explain to someone messaging you from Rome at 9 in the morning why you aren't responding from Boston (where it is 3 a.m.). Or perhaps it might explain why the quality of the response at that ungodly hour seems a bit strained.

- *Location.* I am here — at least for now. You can adjust the location (and the time zone) to reflect your travels. Attention app developers: come up with a utility for the BlackBerry PlayBook to update this information on-the-fly.

- *PIN Barcode.* The BlackBerry PlayBook operating system produces a barcode (shown in Figure 6-7) that can be photographed by another PlayBook or by a BlackBerry smartphone running a current operating system; the barcode contains information to automatically populate a contacts listing on the second device.

Contacts over the Bridge

If you connect your PlayBook to your BlackBerry smartphone using BlackBerry Bridge, your BBM contacts will show up on the tablet even though they still live on the phone. Any changes, deletions, or additions you make on your tablet will show up and be stored on your phone.

Figure 6-7: Your personal profile in contacts shows many ways for people to get in touch with you, including a barcode that you can scan with a PlayBook or current model BlackBerry smartphone.

Contacts as a PlayBook app

The promised native version of BBM will work with contacts stored on the BlackBerry PlayBook itself or be accessible from a remote site using WiFi or (on some models) a cellular data link.

If you can't find a message that you started but didn't send, it's probably saved in your message box as a draft. If you have multiple e-mail accounts feeding into your BlackBerry device, either look in each account or change the message setting to aggregate all messages from all sources into one inbox/outbox.

Penciling You in via the Calendar

Like nearly all of the various standard apps on the BlackBerry, the calendar is simple and to the point. At its most basic level, you navigate to a date, click a time slot, and then add the details of an appointment, meeting, or event.

When you tap anywhere on any day, you can fill in the details of an appointment. You will have an opportunity to set the date and time for the event further down on the screen; this small matter of design is actually quite helpful since it saves you the time and trouble of navigating to a particular date in order to enter an activity.

Adding an attendee to the event will automatically draw details from contacts (if that person is included in that list). After you save an appointment, an e-mail or text message automatically goes to all attendees whose contact information you have; the invitees can accept, tentatively accept, or just flat-out decline your kind invitation.

What a view

The calendar on the PlayBook offers three views:

- ✔ **Day** view is all of your appointments for one selected day. The default setting is for a work day of 9 a.m. to 5 p.m., as if that is something any of us pays attention to anymore. On your BlackBerry smartphone, you can press the Menu button and then select Options to adjust the standard working day. Changes that you make to the time period on the phone are reflected in the display shown on the PlayBook. See Figure 6-8.

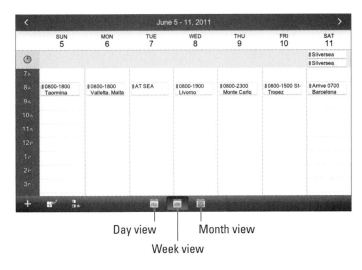

Day view   Month view

Week view

Figure 6-8: The daily view shows full details. Add items directly to a particular date, or create one on another day and move the event.

- ✔ **Week** view shows a seven-day summary view of your appointments, like you see in Figure 6-9. Again, you can adjust the way the week is displayed by changing the options shown on a BlackBerry smartphone. For example, you can choose any day to be the start of your week; that would work well with people who work Sunday to Thursday, for example.

Figure 6-9: The week view of the BlackBerry Calendar includes the first few lines of information about scheduled events; tap any item to see a full day.

✓ **Month** view shows every day of the month, but only indicates that there's an appointment for individual days; you have to tap a particular date to open the Day view. See Figure 6-10.

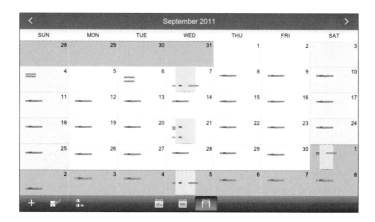

Figure 6-10: The monthly view shows only that particular days have scheduled events or reminders; tap any date to expand its listing.

Switch among the three views by tapping any of the three icons below the main screen. They all show a calendar, but the one with a single green box means one day, the one with seven days of green boxes indicates a week, and the one that is fully green means a display of the entire month.

The calendar on the BlackBerry smartphone includes a fourth view, called Agenda, that isn't tied to a particular day, week, or month. Instead, it presents your upcoming appointments in a list. This view wasn't carried over to the PlayBook in BlackBerry Bridge mode, although that may happen in future updates to the operating system.

Changes you make on the tablet are saved to your smartphone. (Remember: the calendar resides on the BlackBerry, not on the tablet.)

Calendar essentials

Here are your calendar essentials:

- ✔ *To create a new event,* tap the icon at the bottom left. Then enter details (name, subject of event, location) into the New Appointment screen.

- ✔ *To specify the duration,* tap the All Day check box or enter a specific time for Start and End. The system will assume that the time zone for the event is the same as currently set for your BlackBerry phone; if it is not, you can change the zone.

- ✔ *To set a reminder alarm,* choose amongst a number of advance notification times.

- ✔ *To send a notification message,* click Email All Attendees. When you enter the names of attendees, the system assumes they're in your contact list; if it finds a match, it puts the name on the list.

- ✔ *To modify an event,* tap the edit symbol at the bottom right, alongside the X for delete. (It's a somewhat unfortunate design to have the edit button next to delete, but then again, you are prompted with an "Are you sure?" message if you accidentally tap the delete icon.)

Concocting Documents That Go

In This Chapter

▶ Understanding Documents To Go

▶ Using Word To Go

▶ Using Sheet To Go

▶ Using Slideshow To Go

▶ Converting files from other computers

*O*ne of the truly amazing features of recent-model BlackBerry smartphones was the ability to download and use an app that brought the essential functionality of Microsoft Word and Microsoft Excel (and a bit of Microsoft PowerPoint) to the small screen. The app was called Documents To Go, and users liked it so much that Research in Motion bought the program. The BlackBerry PlayBook, in its initial launch, includes the standard suite of Documents To Go.

Understanding Documents To Go

Documents To Go includes three programs:

✔ **Word To Go.** This utility lets you open an existing document created in Microsoft Word (or in a compatible program saved as a DOC or DOCX). You can edit the file and then re-save it on the PlayBook; or you can transfer it by USB cable, Bluetooth, or WiFi, or as part of an e-mail to another device. You can also create a new Word document on the BlackBerry PlayBook and transfer it the same way. See Figure 7-1 for an example.

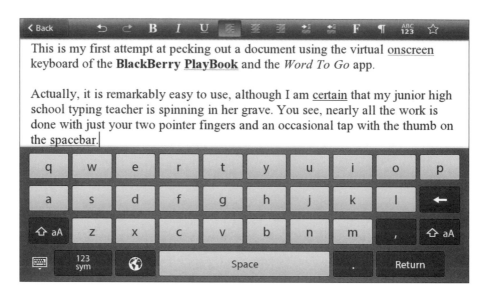

This is my first attempt at pecking out a document using the virtual onscreen keyboard of the **BlackBerry PlayBook** and the *Word To Go* app.

Actually, it is remarkably easy to use, although I am certain that my junior high school typing teacher is spinning in her grave. You see, nearly all the work is done with just your two pointer fingers and an occasional tap with the thumb on the spacebar.

Figure 7-1: Typing on the virtual keyboard isn't as easy as using a full-sized keyboard but is superior to a tiny smartphone keyboard.

- ✔ **Sheet To Go.** You can open an existing spreadsheet created in Microsoft Excel (or in a compatible program capable of saving files in XLS or XLSX format). The file can be edited and then re-saved on the PlayBook or transferred by USB cable, Bluetooth, WiFi, or as part of an e-mail to another device. You can also create a new Excel document on the BlackBerry PlayBook and transfer it in the same way.

- ✔ **Slideshow To Go.** The version allows you to view and display a *basic* presentation created in Microsoft PowerPoint (or in a compatible program that can save files in PPT or PPTX format). Unlike the other apps in Documents To Go, you can't edit a PowerPoint presentation or create a new one on the BlackBerry PlayBook. And a number of advanced features of PowerPoint — including transitions between slides, embedded audio and video, and animation of images and other elements aren't supported. This limitation *may* change with later releases of the PlayBook operating system.

Preaching about Word To Go

To load the word processing app, go to the BlackBerry PlayBook's home screen and tap the Word To Go icon. The first screen will list recent documents, which is a shortcut to files you've worked with previously.

About printing

The BlackBerry PlayBook, as first delivered by Research in Motion, doesn't directly connect to a printer. If you need to make a hard copy of a document, transfer it to a computer using the USB cable or a wireless Bluetooth or WiFi link. Another option is to send a file by e-mail and open that message on a computer with an available printer.

Here are the options in more detail:

- ✔ **Open a Recent Document.** Select one of the DOC or DOCX files listed and tap it to load it.

- ✔ **Delete a Recent Document.** Tap the pencil icon in the upper right. A trashcan icon appears alongside all the files in the Recent Documents listing. When you tap the trashcan next to the doc that has to go, you're given one last chance to confirm.

- ✔ **Create a New Document.** Tap the New Document button along the lower edge of the screen. The keyboard appears, along with a space to view your work. Icons to change font and other goodies appear across the top of the screen.

- ✔ **Open a Document.** Tap the Browse button at the bottom of the screen to see any files the app can find in your PlayBook's memory.

If your BlackBerry PlayBook is connected by Bluetooth to a BlackBerry smartphone, you also see a tab at the top of the Browse screen that shows the contents of the SD flash memory card installed in the phone.

Linking the BlackBerry PlayBook to a BlackBerry smartphone using BlackBerry Bridge (a whole bunch of fruit in that sentence) allows you to extend the tablet's storage space. On my BlackBerry Bold 9700 phone I have an 8GB SD flash memory card; all of that space is available to the tablet using the Bluetooth connection.

Creating a new document

Once you get underway you will find it remarkably familiar to its big brother, Microsoft Word. The bottom half of the screen shows the keyboard. The upper portion is blank. Just start typing. The first letter of a new sentence is automatically capped. If you need to add caps (I would), tap the aA button shown next to this paragraph. Other functions are given in Table 7-1.

Depending on your agility as a two-finger typist and the acuity of your eyes, you may prefer to work in portrait mode; just rotate the tablet 90 degrees to see a smaller keyboard and a larger blank screen.

Table 7-1	Typing in Word To Go	
To Do This...	*Do This...*	*...With This Icon*
TYPE IN ALL CAPS.	Press and hold the aA button for a second or two. Go back to lowercase by tapping the button.	⬆ aA
Change the keyboard to the first level of symbols, which includes numbers and the most commonly used grammatical symbols.	Tap the 123sym button.	123 sym
Change the keyboard to the second level of less-frequently used symbols.	Tap the blue circle button. Tap the ABC123 button to see the lowercase keyboard.	ABC 1 2 3
Add **boldface** emphasis to a word you are about to type.	Tap the **B** icon at the top of the screen. To make text not bold, tap the **B** icon again.	B
Add *italics* to text.	Tap the *I* icon.	I
Add underline to text.	Tap the U icon to turn on either type of emphasis; tap on the same icon once again to turn the emphasis off.	U
Change the font style.	Tap the F icon.	F
Adjust the paragraph settings.	Tap the ¶ icon. You can change alignment there.	¶

To Do This...	Do This...	...With This Icon
Get a count of the number of words, characters, and paragraphs in the file.	Tap the ABC123 icon. See Figure 7-2.	**ABC 1 2 3**
Save your work.*	Display the menu bar by swiping down from the top bezel. Tap Save and type a filename.	

If your BlackBerry PlayBook is linked by Bluetooth to a BlackBerry smartphone, you can choose between saving the file on the tablet or in the smartphone's flash memory card.

You can consult a quick description of Word To Go icons by tapping the Help button; get there by swiping down from the top bezel.

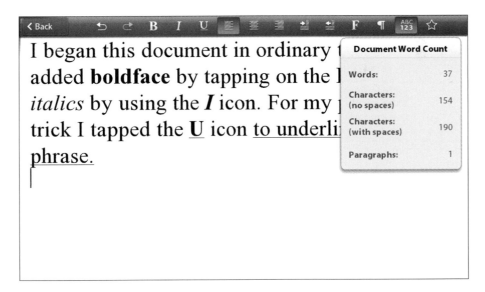

Figure 7-2: The document word count tells you the number of words, characters, and paragraphs in your manuscript; this can help you in planning speaking time or page count for printing.

Editing an existing Word document

To change or add to an existing Word document, open the doc in Word To Go. You can choose a recent document or tap Browse to search your BlackBerry PlayBook (or a linked BlackBerry smartphone) for a DOC or DOCX file. When the file is open, move through the document by swiping up from the bottom of the screen; the speed of your swipe will determine how much of the text will move.

TIP

Word To Go shows horizontal lines across the bottom of what would be pages, but numbering (as well as headers, footers, and comments) doesn't show up.

To work with the existing document, do one of the following actions:

✓ Press and hold your finger for a second anywhere in the text. A set of markers will appear in the text and a pop-up appears displayed, as seen in Figure 7-3. You can move the two markers to highlight a single word, a sentence, or one or more paragraphs. Then tap one of the options in the pop-up:

- **Cut**
- **Copy**
- **Paste**
- **Cancel Selection**

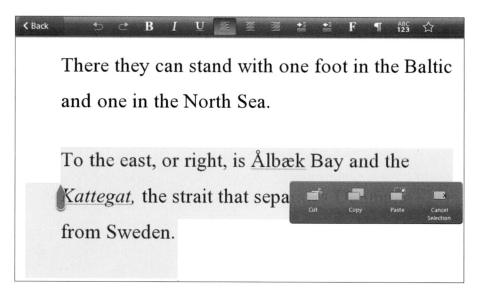

Figure 7-3: Holding a finger on the screen adds a marker to the document; then choose a block of text to cut or copy, or to change font or style.

- ✔ Tap a word to see if Word To Go offers an alternate spelling. This is not *quite* the same as a full-featured spellchecker, but it does accomplish some of the same tasks. If the app has some suggestions that doesn't mean the word is wrong. If you want to make a change, tap one of the alternates.

- ✔ Tap anywhere in the document to place a marker. Move it by touching it and dragging it elsewhere. From the marker, you can insert new text. You can also use the ← key to delete text to the left of the marker. All of the font, paragraph, and symbol functions that are offered to create a new document are also available to you in editing.

- ✔ When you're finished editing the document, display the option menu by swiping down from the top bezel.

- ✔ Tap Save to replace the previous copy of the document with the edited version; it's stored in the same place with the same filename. Tap Save As to give your work a new name. The file is usually stored on your PlayBook, but if you have a BlackBerry smartphone linked to your tablet, you can tap Save To and have the new file stored in the smartphone's Flash memory.

In general, it is good practice to use Save As when you change a document. This preserves the original version and makes a new copy; you can always go back and delete the originals once you're satisfied that the new work is an improvement on the old.

Doing the Wash with Sheet To Go

The PlayBook's spreadsheet app (with an unfortunate name that sounds like the description of a wanderer in search of a bed) works with XLS or XLSX files, and has most full spreadsheet functionality. It certainly works well for basic calculations and display of tables; it isn't as adept as a desktop or laptop version when dealing with multiple-page spreadsheets.

To open the spreadsheet app, go to the PlayBook's home screen and tap the Sheet To Go icon. The first screen lists recent documents, which is a shortcut to files you've worked with previously. (See the previous section, "Preaching about Word To Go," for how to open a recent file, create a new one, or browse for an existing one on your PlayBook or on an attached BlackBerry smartphone.)

In my line of work I use spreadsheets for two purposes: for numerical tracking of things like expenses and income, and as a handy tool to maintain sortable lists and tables. You can see one of my tables in Figure 7-4, as well as the cell formatting options.

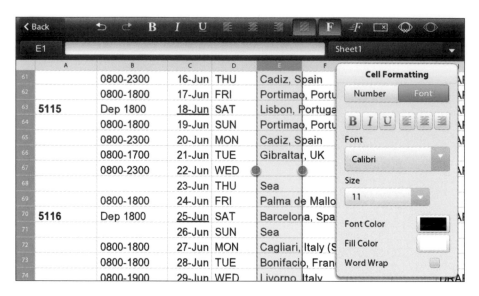

Figure 7-4: I tapped the E column to highlight it and am ready to adjust the font, size, and type color.

Here are some special Sheet To Go commands:

- **Create a new spreadsheet.** Tap New Document from the opening screen.

- **Open an existing spreadsheet.** Tap Browse and then tap one of the displayed spreadsheets. If you have an attached BlackBerry smartphone, you can browse for compatible spreadsheets stored in that device's flash memory.

- **Save a spreadsheet.** Swipe down from the top bezel. Tap the Save icon. Tap Save As to give your work a new name. The file is ordinarily stored on your PlayBook. If you have a BlackBerry smartphone linked to your tablet, you can tap Save To and have the new file stored in the phone's flash memory.

- **Change the font for text or data.** Tap the F icon and make selections; see the options listed in the previous section about Word To Go.

 Change number formatting. Tap the quick format icon, which looks like an F with wings. For an example, see Figure 7-5. Here you can choose amongst the following styles for a cell:

  - **Number** treats the contents as a number.

  - **Time** treats the contents as a time of day.

- **Percentage** treats the contents as a percentage.

- **Text** treats the contents as text, even if it has digits (important if a column holds product IDs, flight numbers, or the like).

- **Currency** treats the contents as currency.

- **Date** treats the contents as a date.

Figure 7-5: Quick Format applies rules that affect the display and processing of specific categories of data in a spreadsheet.

✓ **Hide a column or row.** Tap the letter (for the column) or the number (for a row) you want to hide. Then tap the closed-eye icon. To reveal a hidden column or row, tap the open-eye icon in the bar at the top of the sheet.

✓ **Delete a column or row.** Tap the letter (for the column) or the number (for a row) you want to delete. Then tap the delete icon.

✓ **Clear the contents of a single cell.** Tap on a cell to highlight it; it will be marked within a box with two blue circles at opposite corners. Then tap the delete icon.

✓ **Change the font, size, color, or fill color for a font style to a row, column, or cell.** Tap the letter (for the column), the number (for a row), or an individual cell to highlight. Then tap the F icon to display the Cell Formatting box and choose options there.

- **Wrap the contents of a single cell or all cells in a row or column.** Tap the letter (for the column), the number (for a row), or an individual cell to highlight. Then tap the F icon to display the Cell Formatting box. Tap the Word Wrap check box.

- **Apply a font style to a row, column, or cell.** Tap the letter (for the column), the number (for a row), or an individual cell to apply a highlight. Then tap the B icon for boldface, the *I* icon for *italics,* or the U icon to apply underline. You can also combine two or more of these attributes.

The Help screen for Sheet To Go lays out most of the basics.

Flipping over Slideshow To Go

Things may change in months to come, but the current Slideshow To Go manages to do two things at the same time: it both impresses and disappoints.

I spend more than half of each year speaking publicly all over the world. I can (modestly) state that I am a PowerPoint Ninja, able to make that Microsoft presentation package jump through hoops, juggle flaming bowling pins, and otherwise amaze, astound, and entertain my audiences. These things get me excited:

- It can display a basic PowerPoint presentation in high resolution and full color on your BlackBerry PlayBook screen. See Figure 7-6 for an example.

- That same image can also be output from the little tablet to a high-definition television (or some models of video projector) so you can put your images or your slides up on the big screen.

- You can have the show presented on that second screen or projector while the BlackBerry PlayBook displays notes and thumbnails of upcoming slides (a perfect assistant for a public speaker).

Here, then, is what has left me thus far disappointed about Slideshow To Go:

- The presentation doesn't include most of the fancy bells and whistles available in current editions of PowerPoint 2010 including transitions, SmartArt, and moving elements in the slide.

- The show doesn't include embedded audio and video. All slides are static, without motion.

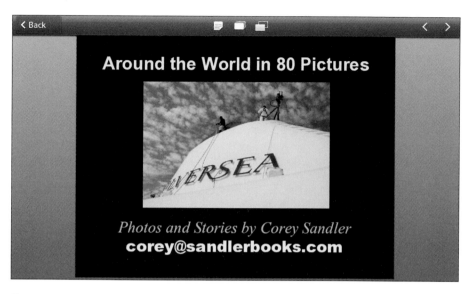

Figure 7-6: A Slideshow To Go presentation can be presented on your PlayBook tablet or output to a high-definition television or projector.

- My presentations typically include more than one image on a slide, with the picture changing automatically or when I click for a change at a key moment in my talks; Slideshow To Go ignores all of this and places all images, one atop another, on the screen.

- Most curiously, unlike Word To Go and Sheet To Go, the Slideshow To Go app doesn't let you create a new presentation on the BlackBerry PlayBook or edit an existing one.

There is one way to use the BlackBerry PlayBook as a player for a fully edited and complete PowerPoint presentation: record a presentation as a video and then use the tablet's player to present it. This doesn't, however, allow you to edit the show and generally results in a lower-resolution version.

Slideshow To Go has only a few available commands:

- **Open an existing slideshow.** Tap Browse and select one of the displayed presentations. If your BlackBerry smartphone is attached, you can also browse its flash memory for compatible files. See Figure 7-7.

- **Delete a slideshow.** From the list of recent presentations, tap the pen icon and then tap Delete next to the slideshow you want to remove.

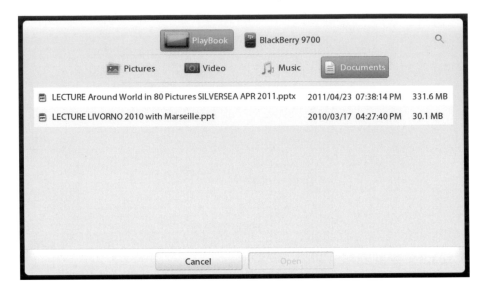

Figure 7-7: If you have a BlackBerry smartphone linked to your BlackBerry PlayBook, the Browse command can look for slideshow, sheet, or Word documents on the phone as well as in the tablet memory.

✔ **Display lecturer's notes.** Display the slideshow onscreen, and tap the leftmost icon to display the Notes screen at the bottom of the screen. Here you can read any notes you made when you created the presentation on a desktop or laptop computer. You can't add notes from the BlackBerry PlayBook's keyboard.

✔ **Display thumbnails of slides.** Display the slideshow onscreen, and tap the center icon to display thumbnails of the current and upcoming slides along the left side of the screen. In Figure 7-8 you can see a slideshow with both notes and thumbnails displayed. You can't add, delete, or rearrange slides on the BlackBerry PlayBook.

✔ **Go to Presenter mode.** Display the slideshow onscreen, and tap the rightmost icon to go to Presenter mode. Connect a micro-HDMI cable to the port on the BlackBerry PlayBook and connect the other end to a 1080p high-definition television or video projector. The show can mirror exactly what you see on the tablet, or can display the completed show while the BlackBerry PlayBook displays notes and thumbnails (or even a completely different application). See Figure 7-9 for the presenter mode request.

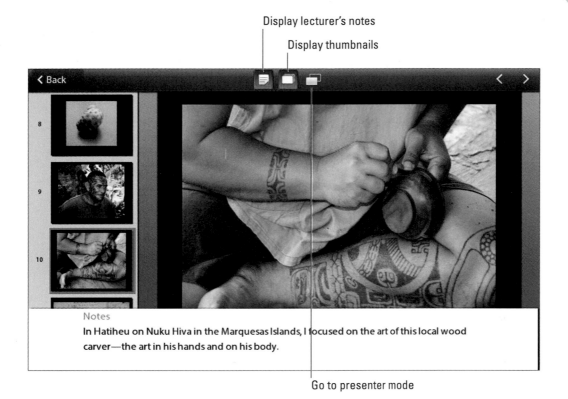

Display lecturer's notes

Display thumbnails

Notes

In Hatiheu on Nuku Hiva in the Marquesas Islands, I focused on the art of this local wood carver—the art in his hands and on his body.

Go to presenter mode

Figure 7-8: A Slideshow To Go document with presenter notes and thumbnails available for reference for the speaker.

✓ **Save a copy of a presentation.** Despite the fact that you can't edit a presentation, you can save a copy of it on your BlackBerry PlayBook or on an attached BlackBerry smartphone. Why would you want to do this? If you loaded the presentation from the smartphone, you could store it locally on the PlayBook (or the other way around).

The Documents To Go suite was built around the specifications of Microsoft Office files: Microsoft Word, Microsoft Excel, and Microsoft PowerPoint. It will work with current versions of that software, which generally means the Office 2010 and Office 2007 or XP editions. You can, though, bring in word processing, spreadsheet, or presentation files created by other programs that are capable of creating compatible files. As one example, the Apple iOffice suite can do this; its Keynote software can save a presentation as a PPT file, which will run under Slideshows To Go. To do that, choose Share⇨Export and click PPT (PowerPoint).

Figure 7-9: If you tap the presenter mode icon, the PlayBook sends a signal through the HDMI port. You can adjust the settings for high-definition video from the control panel.

Mastering PlayBook Utilities

*T*ime is money, or so said Poor Richard, better known under his real name of Benjamin Franklin. It's one of those aphorisms that seems so obvious. But perhaps because it also seems so correct. Franklin would have very much enjoyed owning a BlackBerry PlayBook, not just because of its inventiveness but also because it does a fine job of helping someone with limited time make the most of limited money.

This chapter looks at six important apps dedicated to exactly that: the multi-faced clock and timer suite, the amazingly capable calculators and unit converter, a mapping tool that connects from the PlayBook to satellites in space and back, a personal meteorologist, an electronic equivalent of the string-around-the-finger reminder, and a way to see and be seen as you chat over the Internet.

ideo Chat

friends, family, and colleagu

someone, click the icon be

s.com

Who Knows Where the Time Goes?

With this high-tech analog-look or digital-look clock you can:

- ✔ Use it as an alarm.
- ✔ Create more than one clock, label each, and set them to differing time zones. (You can see three clock faces on the screen and scroll left or right to view more.)

⊯ Use it as a stopwatch.

⊯ Use it as a countdown timer. See Figure 8-1 for the basic display of clocks and timers.

You can set any one of the clocks as your home time, which is quite helpful when you travel. Then you can assign each and every clock with an alarm time. Want to wake up at 8 a.m. in Rome, then be reminded to call the family six hours later when it is 8 a.m. in Boston? No problem.

Figure 8-1: Don't forget to clock in.

Here are the controls for the clock, stopwatch, and timer:

⊯ **Edit a clock.** Tap the clock face. At the top of the control panel, make sure Clock is selected. See Figure 8-2 for the settings panel.

• **Name.** Tap in the open box and type a name for the clock. Most users name one clock "Home" and others with the names of cities they visit or places with which they have business dealings.

• **Time Zone.** Choose from zones that cover nearly every place on the planet. There's even a plus 5.75-hour setting for Kathmandu.

- **Clock Face.** Select between traditional analog, a simple silver on white display, or the electronic blue-green numbers of the digital display.

- **Set as Home Clock.** You can select one of the clocks as your home clock, giving it the prime location on the display.

Figure 8-2: The clock settings panel includes a place to assign a name, time zone, and choose between analog or digital display.

✔ **Add a new clock.** Swipe down from the top bezel and tap New Clock. Set the options, and then tap away from the options panel to close the settings.

✔ **Delete a clock.** Tap a clock and then tap Delete. (You can't delete the original clock, or one that you've marked as your home clock.)

✔ **Display the date.** Swipe down from the top bezel and locate the Date switch at the right side. Slide it to On to show the month, date, and year; slide it to Off to suppress that display.

✔ **Set an alarm.** Tap any clock you have set up, and then tap Alarm. Roll through to select the hour and minute, and be sure to *choose a.m. or p.m.* as needed. You can also choose from several appropriately annoying sounds. In Figure 8-3, I'm setting an alarm on my home clock.

Figure 8-3: You can set an alarm on any of the clocks you've put in place on the BlackBerry PlayBook.

- ✔ **Time an event on the stopwatch.** Tap the stopwatch. Tap Start to begin timing; tap Stop to end timing. You can estimate the time looking at the analog position of the second hand, or read a more precise time by looking at the digital readout above the Start/Stop button.

- ✔ **Time a lap or a segment of time on the stopwatch.** While the stopwatch is active, tap the Lap button. The timer under the Start/Stop button keeps running but the timer under the Lap button resets to 0. When you tap the Stop button, you'll have a total elapsed time above Start/Stop and a Lap time to its right. To time a new event, tap Reset.

- ✔ **Set the timer.** Tap the timer. Then roll through the hours and minutes dials to choose the allotted time. (The default setting is 10 minutes, but you can set the time for as many as 23 hours and 59 minutes, or as little as 1 minute.) You can choose the alarm sound. Then tap Start.

When any of the clocks, or the stopwatch, or timer have been set with an alarm, you can close or minimize the screen and perform other tasks; the BlackBerry PlayBook will keep track of the various timers in the background and interrupt you with any asked-for alarms. In Figure 8-4, an alarm pops up on a section of the home page.

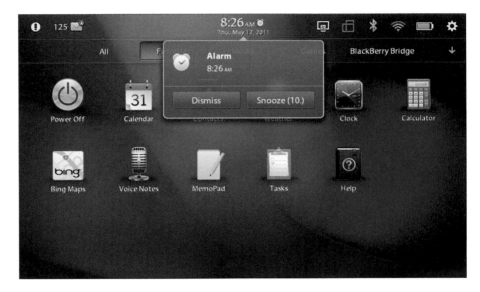

Figure 8-4: Any alarm from any of the clocks or from the timer will run in the background as the BlackBerry PlayBook performs other tasks.

Counting and Calculating

Another simple but very elegant PlayBook tool is the built-in calculator, which can help you balance your checkbook, figure the tip for dinner, perform complex scientific math, or convert from just about any measurement of size, volume, or energy to another.

To switch between the four built-in calculators, swipe down from the top frame or bezel. Then tap one of the following:

- Standard
- Scientific
- Unit Converter
- Tip Calculator

Standard

You'll recognize the number key pad and most of the operators. There are also memory keys:

- **MC** clears the current memory register.
- **M+** adds the current result to the memory register.
- **M-** subtracts the current result from the memory register.
- **MR** recalls the value in the memory register and pastes it into the current calculation.

Scientific

Remember when you needed to buy an expensive special-purpose scientific calculator for trigonometry class? Don't you wish you could get that money back? Here are just some of the operators available in the scientific calculator:

- **Rad**
- **Deg**
- **Sin / Cos / Tan**
- **p**

Unit Converter

This is one of my favorite of all of the built-in apps of the BlackBerry PlayBook. You can perform simple conversions, like figuring out that 100 km/hr is not quite as fast as it sounds, equaling only 62.137 mph or a mere 53.996 knots on the water. See Figure 8-5 for a view of the app doing a simple temperature conversion.

You work the converter like an old-fashioned slot machine, except that you get to select the position of the reels using your finger; if you figure out a way to do that in Las Vegas, please let me know. Select a type of measurement in the first column, the source measurement in the second, and the conversion output in the third. Here are the available inputs and outputs:

- **Angle.** Degrees, gradians, and radians.
- **Area.** Square area for millimeters, centimeters, meters, kilometers, inches, feet, yards, miles, hectares, and acres.

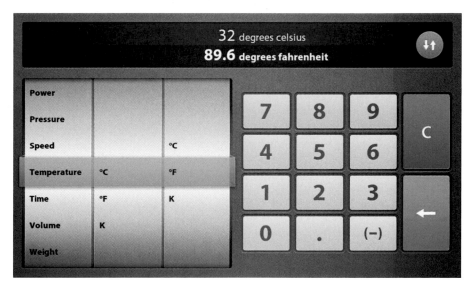

Figure 8-5: From the land of Fahrenheit, 32 degrees sounds cool, until you look at the same value in Celsius in the Unit Converter calculator.

✓ **Data.** Bits, kilobits, megabits, gigabits, terabits, bytes, kilobytes, megabytes, gigabytes, and terabytes.

✓ **Energy.** BTU, calories, kilocalories, ergs, ft lbf (foot pound-force), joules, Nm (Newton metres), Wh (watt hours), and kWh (kilowatt hours.)

✓ **Length.** Millimeters, centimeters, meters, kilometers, inches, feet, yards, and miles.

✓ **Power.** BTU/min, ft lbf/min, ft lbf/sec, horsepower, kW (kilowatts), W (watts), and Nm/s.

✓ **Pressure.** atm (atmospheres), bars, mm Hg (millimeters of Mercury), kgf/cm² (kilogram force per square centimeter), Pa (Pascals), psf (pounds per square foot), and psi (pounds per square inch.)

✓ **Speed.** Knots, m/s (meters per second), km/h (kilometers per hour), ft/s (feet per second), and mi/h (miles per hour.)

✓ **Temperature.** Centigrade, Fahrenheit, and Kelvin.

✓ **Time.** ns (nanoseconds), ms (microseconds), ms (milliseconds), seconds, minutes, hours, days, weeks, and years.

✔ **Volume.** cu in (cubic inches), cu ft (cubic feet), cup, US fl oz (US fluid ounce), gal (Imp), gal (US), liters, cubic centimeters, cubic meters, pt (Imp), pt (US), qt (Imp), qt (US), tbsp (tablespoon), and tsp (teaspoon).

✔ **Weight.** mg (milligram), g (gram), kg (kilogram), t (ton), oz (ounce), lb (pound), and st (stone).

The weight conversion identified as tons appears to refer to metric tons, although it isn't identified as such in the original release of the BlackBerry PlayBook operating system. And in any case, the calculation for tonnage doesn't precisely match a conversion into U.S. pounds or any other measure I can find.

Tip Calculator

Although you could do the same math using the standard calculator, the tip app adds a few extra wrinkles. To figure a tip, do the following:

1. **Enter the bill amount.**

   Many people consider the bill amount *before* taxes, although that's a relatively small downward adjustment of the gratuity.

2. **Enter the number of people who are splitting the bill.**

   If you're treating, leave this value at 1; otherwise, the calculator will help you divide the total amount, including tip.

3. **Enter the percentage of tip.**

   In most places the standard gratuity is 15 percent; you can adjust the amount up or down by entering a whole number here. (You aren't allowed to enter a decimal value, like 17.5 percent.)

4. **Choose whether to round up the amount:**

   • Tap the field to have the calculator round the amount up to the next whole dollar.

   • Set it to None to get a precise amount.

5. **Tap the ← key.**

   At the bottom, you will see the total amount the calculator recommends. Above that you can see the individual values for the amount per person and the total amount of the tip. See Figure 8-6 for an example.

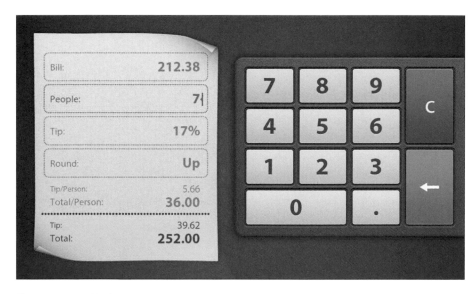

Figure 8-6: The Tip Calculator not only figures the gratuity but also does the heavy lifting: figuring out each person's share of the bill.

Mapping Your Way to Success

For entertainment, I have been known to pick up a road map or an atlas and study it for hours. And when I travel to places unknown, I step up the pace of study. So what's the BlackBerry PlayBook going to do about it? How about offer a nearly global database of street maps and satellite views? And then, how about using the built-in basic GPS (or the more advanced BlackBerry smartphone GPS and link up via BlackBerry Bridge)?

Bing Maps needs downloads from a huge collection maintained by Microsoft. It will only work when your BlackBerry PlayBook has a connection to the Internet, either through a WiFi link or by Bluetooth and through a BlackBerry smartphone.

When you open Bing Maps, you can tap the small blue compass icon in the upper-right corner of the screen; this brings up a report on your present latitude and longitude. (Sometimes the app will take a few minutes before it can figure out where you are; again, this may be a bit of early-release roughness that will be smoothed out over time. And the 3G or 4G cellular versions of the PlayBook may have more advanced GPS hardware built in. Stay tuned.) Bing

Maps wasn't developed specifically for the BlackBerry PlayBook and thus its icons, buttons, and controls don't follow the same standards you'll find in many other apps. However, it's easy enough to use.

Here are some navigation tips.

Explore your current location

Tap the blue compass icon to allow the app to determine where you are. Your latitude and longitude appear along the left side of the screen, and a map or image is shown in the main portion of the screen; an example is shown in Figure 8-7.

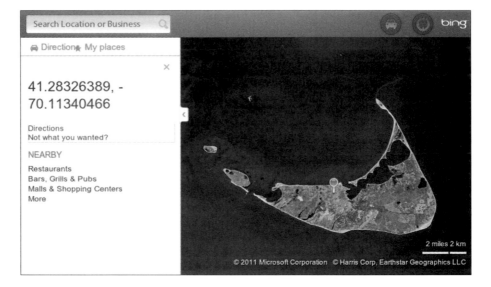

Figure 8-7: This Bing Map reports my current location, sitting at my desk on the island of Nantucket, somewhere beneath the push pin on the satellite map. My keyboard's latitude and longitude appear in the left panel.

Adjust the view

Swipe down from the top bezel and choose one of the following views:

- **Auto.** This selects the best available view for the area; in most built-up areas, this will show a detailed road map.
- **Road.** Displays the road map where available.

🖝 **Aerial.** This view overlays high-resolution satellite views along with highlights for major roads and landmarks. The overhead view of my home even shows our little red car parked out front.

🖝 **Bird's-eye.** Another form of aerial view, this one uses images captured by low-flying aircraft and taken at a slight angle, which allows showing more detail of buildings and elevation.

🖝 **Turn the image.** Tap the compass heading above the image to rotate the view between northern, eastern, southern, or western orientations.

🖝 **Expand the view.** You can move in any direction on the map by touching the image and moving your finger. To zoom in, pinch out by touching with your pointing finger and thumb (or any other pair of digits you can manage) and moving them apart from each other.

Search for places nearby

Tap the Nearby tag and then choose from the travel essentials: restaurants, hotels, shopping, and other commercial sites. The listings aren't at all comprehensive. You may want to use the web browser for further research before making a commitment for the evening. In most cases, you can ask Bing Maps to figure out driving directions from your current location to a business or other place you choose.

Switch to a map view to pinpoint locations

You don't have to limit yourself to exploring the area surrounding your PlayBook's current location. You can navigate to another part of the world by moving the map beneath your fingers, or enter a location in the search box at the upper-left corner of the app. In Figure 8-8, I have asked Bing Maps to show me the city of Civitavecchia, the ancient port of Rome in Italy. With the road map on the screen, I then asked for listings of hotels and accommodations.

Get driving directions

When you tap Directions you can do two things:

🖝 Add the current location as a starting or ending point. Tap the arrows icon to switch between the two.

🖝 Enter addresses using the PlayBook's virtual onscreen keyboard.

Mass transit directions are currently available in about a dozen major cities. Note that the quality of driving or walking instructions will vary; in first-world countries, the maps and directions will generally be first-rate. In other parts of the world, not so much.

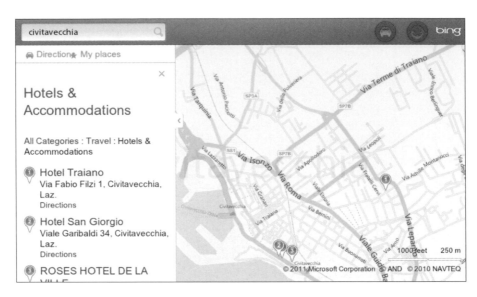

Figure 8-8: After I asked Bing Maps for hotels near my destination, I was able to quickly judge their relative distance to the port, my ultimate goal.

Carrying an Umbrella

I'm not one who generally pays a great deal of attention to the weather forecast; I figure I can just glance out the window or open the door and stick out my hand to determine if I need to carry a bumbershoot or put on a pair of snow boots. My wife, though, requires at least 72 hours notice of pending inclemency so that she can begin preliminary planning for the clothing she will wear.

Happily, the BlackBerry PlayBook provides a quick app that gives you the current weather conditions as well as forecasts, satellite maps, historical data, and the other information some find essential. The app, supplied with the tablet, is helpfully called Weather. When you tap it (a WiFi or other connection to the Internet is required), you arrive at a site maintained by Accuweather.com. The first time you visit, you're asked to enter your home city's Zip code; on later visits you can ask for a report on out-of-town locations. Today's report — note the chilly air in mid-May on our island; summer beach days usually arrive closer to the Fourth of July — is shown in Figure 8-9.

Figure 8-9: The basic display from AccuWeather.com reports the current temperature and conditions, along with predictions for the remains of the day.

When severe weather is in the offing, it's worthwhile to visit AccuWeather and look at the weather maps; one of the most useful puts radar imagery on top of a satellite picture. Zoom in to your region to see storms, color-coded by severity. Click Play to put the images into motion so you can see the direction the storms are headed.

Going to the source

The fact that AccuWeather has its own app on the Blackberry PlayBook doesn't mean you can't find weather information elsewhere. Speaking for myself, I am a big fan of the no-nonsense approach of the National Weather Service: your tax dollars at work. In fact, most of the commercial services rely at least in part on the satellite imagery and advanced technology of the NWS, which is part of the National Oceanographic and Atmospheric Administration.

To go directly to the NWS site, launch the browser of your PlayBook and go to www. noaa.com. From the main page, enter the name of your city or its Zip code, or enter the name of another location in the United States for which you want the meteorological details. The basic page gives current conditions along with a detailed 7-day forecast. You can also request an hourly weather graph with information including wind, rain, snow, and humidity predictions.

Note to Self . . .

The prosaically named Voice Notes is as simple as can be to use: Click the Voice Notes app to open it.

Record a memo

Follow these steps:

1. **Tap the red O recording button.**

   It's below the image of an old-style microphone.

2. **Speak in a normal voice at the tablet.**

   The BlackBerry PlayBook has a pair of microphones hidden away on the top edge. Press the pause button to temporarily halt recording.

3. **Press the square stop button when your dictation is done.**

   See Figure 8-10 for a recording in progress.

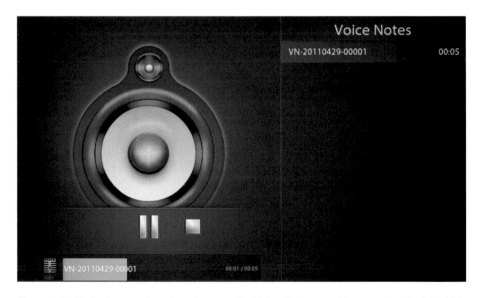

Figure 8-10: It's just you and a microphone on the Voice Notes app. Files are stored with a VN prefix that also embeds the date of the recording.

The microphones on the BlackBerry PlayBook record a single (monaural) channel of sound, but the presence of a pair of them allows the electronics to do some fancy processing to reduce echo and background noise.

Play back a recording

To listen to the contents of a voice recording, visit Voice Notes and tap the file you want to hear. Pause or stop at any time.

Delete a recording

To remove a voice note, follow along:

1. **Open the app and swipe down from the top bezel.**
2. **Tap the pen icon.**
3. **Tap in the check box next to one or more files you want to remove.**
4. **Tap Delete to complete the task.**

   See Figure 8-11 for an example of a deletion about to happen.

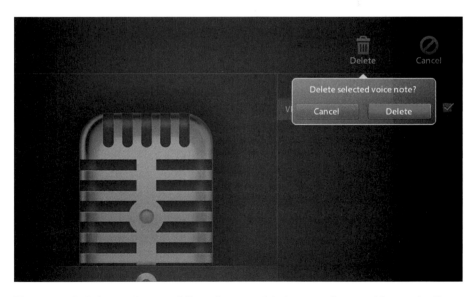

Figure 8-11: Deleting a voice note follows the same deletion procedure used for nearly all BlackBerry PlayBook apps.

Voicing dreams

I am quite confident that what we've got here is the first step in what will become a more complex and useful tool. The ability to record and store digital copies of voice may well lead to advanced apps like these:

✔ **Dictation software.** Speak words, sentences, or numbers to be processed by voice recognition software and entered into notes, word processing documents, spreadsheets, or used as commands for the operating system.

✔ **Oral response to web or app queries.** "Please state your name to access your account information."

✔ **Spoken guidance for complex apps.** "PlayBook: please calculate a route from Boston to Montreal with a stopover in Concord, New Hampshire."

Feeling Video Chatty

One of the Holy Grails of communication is live video conferencing from a tiny handheld wireless device. And to be more specific: to be able to call *from* anywhere *to* anywhere. And while I'm at it, to connect with another person *regardless* of any hardware differences at each end. The not-so-good news: what we've got is about half a loaf. The app, at least in its initial version, only works from one BlackBerry PlayBook to another BlackBerry PlayBook. It won't work from your tablet to a BlackBerry smartphone or from your tablet to a PC or other device.

Video Chat allows you to speak with and see another person or another place in real time. Using a WiFi connection from your PlayBook, it sends live video and audio from your tablet and gets the same from another; see Figure 8-12. That's way cool: you can conduct a business meeting without having to go through a strip search at the airport; you can conduct a pseudo-intimate conversation with a loved one or family member.

You can switch from the front-facing camera (the one that is located just above the touchscreen) to the rear-facing camera (the one on the back of the tablet). The conversation uses the built-in microphones, so no extra hardware is required.

Photo courtesy of Research in Motion

Figure 8-12: A video chat in session shows video from the person you have called, plus a small image of the video you're sending.

Using Video Chat

Here's how to use the app:

1. **The first time you initiate a video chat, enter the BlackBerry ID for the person you want to chat with.**

   See Figure 8-13. Before you place your call, you can tap on the camera icon in the upper-right corner of the Video Chat app for a preview of how you will look to the recipient; think of it as an electronic mirror to adjust your makeup, check your shave, or fix your hair.

2. **Initiate a video call by tapping the ID in your contacts list.**

   The person you seek to chat with gets an on-screen pop-up notice. The recipient can accept a video or voice call, or decline the call. Users can also set a Do Not Disturb flag on their device so all incoming calls are ignored until the sign is removed.

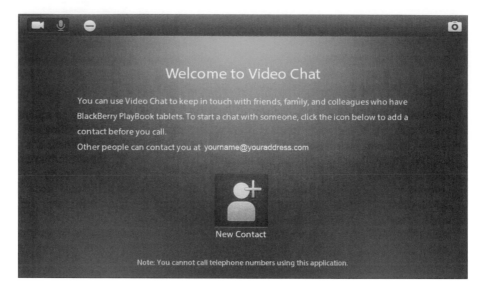

Figure 8-13: You set up Video Chat by adding a new contact within the app.

While a call is underway, you can switch cameras from front to rear so that the viewers at the other end can either see you talking to them, or see what you're seeing on the other side of the tablet. Either end can mute or unmute the audio while a call is in progress, or choose to accept an incoming call for voice only.

Thus dealing with wardrobe malfunctions, or perhaps the complete absence of wardrobe, I suppose.

 Some IT departments may have set up security that interferes with using the Video Chat feature. So, too, some WiFi routers may introduce problems because of security firewalls. You can seek the assistance of RIM's support team if you have this sort of problem, but in the end you may have to change security settings on your own equipment to allow video chatting to take place.

Adding or editing a contact

You aren't required to add a contact to conduct a video chat. However, adding a BlackBerry ID to your contact list means you can skip typing that address each time you want to connect using this app.

To work with the contacts, after you set up a video chat (or after you complete a session), choose from these actions:

Add a contact

Follow these steps:

1. **Click New Contact.**

2. **Enter the contact information, as shown in Figure 8-14.**

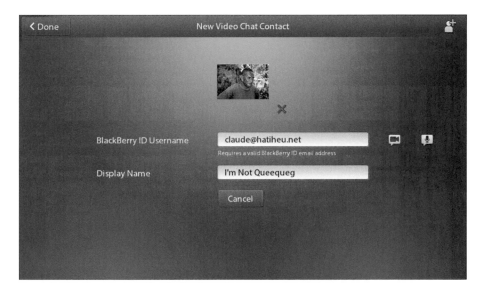

Figure 8-14: New Video Chat Contact requires a valid BlackBerry ID address and a Display Name. You can choose to add a photo to help you put a face to the name before a chat begins.

Add a contact from your chat history

Follow these steps:

1. **Tap the clock icon (which is your history).**

2. **Swipe down from the top bezel.**

3. **Tap the pen icon.**

4. **Tap a contact.**

5. **Tap the + icon to add the information.**

Change a contact

Follow these steps:

1. **Tap the contacts icon (a human bust).**
2. **Swipe down from the top bezel.**
3. **Tap the pen icon.**
4. **Tap a contact.**

Delete a contact

Follow these steps:

1. **Tap the contacts icon (a human bust).**
2. **Swipe down from the top bezel.**
3. **Tap the pen icon.**
4. **Tap a contact.**
5. **Tap the trashcan to delete the contact.**

Add or change a contact picture

Follow these steps:

1. **Tap the contact picture.**
2. **Tap a new image.**
3. **Zoom and position the new image.**
4. **Tap Done.**
5. **Tap Back.**

Turn on Do Not Disturb

Follow these steps:

1. **Swipe down from the top bezel.**
2. **Tap the gear icon.**
3. **Set Do Not Disturb to On.**

    If it's already on, set it to Off to accept calls.

Orbiting BlackBerry App World

In This Chapter

▶ Shopping at App World

▶ Performing advanced shopping tricks

▶ Supporting apps from elsewhere

The marketing plan for RIM's tablet — just as it was for the Apple iPad and the personal computer before it — faced a cart-before-the-horse sort of problem. It was difficult to get developers to spend large amounts of time and money to write programs — we call them *apps* now — before there were many units of the PlayBook already in the hands of consumers and professionals.

At the same time, it's challenging to get people to spend money on a fancy new piece of equipment before there's much in the way of apps to run on it. (Although it is an irrefutable fact that Apple is way out in front of all other tablet makers when it comes to the number of apps available for the iPad, it is also true that there were almost none available when that device first hit the market.)

Introducing BlackBerry App World

REMEMBER

You can get to BlackBerry App World directly from your BlackBerry PlayBook by tapping its icon on the home page; see Figure 9-1. You need a WiFi connection to download apps; cellular radio versions of the tablet may allow the same, although you could wind up paying charges.

Figure 9-1: The BlackBerry App World icon is a direct link to RIM's storefront for add-on software for your tablet; the icon is the first one on the second row in this portrait mode view of the home page.

If you're using a cellular radio version of the BlackBerry PlayBook be sure you understand the details of the contract you have with your cellular provider. Unless you have a truly unlimited data plan, you may be billed for data usage in consulting BlackBerry App World or downloading apps from that site.

The process began with the current generation of BlackBerry smartphones. Some of the first apps were pretty minor — little calculators or minor games — but over time, they became more sophisticated and included investment trackers that tied into stock tickers and bank accounts, mapping and touring tools that use the GPS already on the phone, and more.

The storefront is now known as BlackBerry App World. And with the introduction of the BlackBerry PlayBook, it has expanded its offerings to include apps for the tablet. Some of the products are free, supported by advertising, or given away in hopes of enticing you to upgrade to versions with a wider range of features. Apps that are sold (such as simple tools) usually begin at 99 cents and rise from there; based on the history with smartphones, only a handful of highly specialized apps are likely to have prices above $20.

A number of app makers also let you download a free trial of their product. In some cases this is a limited version (perhaps allowing only a certain number of uses, or remaining active only for a short period of time). In other situations, the trial might consist of an edition that allows you to sample its features but not save or transmit any final work.

As this book goes to press, BlackBerry App World is the only way to add new apps to your BlackBerry PlayBook. However, it seems likely that other sellers will find ways to get their products onto your tablet, just as they already do for BlackBerry smartphones. And in some cases, providers such as airlines or banks may be able to offer direct downloads to a PlayBook.

Here's what you need to shop for and download PlayBook apps from BlackBerry App World:

- **A BlackBerry PlayBook.** You anticipated that one, right?

- **A BlackBerry ID.** You'll register for one as you set up and configure your tablet. You need it to receive OS updates, technical support, and (I hope you don't need it, but) repair or replacement of a tablet under warranty. The App Store uses your BlackBerry ID to keep records of your downloads, making it easy to restore them if necessary.

- **A credit card or checking account.** The store will happily bill you through a personal or business credit card, or you can use the facilities of PayPal, which also allows payment by direct withdrawal from a bank account.

If you're shopping for apps from a BlackBerry PlayBook equipped with a cellular radio, your provider may let you make a purchase by simply agreeing to add the charge to your wireless bill. (This is an excellent argument for requiring a password for use of your PlayBook, unless you are willing to allow anyone who uses your cellular tablet to purchase apps with the tap of a finger.)

Shopping at App World

As anyone who has ever visited a shopping mall (a real one, with a parking lot and a food court and teenagers engaging in mating rituals) knows there are two types of shoppers: targeted buyers and browsers. A targeted buyer comes into a store already knowing what he or she wants to buy. A browser is someone who is willing to buy, but doesn't yet know what.

No parking lots, food malls, or real teenagers lurk at BlackBerry App World. It's a virtual storefront, the sort of business that has become extremely successful for companies like Amazon, iTunes, and other online enterprises.

At App World, though, you can shop or you can browse. Buttons on the front page of the shop take you to the newest, top free, top purchased, or recently updated apps.

Allow me to explain how:

Targeted shopping

You know what you're after. Go here:

1. **Tap Categories at the top of the screen.**

   See Figure 9-2. You can jump directly to business, finance, news, photo & video, travel, sports, or other collections.

2. **Tap one of the categories to open subgroups.**

3. **Tap a subgroup to see apps you can download to your tablet.**

Another way to look for something specific is to tap the search window in the upper right and enter a keyword. For example, as shown in Figure 9-3, I entered *flight* and was given 11 choices related to that subject.

Browsing

If you're the sort who responds to a salesperson's offer to help, "Just looking," then you're a browser. In Blackberry App World, the opening screen is called Featured, and it offers new or top-selling apps of all sort. You can scroll through them by flicking the list left or right.

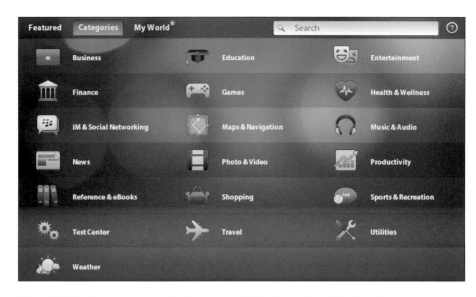

Figure 9-2: Tap Categories from the front page of BlackBerry App World to shop for apps of particular types.

Figure 9-3: You can look for an app by title or a keyword by using the search window on the site.

My World

You have BlackBerry App World, and then you have My World. Well, *your* My World (shown in Figure 9-4). You can find the details of any apps you've purchased or downloaded for free from the site. (Also included are apps provided to you by BlackBerry as part of the operating system.)

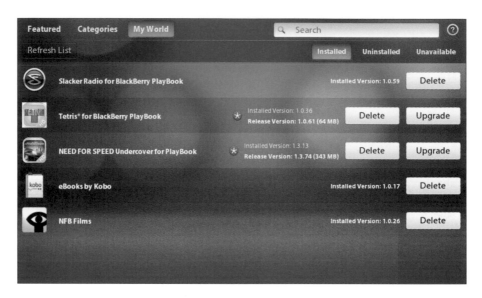

Figure 9-4: In the My World section you can delete or update any apps you've already downloaded.

Alongside each of the apps is information about the version number; when an update is ready, you will see it noted here. Finally, at the right side of the screen, a Delete button is there for each installed app. If you delete an app, it's removed from your BlackBerry PlayBook, but the record of your download is maintained by a computer at the store. Tap the Uninstalled button to see the details of any app you took off your device; tap the Reinstall button to put it back in place on the tablet.

You can use the Delete and Uninstalled panels to help determine if an app is the source of problems on your tablet. Delete a suspect app and then restart your tablet by shutting it down and then bringing it back to life. If you reinstall a deleted app, you can do so from the Uninstalled panel without having to pay a new fee.

Advanced app shopping

These extra features are available in the store:

- ✓ **Download a trial or lite version.** If a limited-time or limited-feature trial edition of an app is available, look for a button that says Download Trial. Be sure you understand the limitations that go with the trial period.

- ✓ **Update an app.** Go to My World and examine the list of installed apps. If you see an Upgrade button, tap that and follow the instructions. In most cases, minor updates are offered for free to registered purchasers. Major upgrades may require an additional fee.

- ✓ **Delete or remove an app.** Go to My World and examine the list of installed apps. Tap Delete to remove it from your tablet; see Figure 9-5.

- ✓ **Update your BlackBerry ID account information.** Load the web browser and go to https://blackberryid.blackberry.com/bbid/login/ and follow the instructions there.

- ✓ **Change the payment method.** Because your BlackBerry PlayBook automatically signs in to the BlackBerry App World, you have to change your method of payment from a different device. It's easier from a PC or Mac personal or laptop computer.

Figure 9-5: You're given the chance to confirm the deletion of an app before you proceed to remove it.

1. **Use the computer's browser and go to** appworld.blackberry.com/ webstore.

2. **Click the Sign In link in the upper-right corner.**

3. **Enter your BlackBerry ID username and password and click Login.**

4. **Click My Payment Options in the upper-right corner of the Featured Items page.**

5. **Select the method of payment you want to use and then click Next.**

6. **Fill in the requested information for credit card or bank account.**

7. **Confirm your choice.**

Supporting Third-Party Applications

Nearly all the apps available at BlackBerry App World are developed and sold by companies other than RIM; they use the BlackBerry storefront to get their wares in front of you, and Research in Motion handles the mechanics of downloading and installing the software. (RIM, of course, takes a portion of the sales price for its trouble.)

For an app to be listed in BlackBerry App World, it has to be RIM tested and approved. This helps assure that the app won't cause you any problems (aside from trying to beat your Scrabble partner), and that the product delivers on its performance promises. Nothing is wrong with that sort of arrangement. It does, though, add an extra layer of complexity if you have a problem or a question about an app from a company other than Research in Motion.

To get help, try this:

1. **Go to BlackBerry App World and locate the listing for the app in question.**

2. **Tap the Support button in the upper-right corner of the screen.**

   The e-mail address for the developer will appear. In some cases you will also see the web address for the developer.

3. **Send them a message and wait for a response.**

Waiting for Android

As the installed base of PlayBook tablets grows, many developers who participate in the iPad market are expected to adapt their product to run on the BlackBerry device. In the meantime, Research in Motion came up with two clever ways to greatly increase the number of apps that can run on its tablet.

✔ First of all, developers who produced apps for BlackBerry smartphones were given tools to help adapt those products to run on the BlackBerry PlayBook; that isn't a minor task since the tablet has a much larger viewing surface and also uses touch-screen gestures. The other issue is that BlackBerry smartphones run a RIM operating system developed for that device, while the BlackBerry PlayBook uses a Tablet OS based on QNX that is not directly compatible. But we can expect the flow of apps from the phone to the tablet to pick up speed as the PlayBook grows in use.

✔ RIM arranged for the tablet OS to run an emulator for Android apps. An *emulator* is a piece of software that adapts one OS to work with programs written for another. For example, most Apple personal computers can now run Microsoft Windows as well as programs written for that operating system.

Now about Android: this is the operating system developed by Google and used by a wide range of tablets and some smartphones. By developing an emulator, the BlackBerry PlayBook can run its own secure operating system *and* work with the growing number of programs written for Android devices. As this book goes to press, RIM has demonstrated its emulator at conferences for developers and promised its release sometime soon. RIM says that programmers won't have to make major changes to their apps, but mostly changing any use of physical buttons on Android devices to instead be replaced by buttons on the PlayBook touchscreen.

Part III
PlayBooking Around

The 5th Wave   By Rich Tennant

"What I'm doing should clear your sinuses, take away your headache, and charge your PlayBook."

In this part . . .

Most Canadians I know are so very hard-working and earnest, but when it comes time to enjoy themselves, somebody's going to end up wearing a moose head. All work and no play makes for a dull digital electronic tablet, which is certainly not the case when it comes to the BlackBerry PlayBook. In Chapter 10, the hills come alive with the sound of music — digital files you bring to the PlayBook. Chapter 11 shows you how to use the built-in high-definition still and video cameras (one in front and one on the back). You also see how to use the tablet's screen as a picture frame or as your own private HD multi-plex. Just bring popcorn. Also, have you read any good books lately? Sure you have, and you can swipe through an entire library on the screen of your PlayBook; I show you how in Chapter 12.

10

Playing Music, Podcasts, and Games

In This Chapter

▶ Banding together for music

▶ Loading music files on your PlayBook

▶ Shopping for music

▶ Opening a PlayBook radio station

▶ Listening in on PlayBook podcasts

▶ Playing by the PlayBook

I'm getting on in years. As a child, my father had me (briefly) convinced that there was an orchestra hidden inside the big wooden box that held the family radio. I've been around long enough to remember when the first portable radios arrived; they were about the size of a loaf of bread and they required an electric outlet and rabbit ears (not the listening appendages of a bunny, but a pair of long aluminum wands that served as an antenna). These big boxes were eventually followed by slightly smaller ones that used early transistors and a whole bunch of batteries. The pace of change began to pick up and radios got smaller, to about the size of a paperback book. And then came the first personal music player: the Walkman, which allowed us to play tape cassettes that we bought at a record store or made on our own home tape recorders. But enough about ancient history.

The BlackBerry PlayBook is the greatest professional-grade music and video player ever offered. It can match the iPad feature for feature, and it's coupled with the enhanced security and dependability of the BlackBerry smartphone. This chapter looks at the PlayBook's ability to sing and talk: music and audio podcasts. It explores how to load some of your own music collection on to the tablet and you see how to use an online music store to purchase tracks of the latest or greatest music.

PlayBook Audio File Standards

The BlackBerry PlayBook can make music from four common file formats. Three of the four use compression to make the files smaller; with that compression comes a bit of fidelity loss, although whether or not you can detect the difference may depend upon

- ✔ The quality of your own hearing
- ✔ Your personal degree of pickiness about tiny defects or reduction of audio range

Touch and drag the volume bar to adjust the volume.

Later in this chapter I explain how to obtain files to use on your PlayBook or convert existing files to the proper format. First, though, take a brief look at four file formats that the tablet can use.

- ✔ **MP3** is the most common standard for compressed music and other audio on digital audio players.

  The designers came up with a way to reduce the size of an audio file by applying less accuracy to portions of the music that are deemed to be beyond the auditory resolution of most people. I'm not talking about dog whistles or low-frequency rumbles here, but instead acknowledging that most people can't easily distinguish — or don't much care about — tiny differences in frequency in some parts of music. As a compressed file, it uses (in dweebish technical terms) a *lossy algorithm*. That means that on some level, to some ears, in certain situations, the quality of the playback is less than perfect and certainly not as good as the original version before compression.

  Does that mean that you won't like the sound you hear from an MP3 file? You probably won't notice, and if you do, you can console yourself with the fact that you can get about 11 times as many tracks on your PlayBook using MP3 as you could if you used full CD files.

- ✔ **AAC** format includes .m4a, .m4b, .m4p, .m4v, .m4r, .3gp, .mp4, and .aac files. Advanced Audio Coding improves on the MP3 format and people generally think it delivers an improved sound.

10110011 is the loneliest number

Computers, including the BlackBerry PlayBook, store things like music and video (as well as everything else) as collections of numbers. Computer hardware and software work together to sample music and assign tiny fragments to numerical values representing the frequency of sound. Among the many bells and whistles of the PlayBook are electronic circuits that can convert those numbers back into tones

that can be played back through a surprisingly decent pair of tiny speakers on the left and right sides of the tablet or, even more impressively, through a headset that plugs into a jack or connects wirelessly to the tablet. And to really rattle the china in your neighbor's dining room, hook up the PlayBook to a home entertainment system using either the headphone jack or the ultra high-fidelity HDMI connector.

Like MP3, it uses a lossy compression algorithm. AAC has been adopted as the standard audio format for Apple's iPhone and iPad as well as a number of game machines and mobile phones from Nokia and Sony Ericsson and Android-based phones and tablets.

- **WMA** is Microsoft's version of a lossy compression scheme; according to Microsoft the quality of tracks recorded in this method is better than that of an equivalent MP3.

- **WAV** (Waveform Audio File Format) recordings aren't compressed and are — to some ears — about as close as a digital recording can get to representing the actual sound of an analog sound. WAVs are, of course, much larger than MP3, AAC, or WMA files.

Loading Music Files on Your PlayBook

You can load music files onto your PlayBook three ways:

- **Drag them across from your computer.** If you connect your PlayBook using the USB cable, use the tablet's internal memory as if it were an attached disk drive. I discuss this method in Chapter 2. Locate music files on your computer (in MP3, WMA, AAC, or WAV format) and drag them across to the PlayBook folder called MUSIC. That's all you need to do; as long as the files are in one of the usable formats, they'll be ready for playback.

Consider renaming files so they're easier to recognize in the music player. Give them a name that includes the artist and some (or all) of the title.

If you want to burrow deeper into your computer's OS, go to the file's properties and choose Advanced; and there you should be able to specify more information, including the name of the album or source. If you buy a file from an online music store, the file will likely come with this information already included.

✔ **Sync up.** Use the sync process to assure that you have the same set of audio files on your PlayBook as you have on your personal or laptop computer (or on your BlackBerry smartphone, if you choose). I discuss the sync process in Chapter 6.

✔ **Get the whole shebang.** Get crazy. Go old school. Buy entire albums from the Music Store, reachable directly from the PlayBook. You can, of course, buy individual tracks as well.

Playing Music from the PlayBook

Opening the music player and picking a tune is as simple as a tap dance — simpler, actually, since it doesn't require special shoes or a sense of rhythm.

Launch the music player

Follow these steps:

1. **Go to the home screen and tap the Media button in the status bar.**

2. **Tap Music.**

   You can also tap the All button in the status bar and scroll through all of the available apps to find Music. You'll see the number of songs, albums, and playlists on your PlayBook; see Figure 10-1.

Play a specific track

Tap the track title to automatically begin playback of the music. If you have more than one screen full of tracks, swipe up on the touchscreen to show additional individual tracks. The contents of my All Songs folder are shown in Figure 10-2. From the status bar you can do the same: Tap the fast forward, rewind, or pause buttons, or the button that looks like the one next to this paragraph.

Jump to a specific song or album

Follow these steps:

1. **On the All Songs or Album screen, swipe up from the bottom-left corner.**

2. **Type the first letters of the song or album.**
3. **Click Return to jump to that section of your music list.**

Figure 10-1: The opening screen of the music player shows your library. Tap one of the folders to see all songs or those categorized as a particular artist or genre or from a specific album.

Figure 10-2: The All Songs folder includes every track stored in your PlayBook, sorted in alphabetical order.

You can see the next scheduled track in a playlist: Tap ^ beside the album art of the song that's currently playing.

Search your music

Follow these steps:

1. **Tap Search All.**

2. **Type the title or artist you're looking for.**

Switch to a different music category

Follow these steps:

1. **Swipe down from the top frame.**

2. **Tap a category.**

Create playlists

The BlackBerry PlayBook comes with a single empty playlist that can hold your absolute most favorite tracks. If you'd like to have more than one playlist (you're a person of many moods), set them up in a computer-based music library such as Windows Media Player or iTunes; from there you can transfer the playlists to the PlayBook and sync up using the BlackBerry Desktop Software.

Add a song to the playlist

Follow these steps and check out Figure 10-3:

1. **Tap a song, artist, album, or gcnrc.**

2. **Swipe down from the top frame.**

3. **Tap Edit.**

4. **Tap Add.**

Delete a song from a playlist

Follow these steps:

1. **Tap PlayBook playlist.**

2. **Swipe down from the top bezel to display the pen icon; tap it.**

3. **Tap one or more songs, or tap the Select All button.**

4. **Tap Remove.**

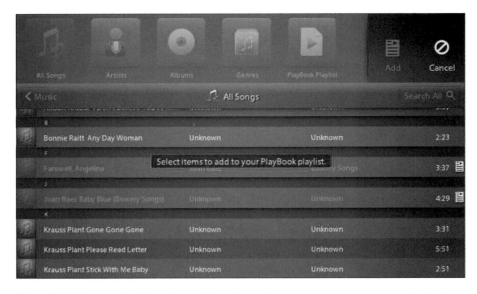

Figure 10-3: Manage playlists using certain other software programs on a personal or laptop computer.

Add playlists from your computer

Follow these steps:

1. **Connect your BlackBerry PlayBook tablet to your desktop or laptop computer using a USB cable.**

2. **On the computer, allow the BlackBerry Desktop Software to open automatically.**

   Or you can manually load it.

3. **Click Music.**

4. **Complete the onscreen instructions.**

   You'll add playlists that you created using a music library such as Windows Media Player or iTunes. An example of a ready PlayBook playlist is shown in Figure 10-4.

Synchronizing music with your computer

Current versions of BlackBerry Desktop Software, available for free from blackberry.com (or from your cellphone provider if you use a BlackBerry smartphone), allow you to synchronize the media (music, videos, and photos) between your computer and your tablet. That means if you buy something new, you can load it onto your tablet as well.

Figure 10-4: This playlist of seven of my favorite pieces of music is ready. If you can figure out the common thread between Bob Dylan, Alison Krauss and Robert Plant, Leonard Cohen, and Frederic Chopin you're my kind of audiophile.

As this book went to press the most up-to-date version of BlackBerry Desktop Software was 6.0.2. It supports the BlackBerry PlayBook as well as most current models of BlackBerry smartphones.

Here's how to synchronize music from your computer to the PlayBook:

1. **Connect the BlackBerry PlayBook to the computer using the supplied USB cable.**

   The desktop or laptop computer will recognize the PlayBook and automatically launch the BlackBerry Desktop Software. If this doesn't happen, locate the software on your computer and manually launch it by going to Settings and clicking the box instructing the software to automatically start when it detects the attachment of a BlackBerry device.

2. **In the BlackBerry Desktop Software, click Music.**

3. **Select one of the following options:**

   • **Synchronize your entire music library.** Select the All Music check box. (The system will consider any file stored in one of the acceptable file formats as music; some systems store sound effects and notification tones as WAV files, for example, and these would be transferred to your PlayBook as if they were music as well.)

- **Synchronize specific playlists.** Select the check box next to one or more playlists already established on the computer.

  - **Synchronize specific artists or genres.** Select the check box next to one or more artists or genres already established on the computer.

    - **Synchronize a random selection of music not already assigned to a playlist.** Select the check box next to Random Music.

  4. **Click Sync.**

Shopping at the Music Store

Ah, I feel like such a geezer once again. I remember when you used to have to visit a record store. (You do know what a record is, right?) An album usually had about 14 tracks, divided between side A and side B; there were also smaller 45rpm singles that contained the latest hit songs from top artists. Many record stores had listening booths where you could sample some of the music before making a purchase. Or you could wait for the recommendation of your favorite deejay on the radio.

You can download content from 7digital or other online stores across a WiFi connection. If you buy something using a cellular data link, make sure you understand the details of your contract with that provider. There may be additional charges for data, especially if you're roaming away from your home market or traveling in a foreign country.

The records, of course, were *analog* recordings. If you looked closely you could see the tiny squiggles in the tracks that would be converted to music by the needle in the record player arm. Because the needle actually touched the record, every time the music was played the quality would be reduced just a bit. If the record got scratched or if your kid brother left the vinyl in the window on a summer day, the music might become completely ruined. The point of this reminiscence is to contrast the physical medium of the record with its analog recording to the electronic replacement of a digital file. No matter how many times you play a digital file, it will always sound the same. And because it's just a string of 0s and 1s, you can easily move or copy it from place to place (within the bounds of copyright laws).

Besides syncing a file that's on your computer to the storage memory inside your BlackBerry PlayBook, you have another way to add music to your portable tablet: buy it from an online seller. The official supplier of music for the BlackBerry PlayBook is a British company called 7digital. (Over time, other companies may come up with delivery systems to deliver tracks to your tablet.)

You can look at pre-selected groupings of music by artist, or you can use the search bar in the upper-right corner to hunt down specific albums or tracks; see Figure 10-5 for the results of my hunt for the discography of Emmylou Harris.

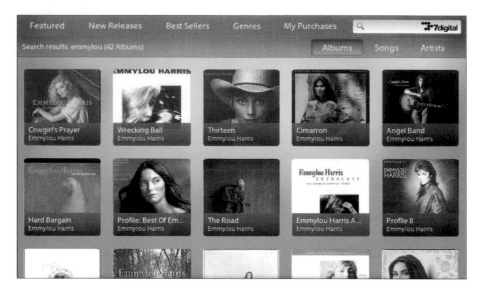

Figure 10-5: The results of an artist search on the 7digital music store. You can tap an album cover to see the tracks and listen to samples.

The PlayBook comes with an app that connects to 7digital. As The Beatles almost said, "All you need is a credit card." Actually, you can visit the music store any time you want just to browse through its collection. For nearly all artists, you can tap an individual track and hear a 30-second sample of the music. But in order to make a purchase, you need to set up a 7digital account. Visa, MasterCard, or American Express, please.

Before you buy or download music (or any other content), make sure the time and date on your BlackBerry PlayBook are correct. Incorrect settings could cause problems with the licensing of the content; in legal terms you aren't buying ownership of music or other content but instead buying a license to use them on your device.

The music store has some other options. They're described in the following sections.

Sign in to your 7digital account

Follow these directions:

1. **Swipe down from the top bezel.**

2. **Tap the gear icon to display options.**

3. **Tap the Sign In button.**

   The Secure Sign In screen is shown in Figure 10-6.

Figure 10-6: If you haven't already established an account with 7digital, they will be glad to oblige. Once you've set up sign-in information, you have to enter a credit card to buy anything.

Buy a song or complete album

You can preview a song before you buy it: just tap the song. If what you hear has you bobbing your head, buy it!

1. **Tap the name or picture for a song or album.**

2. **Tap the price button.**

   A page from one album, ready for purchase, can be seen in Figure 10-7.

3. **If asked, enter your login information and click Sign In.**

4. **Confirm your payment method.**

5. **Tap Buy Now.**

Adjust settings for your 7digital account

For further information about the terms and conditions of a 7digital account, visit their website at 7digital.com.

Follow these steps:

1. **Swipe down from the top bezel.**

2. **Tap options.**

   You'll see a screen like the one in Figure 10-8.

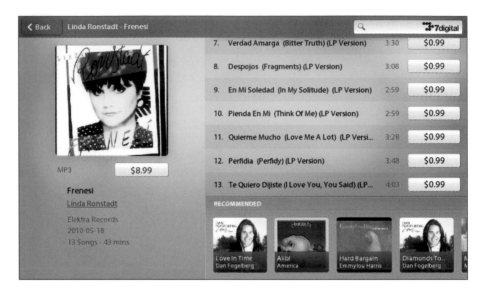

Figure 10-7: If you're in a frenzy for Frenesi, a Spanish-language album by Linda Ronstadt, you can buy the entire album with the tap of a button.

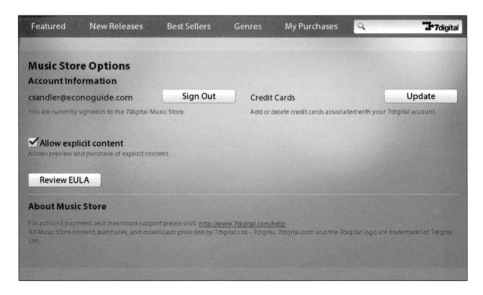

Figure 10-8: On the Music Store Options screen you can add or change credit cards and allow or disallow the preview/purchase of explicit content.

3. **To turn off explicit content, clear the Allow Explicit Content check box.**

4. **To add or change your payment method, sign in to your account, make changes, and tap Update.**

Access your previously purchased music

If you accidentally delete some music, the license lets you download previously purchased music as many as three more times.

1. **Tap the Music icon.**

2. **Tap My Purchases.**

3. **Follow onscreen instructions to re-download your music or video files.**

Exploring the music store

When you visit the music store from your BlackBerry PlayBook, you will be traveling from your tablet out onto the Internet to the 7digital website.

Here are the store's major components:

- ✓ **Featured.** A scrollable overview of selected current or promoted albums and tracks available for you to buy. Tap the album cover to learn more about the tracks and to make a purchase.

- ✓ **New Releases.** Recent additions to the store.

- ✓ **Best Sellers.** A changing selection of the top albums and tracks, based on sales figures.

- ✓ **Genres.** A reorganization of the store's offerings, divided into about 100 different categories, from hip hop to Hindi and most everything in between; see Figure 10-9.

- ✓ **My Purchases.** A listing of albums or individual tracks purchased under a particular account. You can check the progress of current downloads to your PlayBook, and (within the terms of the license agreement) re-download music that you may have accidentally deleted.

Pre-ordering music

One definition of a *serious* music fan is someone who can't stand the thought of being a single beat behind the release of a new song or album. If that describes you, BlackBerry has a solution: pre-ordering music before it is officially available for sale. Some — not all — albums or tracks will be listed on the 7digital website days (or even weeks) ahead of the official release date. You'll know exactly when the music will flow to your BlackBerry PlayBook.

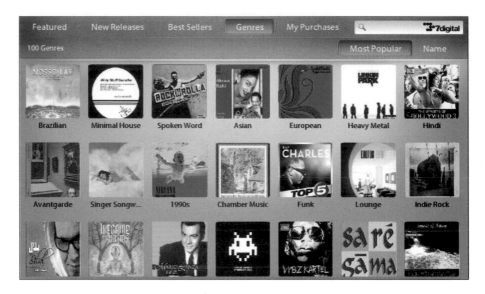

Figure 10-9: The music store genres are one way to find other tracks or albums that fit your taste. 7digital offers a quite extensive library, with some unusual genres.

If you order pre-release content, the purchase will appear under Pre-Orders in the My Locker section of your account on the 7digital website, and under the My Purchases section of Music Store.

Converting your own music

The CDs in your personal library are recorded as digital files, which is a good thing; they will likely last for years because the laser beam in a CD player doesn't physically touch the tracks. And generally, you can make whatever *personal use* you want of the music you own. You can listen to the tracks, invite friends over to a party and dance to the music, and even make copies *as long as you don't re-sell or redistribute those copies.*

But CDs use a file format that most digital music players, including the BlackBerry PlayBook, don't support. If you want to play some of your personal CDs on the PlayBook, you'll need to *rip* a copy, which is a rough-sounding term for converting it from the CD format to one of the formats the tablet can use. The most common conversion is from the CD to MP3 or WAV format.

You have to do the conversion on a personal or laptop computer, and you need software for the purpose. Products include Creative Technology's Creative Media Source, Microsoft Windows Media Player, and others. Once you've made the conversion, store the MP3 or WAV files on your computer, bring them over to the PlayBook using the USB cable connection, and store them in the Music folder on the tablet.

Opening a PlayBook Radio Station

Among the many wonders of the Internet is its ability to serve as a conduit for personalized radio stations. Okay, to be technical about it, this isn't radio or broadcasting in the traditional sense. First of all, the signal isn't coming from an antenna over the airwaves to a receiver as it is with a traditional radio. Instead, the music comes from a digital library somewhere *out there* on the Internet and is sent as a *streaming* (or near-continuous) message to you. And this isn't broadcasting. No disk jockey or station manager comes up with a list of music (the stacks of wax, the platters of plenty, the Top Forty) and then sends it out for all to hear. This is, in the very best sense, *narrowcasting*.

With the PlayBook, *you're* defining the category or the style or the particular artist you want to hear, and a computer at the other end of the connection puts together tunes. A number of services are worth considering, but two stand out from the rest.

Accessing Internet stations like Slacker or Pandora across a WiFi connection is generally free, or within the usually reasonable charges assessed by an Internet café or other local provider. If you connect to one of these stations, or download a podcast while using a cellular data link, make sure you understand the details of your contract with that provider. You may have to pay more for additional data, especially if you're roaming away from your home market or traveling in a foreign country.

Slacker Radio

Slacker Radio is included as a standard app with the initial release BlackBerry PlayBook's OS. Just tap its icon from the home screen and set up an account; see Figure 10-10. The basic Slacker account is free; just enter your e-mail address, create a password, and answer a few basic questions to satisfy the advertisers and the legal department. You can use the same account on your PlayBook and on a personal or laptop computer or other device that can access the Internet.

Slacker is an interactive music service available in the United States and Canada. You begin with pre-programmed stations or by choosing an artist's name or title. Once you do that, you can customize (and share) the selection to meet your tastes.

You can pick a station all set to go, based on a particular singer or genre. In Figure 10-11, I've chosen Emmylou Harris as my sweetheart of the rodeo; once the station begins playing I can make a particular song a favorite or ban it from the list. I can pause the music when rudely interrupted by things like a phone call or the boss.

Figure 10-10: What's so slacker about this?

Figure 10-11: Pre-programmed stations on Slacker begin with a particular artist or style and then branch off based on decisions made by music aficionados back at the home office.

You can also create your own stations, beginning with a particular artist or song and adding the names of artists suggested by the Slacker's programmers; the system will also branch out from your specific selections.

The easiest way to create a personal station is to sign on to Slacker on a personal computer at slacker.com and make your selections there; as long as you use the same sign-in name and password on the PC, the same settings will appear on your BlackBerry PlayBook the next time you load the station from there.

Pandora

You can reach Pandora on your own by opening the web browser and going to pandora.com. Recently, Pandora has slightly tightened "free" to mean that you can listen for 40 hours each calendar month without charge. After that, you can pay 99 cents by credit card for unlimited tunes for the remainder of the month.

You can create your own home page icon for Pandora or put its web address in your Favorites folder by tapping the Add to Favorites icon at the top of the screen; see Figure 10-12. Pandora is available as an app for BlackBerry smartphones; it may arrive as a downloadable equivalent for the BlackBerry PlayBook.

Figure 10-12: You can add Pandora (or any other website) to your browser's favorites, or add an icon on your home page by tapping the add-a-bookmark icon (a star with a + sign).

The basic Pandora service is free; you will see advertisements on the screen if you bother to look at it, and the steady stream of songs is interrupted from time to time with short video commercials. Because of restrictions by copyright holders, Pandora is only available in the United States; the system will do its best to identify the location of the WiFi system to which you're located.

Musical DNA

Think of Pandora as your personal electronic disk jockey that starts with a few songs or artists you like and then finds music that's similar or shares certain attributes. (If you like Paul Simon, you'll probably like James Taylor and you may not know how much in common both have with the Everly Brothers and selected songs by Elvis. Or Bob Dylan to Pete Seeger and Woodie Guthrie with side trips to Robert Johnson, Muddy Waters, and The Rolling Stones.)

Pandora is actually a relative old-timer in the world of the Internet, rising out of the Music Genome Project that began in 2000. Over the years a team of musicians and music lovers has been sitting around and listening to recordings old and new, popular and obscure. (What a job! Almost as good as sitting around and playing with the BlackBerry PlayBook for a living.) The experts rate each song for as many as 400 attributes: its musical DNA, or genome, if you like. The details include style, instrumentation, rhythm, tempo, harmony, subject of its lyrics, type of singer, and the secret sauce that makes a song a hit or a flop (for me, but possibly not for you).

You get to create and fine-tune your own stations. You're allowed as many as 100 channels and you can pick just one to play, rotate through them all, or ask the computer to choose pleasing songs at random. Although you can pause playback, you can't rewind or replay a song. There are some other strictures, mostly related to copyright issues, including a limitation on the number of times a particular artist can be played per month. But in theory, you should be hearing enough similar music and musicians to eliminate that as an issue.

Your BlackBerry will display a picture of the album or CD cover as a song plays. And if somehow Pandora casts a swine amongst the pearls, you can remove it from the mix with a click. The more feedback you provide, the better the electronic DJ understands your ear.

Listening In on Podcast Conversations

It's not all about music, though, when it comes to Internet "radio" stations. The Web is filled with thousands of on-demand *podcasts* of talk shows, interviews, and special events.

About that word podcast: if you take it apart, you'll realize that its prefix is derived from the Apple iPod, and its suffix as a shortened version of *broadcast.* In reality, it is neither: you don't need to use an iPod and it's an on-demand medium. When you ask for a segment or a show, it comes to you digitally. Semantics aside, podcasts are an interesting way to use your PlayBook.

On the BlackBerry PlayBook the home page icon called Podcasts shows RIM's managed set of podcast categories you can access with a few taps of the finger. See the categories in Figure 10-13.

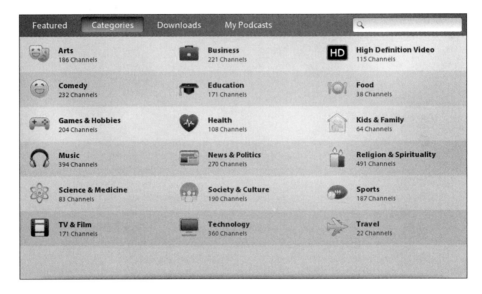

Figure 10-13: From the BlackBerry PlayBook, the podcast icon takes you to a page of featured episodes; click Categories to see available podcasts by subject.

You can also subscribe to many podcasts two ways:

- ✔ Go to the websites of sponsoring stations or organizations.

- ✔ Use the facilities of RSS (Real Simple Syndication) to subscribe to an automatic dispatch of podcasts to your e-mail account. (If you see the RSS icon on a website, explore the site to find out about subscribing to a podcast feed.)

Did you miss a radio broadcast of National Public Radio's *Fresh Air*? No problem: download the podcast and listen to it on your tablet. In Figure 10-14 you can see a list of episodes available from that particular show. Many podcast sources will allow you to listen to a brief preview of an episode before you download the full show.

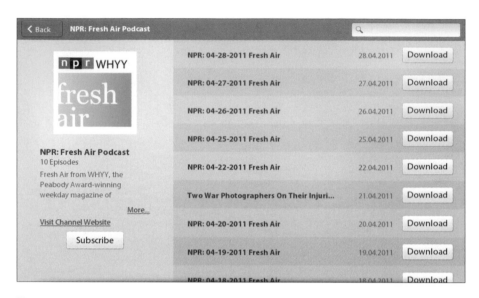

Figure 10-14: Each provider offers episodes. Here, NPR affiliate WHYY shows episodes for its *Fresh Air* interview show. It's a fine production; I'm a regular listener and occasional guest.

Gaming the PlayBook

But can it play *Angry Birds?* For some people, that was the real missing piece from the BlackBerry PlayBook when it hit the stores. But not to worry: a version of the incredibly popular (don't ask me why) game that flew out of Finland in late 2009 and landed on the Apple iPad was winging its way to the tablet as this book went to press.

In case you're not one of the 12 million or so who have bought the game and many millions of others who have tried it, here's the inside skinny: you use a slingshot to launch birds at pigs that sit in, on, or within structures on the screen. The further you progress into the game, the more talented the birds become. But so, too, the pigs become tougher to get at. But in the end, isn't this why the computer and the Internet and the BlackBerry PlayBook were invented?

Don't ask me. I'm too busy playing *Tetris* to sweep away the cobwebs. And then when I get really, really tense (being a *For Dummies* author is not for people who get writer's block or can't meet deadlines), I indulge in my *Need for Speed: Undercover.* The BlackBerry PlayBook comes with two games as part of its basic suite of apps; you can add free games or buy others through the BlackBerry App World store.

Tetris

It's back to the future with *Tetris,* a classic electronic game; the PlayBook version is shown in Figure 10-15. It was actually born in the U.S.S.R. in 1984; I sometimes think of it as the Soviet Union's final attempt at undermining productivity in the capitalist world. Programmer Alexey Pajitnov named the game after the Greek numerical prefix *tetra* and added a suffix from his favorite sport, tennis. And just to add to the mix, the game pieces are known as Tetrominoes.

The game was a staple of early personal computers and then moved on to gaming machines like the Nintendo Entertainment System. Just in case anyone out there hasn't played it, here's the basic idea: a random sequence of tetrominoes of various block shapes fall down into the vertical well. Your assignment is to manipulate the blocks by moving them from side to side or rotating them in 90-degree increments so that you eventually fill a row completely across the screen.

Each time a line is filled, it disappears and any block trapped above the line drops down one or more rows. Playing is relatively easy at first, and then the blocks come faster and the rows build up from the bottom, and then the room starts to spin and sweat breaks out on your brow . . .

The version of Tetris on the BlackBerry PlayBook is similar to the original, except that you manipulate the blocks by tapping and swiping on the touchscreen. And you can use a number of special tools and extra tricks. You can also see the next few upcoming blocks, which is a great deal of help if you can manage to divert your eyes from the well for a few microseconds. The game includes several screens of help, which should get you past the opening sequence. Then prepare to lose hours of productive work.

Need for Speed: Undercover

First of all, this game is a lot of fun. Secondly, it's a great way to show off some of the PlayBook's advanced graphics and controls. See Figure 10-16 for a bit of street action. *Need for Speed: Undercover* is part of a series of racing video games; parent company Electronic Arts has sold more than 100 million copies of the various titles. Perhaps coincidentally (or not) the series was originally developed by a Canadian company in 1994; Distinctive Software was later purchased by EA.

Figure 10-15: I've scored enough points to make it to Level 2, but I'm in a *Tetris* pickle now.

Figure 10-16: Do you feel the *Need for Speed?* This is an exciting and most of all technically impressive game for the BlackBerry PlayBook.

Before the game you can choose a car, adjust its setup, and pick some race tracks. You take hold of the BlackBerry PlayBook (get a good grip, please) and start the race with a tap; then you steer by rotating the tablet left or right. You can apply the brakes and adjust for spinouts, but basically you're trying to keep your car in the middle of the street as it bends one way or another and as cars come at you or across an intersection.

And then there are pesky things like trash cans, cobblestones, median strips, street signs: they're all designed to make things interesting. The game is also accompanied by a frenetic and repetitive soundtrack; you can turn down the music but you're going to want to hear the squeal of tires.

Handle music and sound effects volume this way:

1. **Before starting a race, tap the options icon.**

   The icon looks like a set of tools.

2. **Tap the sound icon.**

   The icon looks like a loudspeaker. Two sliders are available when you click: Music and SFX. The latter is for sound effects including engine noise, squealing tires, and crashes.

3. **Use the slider to reduce or mute the sound volume (or to rev up the noise).**

There is also just a bit of pre-race coaching; see Figure 10-17.

You're definitely going to want to try *Need for Speed: Underground.* But does this sound like a game you might not want to play at your desk when the boss is walking around?

Activate speedbreaker with a single downward swipe anywhere on screen.

Figure 10-17: Spend the time learning the controls for your virtual race car if you hope to ever get out of last place.

Picture This

*H*ere is the gee-whiz good news about the BlackBerry PlayBook: along with all of its other amazing features, its designers have managed to include a highly sophisticated full-color autofocus high-resolution digital camera. *In fact, they put in a pair!* The PlayBook has a 5-megapixel camera neatly hidden on the back of the tablet. And then a slightly lower-resolution camera (a mere 3-megapixel device) is tucked behind the glass at the top of the frame on the front.

Why are there two cameras?

✓ Putting a camera on the back of the PlayBook allows you to frame an image by looking at the large display on the front. If you need to photograph the contents of a whiteboard in a conference room, for example, this would work just fine. So, too, taking a group portrait: hold up the tablet and look at the screen to frame the image.

✓ Adding a camera on the front allows you to snap a self-portrait, something that may be of use to you for social networking or creating a picture icon of your face to attach to e-mail and phone notifications.

Shhh! Don't tell anyone, but the digital camera also can collect a series of still images that can you can play back so fast, one after another, that a human being looking at them will think it's a moving picture. Wait a minute: that sounds very much like the front and back cameras are actually *video cameras.* Well, actually you can go ahead and tell the world; I explain why this is significant in this chapter.

Asking Them to "Say Cheese!"

Taking a photo with the BlackBerry PlayBook is as easy as can be, except that the tablet isn't shaped like a camera (or shaped like a handheld smartphone). First tackle the rear-facing camera, the one on the back of the tablet. You're going to have to deal with the fact that it's slightly awkward to hold up a half-inch-thick 5×7-inch rectangular slab at arm's length and press an onscreen button to take a picture. As much as I admire the design and ergonomics of the BlackBerry PlayBook, this isn't exactly a simple point-and-click procedure.

It's a little bit easier when using the front-facing camera, because you might be able to prop it on your lap or a desk as you frame your handsome visage on the screen. The tricky part with using the front camera is to avoid including your finger in the picture.

When you do press the virtual shutter button on the touchscreen, it takes a second or so before the image is actually collected. The delay allows the internal circuitry to come up with the best exposure level and focus setting, and it lets the auto-stabilization feature reduce blur caused by motion of the tablet itself. And as a bonus, it should give you enough time to get your finger out of the picture.

The internals of the camera are quite complex but the controls for the user are quite simple. In Figure 11-1 you can see the onscreen buttons and sliders. The following sections explain how to use them.

Turn on the camera

If you've created and placed a separate icon for the camera in another location, or if you're using an app that will automatically load the camera, you may have another way to get snapping on your PlayBook. Otherwise, follow along:

1. **Go to the PlayBook's home screen.**
2. **Tap the Media tab.**
3. **Tap the camera icon.**

   Or, from the home screen, tap the All tab and then tap the camera.

Figure 11-1: The onscreen controls for the still camera include turning on or off image stabilization, selecting an aspect ratio, and choosing white balance.

Switch between the front-facing and rear-facing camera

The standard setting is to use the rear-facing camera.

1. **Tap anywhere on the touchscreen (except on the virtual shutter release).**

   The additional controls appear.

2. **Tap the icon in the lower-right corner.**

   The icon shows a small camera with a pair of green arrows that seem to chase each other around a circle. Tap once to switch to the front-facing camera; tap again to switch back to the rear camera.

It is very appropriate to protect your BlackBerry PlayBook in a soft and padded carrying case. One problem with this, however, is that the case blocks the rear-facing camera. You have to remove the PlayBook from the case and carefully hold it in your hands in order to use the camera on the back.

Zoom in or out on a subject

The camera includes a *digital zoom* that allows you to make a person or object appear three to four times closer. The camera will always start with a wide angle view, which is often quite acceptable for a snapshot.

To zoom in closer, tap anywhere on the screen image (except on the virtual shutter release) to display the controls. Move the slide up toward the + sign to zoom in, or back toward the – symbol to zoom out. Make your adjustments in small increments; the screen view will lag slightly behind your changes. In Figure 11-2, I set the zoom to nearly its longest (telephoto) setting to watch our neighbor's horses on their lunch hour.

Figure 11-2: The zoom digitally enlarges the image, which is less sharp than using an adjustable optical lens.

The zoom on the PlayBook camera — like those on other tablets and on nearly all smartphones and many simple point-and-shoot cameras — is a *digital zoom* and not an *optical zoom*. An optical zoom uses an adjustable optical lens to enlarge or widen the image that comes in to the sensor. A digital zoom works with a non-adjustable lens but instead uses the computer processor to enlarge a portion of the image to make it appear closer. An optical zoom delivers a better quality picture, but if you think about it, where in the world would they stick an adjustable lens in a thin tablet or smartphone?

Geo-tag your image

Geo-tagging marks photos with your approximate location on the planet.

HD:TV

Modern high-definition flat-screen TVs use an aspect ratio of 16:9, meaning they're just slightly under twice as wide as they are tall. The viewable portion of a screen that might be 32 inches wide would be 18 inches tall. Older television sets were 4:3, meaning that a viewable portion of the tube that was 32 inches wide would be 24 inches tall. The wider HD experience works well with movies and sporting events.

1. **Tap anywhere on the touchscreen image (except on the virtual shutter release).**

   The controls appear.

2. **Tap the little compass-like icon in the lower left.**

   Geo-tagging is turned on; a set of radio waves will appear to the right of the icon to indicate that the service is on.

3. **Tap the icon a second time to turn off geo-tagging.**

Geo-tagging uses GPS, WiFi router locations, or cell tower identification to show your approximate spot on the globe. This intriguing feature, as this book goes to press, doesn't yet have applications that use the information it collects. But eventually you should be able to take pictures and then have a program figure out where you were at the moment. Or perhaps you could photograph your keys before you go to sleep at night and in the morning ask the PlayBook to help you find where they are. *Note:* as befits a security-oriented company like Research in Motion, IT managers can disable the geo-tagging function in certain situations.

Show more camera options

To see some additional camera options, swipe down onto the touchscreen from the top frame or bezel. Here are the standard set of custom options:

- **Pictures.** Tap here to look at all photos stored on the PlayBook, including those taken with the camera as well as any uploaded from another source or grabbed using the system's built-in screen capture system.

- **Stabilization.** When turned on, this standard setting allows the PlayBook to correct a small amount of movement of the tablet itself when you take the picture. Tap the icon to turn *off* stabilization if you're interested in making artsy, blurry photos.

✔ **Ratio.** Choose between the standard setting (of a 16:9 ratio) for display on the full width of a PlayBook or an HD television, or select the boxier 4:3 ratio, which fits better with many standard sizes for photographic prints. When you tap the ratio icon, you can switch back and forth between the two options. In Figure 11-3, you can see an image taken with the high-resolution rear camera set at the 4:3 aspect ratio.

Figure 11-3: A photo taken at a 4:3 aspect ratio is better for printing without having to crop; the wider 16:9 aspect ratio matches the shape of an HDTV.

Exposure and white balance settings

The camera can accommodate most situations by adjusting the amount of light or length of exposure. Digital cameras can generally record an image in low light, although to get the greatest amount of detail and accurate color, more light is better than less.

Tap one of the three settings to select one of the available exposure settings:

✔ **Auto.** The operating system and processor will choose the best combination of settings based on what's coming through the lens.

✔ **Sports.** The camera will seek the shortest exposure time possible in order to minimize blur caused by moving objects.

✓ **Whiteboard.** This specialized setting looks for a significant area of the image that is closest to white and assigns that value as white; this is an effective tool to allow photographing notes on a whiteboard in a conference room, notes on paper, or other similar objects.

Taking a picture

That's what it's all about, at least for the moment in this section. Tap the camera icon in the large block on the right side of the touchscreen; after a short delay the image is recorded to the memory of your tablet.

Editing a selection of camera pictures

Follow these steps to make things a bit cleaner:

1. **With the camera app open, swipe down from the top bezel.**

   You can now see what's in the Camera folder, as shown in Figure 11-4. Scroll through the images by sliding your finger left or right in the menu at the top.

2. **Tap any picture and choose from these options:**

   • **Delete:** Removes the photo from the PlayBook.

   • **Set as Wallpaper:** That image is set as the home page background.

Figure 11-4: You can edit the contents of the Camera folder from the camera app.

For many photographers, taking the picture with a digital camera is just the start of the process. You can change contrast, brightness, and color saturation, and can remove unwanted elements. You can upload your images to a computer and use a full-featured program like Adobe Photoshop or the simpler Adobe Elements. Or you can do the work on the BlackBerry PlayBook itself by downloading a photo app from BlackBerry App World.

Grabbing a screen capture

One nice bit of programming, an element of the operating system itself, allows you to *capture* just about anything you see on the screen of the BlackBerry PlayBook. The capture is treated as if it were a photo, stored with pictures taken by the camera. For example, you can

- Capture a web page for later reference (or as confirmation of an order or a price quote).
- Capture a frame from a video or other visual media.
- Capture images for use in a book like the one you're reading right now.

To grab a screen capture, press the – and + buttons at the same time (the volume decrease and increase buttons) on the top edge of the BlackBerry PlayBook.

The full screen is *grabbed* at the tablet's resolution of 1024×600. You can easily use those images in a presentation or slideshow. You can edit the images in any digital photo program, either on the PlayBook itself or on a personal computer. In Figure 11-5, I've shot a screen capture of the camera minimized from the full screen; alongside is the PlayBook's Pictures folder.

Take care to honor the copyright of any material you see on the screen of your PlayBook. In general, it is permissible to make a copy of an image or text for your personal use, but the permission of the copyright holder is required before anything can be repurposed for commercial use.

Using a PlayBook as a Picture Frame

Okay, let me see now: the BlackBerry PlayBook has a stunning high-resolution full-color screen, a large block of flash memory storage, a highly sophisticated operating system, and a microprocessor equal to or better than that in many laptop or desktop computers. Don't you think it would make a great digital picture frame? The answer, of course, is yes. The PlayBook can store and display images just like a digital picture frame can. But much better.

Figure 11-5: To grab a screen capture of anything you see on your BlackBerry PlayBook tablet, press the volume + and − buttons at the same time.

The illogical part of this discussion, of course, involves relative price. You can buy a capable picture frame for somewhere starting near $1, while the price for a BlackBerry PlayBook begins at about $500 and goes up from there. But the beauty of a multipurpose device like the PlayBook is that it can be put to . . . multiple purposes. If you want to show your digital photos (one at a time or in a self-propelled automated show), you have some spectacular ways to do so.

I discuss how to use the USB cable to import photos from a smartphone or a personal or laptop computer (and indirectly from a standalone digital camera) in Chapter 2.

Launching the pictures app

The pictures app is one of the utilities that come as part of the basic operating system for the PlayBook. You can load it one of three ways:

- Go to the home page and tap the All button. Find the pictures app and tap it.
- From the home page, tap the Media button to refine your search. Tap the pictures app.
- From within the camera app, swipe down from the top frame or bezel to display options. Tap the pictures icon.

All three routes bring you to the same place, shown in Figure 11-6. You will see folders holding images from various sources. You're given a choice after launching the app:

- ✔ **Camera Pictures.** Here are stored images taken using the front or rear cameras of the BlackBerry PlayBook as well as screen captures.

- ✔ **Photos.** This folder holds any images you've imported to the PlayBook for display onscreen or output by HDMI.

- ✔ **Wallpaper.** A collection of about 25 generic images, supplied by Research in Motion, that can serve as a background image on your home page.

- ✔ **All Pictures.** If you choose this option, you can select from all images found on the tablet, including those from the camera, screen captures, uploaded pictures, and wallpaper.

Tap any of the folders to open a display of small (thumbnail) images. You'll see the name of the folder at the top, in the status bar; at the right side of the status bar, you'll see the number of images in that folder.

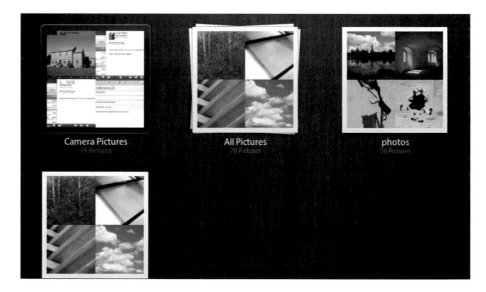

Figure 11-6: Tapping the pictures icon shows folders for all images that the PlayBook recognizes.

You can show your images in larger-than-life living color on an HD screen. Plug a micro-HDMI to HDMI cable (sold separately) into the connector on the PlayBook and into the corresponding port on a high-definition television or projector.

Messing with the folder

Here's what you can do with the Camera Pictures, Photos, Wallpaper, or All Pictures folders:

✔ **Jump to a specific image from your collection.** Swipe down from the top bezel to display the available folders and tap one to open it. Swipe down again from the top bezel to show a scrolling series of thumbnails (as seen in Figure 11-7) and scroll through them with the touch of a finger until you see the one you want to display. Tap it.

Figure 11-7: Can you pick out the two thumbnail pictures of the author, and the two of his wife? Hint: I have no tattoos, and my wife doesn't tend to balance baskets on her head.

✔ **Enlarge a single image to fill the screen.** If an image is smaller than the full screen, simply pinch out. The easiest way to do this is to place your thumb and pointing finger on the image and spread them apart; if the image gets too large, you can pinch in to make it smaller.

✔ **Return an enlarged image to its original size.** The simplest way to reduce an image from an enlarged size to its original size is to tap twice on the picture. Hey, you: get back to where you belong.

✔ **Display a single image.** Tap any of the images to have it fill much of the touchscreen. Depending on the file's size, it may not fill the entire screen. In Figure 11-8, you can see one of my photos as displayed on the PlayBook screen.

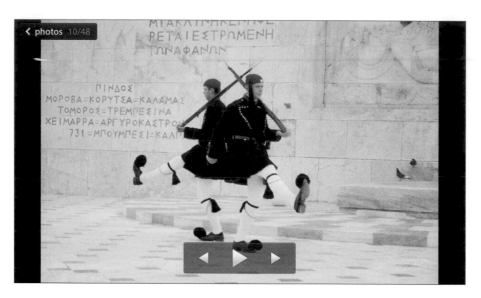

Figure 11-8: When an individual image is displayed, you can start an automatic slideshow.

✔ **Move manually from one picture to another.** You can do this two ways:

- Swipe horizontally from right to left to move to the next image. Swipe horizontally from left to right to move to the previous one.

- Tap an image to bring up a large → play button surrounded on either side by small back ← and forward → buttons. Use the smaller back ← or forward → buttons to move in one direction or another.

✔ **Set up an automatic slideshow.** Tap one of the pictures and then tap the large → play button. The tablet marches through your pictures all by itself, with each one displayed for about two seconds. You can halt the display at any time by merely tapping a picture. Start it again by tapping again, and then tapping the large → play button.

✔ **Set a particular photo as the wallpaper for the home screen.** Display an image you want to use as wallpaper and then swipe down from the top bezel to show available options. Tap the Set as Wallpaper icon in the upper-right corner.

✔ **Delete a specific photo from your collection.** Display an image and then swipe down from the top bezel to show options. Tap the trashcan icon in the upper-right corner. You get the chance to confirm your decision.

Killing the Radio Star: Video

In this section, I tell you how to shoot your own video. In Chapter 8, I discuss how to use Video Chat to use your PlayBook as a webcam or as a two-way videoconferencing device.

The video camera doesn't have electronic image stabilization. To get the best quality videos, take your time and prepare yourself to act like a tripod: stand as still as possible with your legs set a bit farther apart than usual. Tuck your elbows in tight against your sides. If you choose to move the camera/tablet after you begin shooting, do it with a slow and steady motion.

Setting up a video shoot

The video cameras in the BlackBerry PlayBook use the same lenses (and much of the same electronics) as the digital still cameras. Again, the rear-facing camera (the one on the back of the tablet) is the higher-resolution device, providing 5-megapixel high-definition images; the front-facing camera is still quite capable at 3 megapixels.

The video camera has no zoom. The image is shot at the standard wide angle setting. You can make a few minor adjustments to exposure, and you can select the resolution (the amount of detail recorded) for your video.

Start the process as if you were taking a still digital picture. The steps for turning on the camera and switching between rear- and front-facing cameras are the same as those given in the "Asking Them to 'Say Cheese!'" section. To choose the video camera, tap the icon in the upper-right corner to switch between the camera and video camera.

If you use the rear-facing video camera, remove your BlackBerry PlayBook from its protective case. That is, unless you want to shoot a video of life inside a padded carrying case.

To see some additional options for the video camera, swipe down onto the touchscreen from the top bezel. See Figure 11-9. Here are the standard set of custom options:

✔ **Videos.** Tap here to look at all videos stored on the PlayBook, including those taken with the camera as well as any downloaded from another. You can choose All Videos, Downloaded Videos, and Recorded Videos tabs. In Figure 11-10, you can see two clips I downloaded, as well as the very impressive demo reel that comes with the BlackBerry PlayBook.

Figure 11-9: The controls for the video cameras include resolutions from standard to high-definition, plus a choice of white balance.

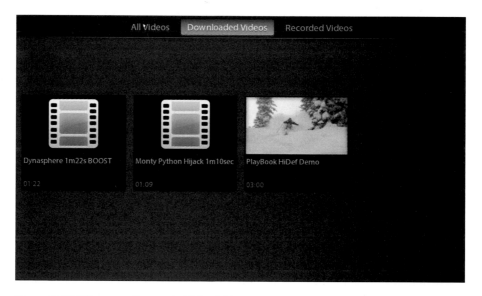

Figure 11-10: When you display the Video folder contents, you can choose among downloaded, recorded, and all videos.

✔ **Resolution.** Tap the rectangle next to Videos to choose a resolution. The BlackBerry PlayBook can shoot and record at the same high resolution used on the most capable of high-definition television sets: 1080p. It can record at a medium resolution of 720p, or standard television definition of 480p. Haven't a clue what those numbers and letters mean? Read the sidebar called "About resolution and interlace."

Videos shot with the BlackBerry PlayBook camera are stored in standard MPEG-4 format, which should be playable or editable on most computer systems. A 1080p recording is much larger than a 480p recording. As an example, using the 5-megapixel rear-facing camera, a 30-second video shot in high-definition will be about 60MB in size, while a standard-definition video of the same length will be about 10MB.

✔ **Delete.** You can get rid of a specific video from your collection by following these steps:

1. **Display the videos and then swipe down from the top bezel.**

2. **Tap the open white square at the lower-right corner of a video to place a checkmark there.**

3. **Tap the trashcan icon in the upper-right corner of the status bar.**

4. **Confirm your decision (or change your mind).**

✔ **Exposure and white balance settings.** The video camera shares the same electronics as the digital still camera; remember that a video is essentially a string of individual still photos that appear one after another. Tap one of the three available settings to select exposure:

- **Auto.** The operating system and processor will choose the best combination of settings based on what's coming through the lens.

- **Sports.** The camera will seek the shortest exposure time possible to minimize blurring.

- **Whiteboard.** This setting looks for a significant area of the image that's closest to white and assigns that value as white; this is an effective tool to allow photographing notes on a whiteboard in a conference room, notes on paper, or other similar objects.

✔ **Shooting a video.** Once you've selected the video camera over the still digital camera, the shutter button is replaced by a silver circle with a red core. Tap the icon to start recording; you will hear a beep and the circle changes to a red square. You'll see a clock running, in seconds and hundredths of a second; tap the red square to stop recording. The video will be stored in the memory of your tablet. Files are recorded on the tablet and automatically named (beginning with the date and then a unique code). For example, a video shot on July 4, 2011, would have filename like this: 2011-07-04T10:40:23.

About resolution and interlace

The PlayBook can record and play back video at three resolutions: 480, 720, and 1080. And it does so without interlace, but instead with progressive imaging. Allow me to explain. First, a very quick primer about television (and computer and tablet screens). The image you see is made up of hundreds or thousands of dots of light (called *pixels,* or picture elements, on a computer). The closer the dots are to each other, the sharper the apparent image; past a certain point human eyes can't discern the gaps between the dots. If you were, though, to carefully bring a magnifying glass near the screen of any electronic display, you should be able to see the dots.

The number refers to the total number of vertical lines that make up the image. An old-fashioned television set as used in the United States, Canada, and many other countries had a vertical image consisting of 480 lines. (Some European standards were slightly higher, delivering 625 lines.) Today's television screens deliver either 720 lines (often called medium resolution) or 1080 lines (high definition). The 720 and 1080 models also have a wider aspect ratio than the near square of the original standard definition sets.

One other detail: the original design for HD used *interlacing,* meaning that the electronics produced half an image and then very quickly went back to draw the other half. This was done to allow a great deal of information to be broadcast quickly without having to double the signal bandwidth; think of bandwidth as the size of the pipe used to deliver data. On a 1080i system this meant that every other line, or 540 lines, were drawn and then the electronics went back up to the top of the screen and filled in the remaining 540 lines. Because it was done so very quickly, the human eye and brain weren't generally able to notice that it was happening (although in certain circumstances, such as something moving very fast across the screen or problems with the transmission itself, some interlaced HD screens produce less-than-perfect images).

On the other hand, a progressive system draws each line one after another, without going back and interlacing missing information. A higher resolution is better than a lower resolution. And progressive is better than interlacing. Why, then, would you want to shoot a video at 480 instead of 1080? If the video is going to be shown *only* on a standard definition television or on a tiny smartphone screen, it's not likely to make a difference and the file size will be much, much smaller.

You can play back the video just as it was shot, or you can become Steven Spielberg or Alfred Hitchcock or Ingmar Bergman: you can edit the files using a full-featured program like Windows Live Movie Maker on a PC or iMovie on a Mac. And there are certain to be editing programs that will be sold as apps to run on the PlayBook itself. A proper editing job might include removing unnecessary portions of a video, cutting from one scene to another, and adding scenes from a different video.

Playing a video

To watch a video on your BlackBerry PlayBook, go to the Videos folder and select one of the files. Then simply tap the image.

The PlayBook comes with a three-minute high-definition video demonstration that is just inches away from unbelievable. I've captured a scene from the video in Figure 11-11. You can pause the image any time by tapping the screen's pause button; start the video again by tapping the → play button. If you tap the circular arrow, the video will loop until you tell it to stop. Adjust the volume by tapping the screen and pressing and holding the slider in the lower-right corner; this is a virtual duplicate of the volume controls on the top edge of the tablet.

Figure 11-11: The video playback controls use VCR-like buttons and also include a volume control.

Viewing videos from other sites

As an Internet appliance (it won't toast English muffins, but it will connect to the web), with the PlayBook you can watch and download videos from many online sites. Check the web pages for your cable television provider, as well as for services like Netflix.com, YouTube.com, and Vimeo.com. Sites like Yahoo make available movie trailers and sometimes short subjects.

This is a fast-changing corner of the Web. Many original sources of programming including major television networks have their own websites where you can watch entire episodes of shows (usually delayed after original broadcast time). Some of these sites include additional material such as interviews with stars and directors, bloopers, and episode recaps.

Some sites, such as hulu.com, blocked free access to video from the BlackBerry PlayBook (just as it does for other tablets), with the hopes of getting viewers to pay for premium access. That policy, and others like it, could change at any time.

The BlackBerry PlayBook includes an app that takes you directly to the mobile version of YouTube.com where you can watch videos without restriction; see Figure 11-12. (You can also go to the same site by entering its address into the tablet's browser. I've discussed the YouTube app in Chapter 5.)

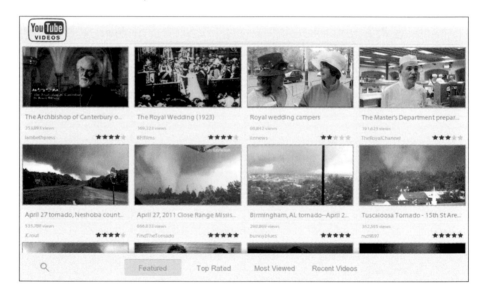

Figure 11-12: The YouTube app, supplied as an app with the BlackBerry PlayBook, takes you directly to a version of the site maximized for viewing on the smaller screen of a tablet.

If you have videos on your personal or laptop computer, you can drag them over to the video folder on your PlayBook when they're connected using the USB cable. The videos must be in MPEG4, WMV (Windows Media), or DixX format; and a number of free or inexpensive conversion programs for your computer can copy videos that you own into one of the compatible PlayBook formats.

NFB PDQ

In yet another Canadian connection, the BlackBerry PlayBook includes an app that goes to the National Film Board of Canada. The NFB, a government agency, produces and distributes documentaries, dramas, and animation in English and French. (The Francophone equivalent is the Office national du film du Canada, or ONF.) Tap the icon and see what's moving and shaking in the nation where the BlackBerry was born; see the accompanying figure for an example.

12

Swiping Through an eBook

*I*t was probably before your time; it was certainly before personal computers. The year was 1947, and the great Jimmy Durante had a hit with the novelty song, "The Day I Read a Book." Here's the refrain: "I'll never forget the day I read a book. It was contagious. Seventy pages. There were pictures here and there, so it wasn't hard to bear. The day I read a book." Oh if The Schnozzle could see us now! The BlackBerry PlayBook comes preloaded with the Kobo Books Reader app.

The Kobo bookstore allows you to purchase a wide variety of current and backlist books and also allows access to a selection of free classics. I tell you in this chapter how you can get free copies of classic books (legitimately!) from sources like Google Books, Project Gutenberg, or Planet PDF. And I also show how to obtain books — including current titles — on loan from your public library.

Reading on the Go with the Kobo

The BlackBerry PlayBook comes with the Kobo Books Reader app; see Figure 12-1 for its welcome page. This electronic portal sells digital books. (Kobo exists in two forms: as an online bookseller and as a separate electronic eReader, like the Amazon Kindle.)

Figure 12-1: The Kobo Books Reader is an app included with the BlackBerry PlayBook.

The Kobo store on the BlackBerry PlayBook is essentially the same as the online bookstores for Barnes & Noble, Borders Books, the Apple iBookstore, the Google eBookstore, and others. You can browse the virtual shelves for current titles, search through thousands of titles by name, author, or subject, and you can make a purchase that's downloaded almost instantaneously to your PlayBook.

Reading a digital book

Reading an electronic book is the same as reading a paper book, only different. There are four very important distinctions:

✔ The version of the book we plan to read does not exist as a physical object. There may be a printed equivalent, or the title may have gone directly from the authors fingertips (with the professional intercession of an editor and publisher) to an electronic file.

✔ The digital process saves trees, paper, and energy because books do not have to be printed and packaged and shipped to the bookstore or directly to your home or office.

✔ You don't need to go anywhere to get a copy of a digital file.

✔ The contents of the file can be corrected, updated, annotated, or archived with the tap of a button.

The Kobo store isn't the only place where you can shop for digital books, but it is the one app that comes preloaded on your BlackBerry PlayBook. You can expect to see other apps from other sellers.

Browsing for a book

This example uses the Kobo store as the model for electronic reading. However, the same principles apply for anywhere else you get a digital book.

1. **Connect to the Internet.**

   Do it by either directly using a WiFi link or indirectly with BlackBerry Bridge to your BlackBerry smartphone and from there to the Web. When cellular radio models of the BlackBerry PlayBook are available you will be able to connect directly to a cellular data link in that manner. See Chapter 4.

2. **Launch the Kobo Books Reader app from the PlayBook's home screen.**

   You'll find it in the Media section (or mixed in amongst all the apps if you choose All).

   Be sure you understand the details of the contract you have with a cellular provider if you intend to use a cell-based data link. Some plans offer unlimited data per month while others run a meter on usage. And all plans can run up very high bills if you use cellular data while roaming on another company's cellular network, especially in a foreign country.

   When the Kobo store opens, you can visit three important sections:

3. **Decide which area you want to enter:**

   • Store

   • Library

   • Search

Store

Store is the simply but appropriately named retail page for books. Here you will find Today's Top 50 (again, simply but appropriately named as a place for current bestsellers). Figure 12-2 shows one day's selection. You can tap Popular Categories to find titles by subject.

Library

The library is where you find the books you've obtained through the Kobo store. This includes titles you bought (speaking on behalf of authors everywhere: thank you very much), as well as classic titles you downloaded for free through Kobo. And you will find previews of books you asked Kobo to send you. Those books follow you from device to device; if you open a book on your BlackBerry PlayBook and later sign in from your BlackBerry smartphone or PC, the content — including the last page you were reading — syncs up.

Figure 12-2: The Kobo store features a daily Top 50 as well as popular categories.

The library offers several views:

- ✔ By Last Read
- ✔ By Author
- ✔ By Title

Figure 12-3 shows the basic bookshelf. If you tap the second icon at the bottom-left corner of the page, you will see a different view of the books in your collection, showing titles and authors, as well as your progress in reading through them, expressed as a percentage of the book read. See Figure 12-4.

Figure 12-3: Each Kobo account has a bookshelf of purchased titles.

Figure 12-4: The alternate view shows the cover, title, and author name for each book, and tells what percentage of each book you've read.

Search

You can enter a name, title, or subject into the Search box in the upper-right corner of the Store page. In Figure 12-5 you can see the results of my hunt for an electronic copy of T.S. Eliot's superb observations on the meaning (or meaninglessness) of life, *Prufrock and Other Observations.* The first version is a free download, the second a presumably more-recently edited and vouchsafed edition from a contemporary publisher. The other two books that turned up in my search for Prufrock apparently have that name buried somewhere in the text; if I'd been more precise in my search they wouldn't have appeared.

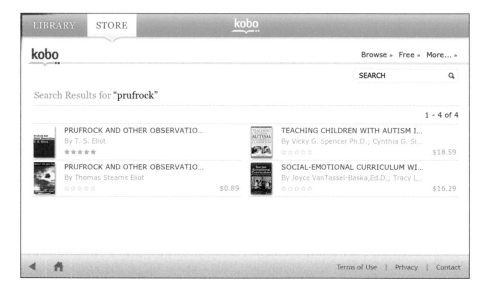

Figure 12-5: The results of a search for a copy of the Prufrock poems by T.S. Eliot.

Buying a book from Kobo

If one part of using the BlackBerry PlayBook has been tested six ways to Sunday, it's user efficiency and satisfaction in the purchasing process. After all, that's where the money is; although Research in Motion makes a bit of money with the sale of each tablet, its business plan also counts on future income from a slice of the sales price of books, music, and apps purchased by users.

When it comes to making a purchase, you need two things:

- ✓ An account with Kobo
- ✓ A credit card

I'll spare you the details of setting up the account, because it's exactly the way you'd expect it to be: name, address, credit card number, login name, and password.

 You can set up an account with Kobo from your BlackBerry PlayBook, a BlackBerry or other smartphone, or from a personal or laptop computer; use the same login and password for the account so you can access the store from any Internet-connected device.

1. **Once your account is in place, go to a book you want to buy.**

2. **Tap its cover.**

   Most titles show a thumbnail of the cover along with a synopsis. For many current books there's a Get Preview link near the book title; tapping that will download a sample from the book. Most importantly is a prominent green button marked Buy Now, as shown in Figure 12-6.

3. **Tap the Buy Now button.**

   I'm sure you know what comes next.

4. **If you haven't already done so in your account, enter your payment and billing information.**

   All the way down at the bottom of the page is a place where you can enter a promo code; once you get a Kobo account, you have every right to expect the occasional special discount offer. These are the things professional shoppers live for; you know who you are.

   Once the buying is done, you're notified that the download is underway. Depending on the file size and your network speed, the book should arrive within seconds or you may have to wait as long as several minutes. Yes, I know that's a huge inconvenience . . .

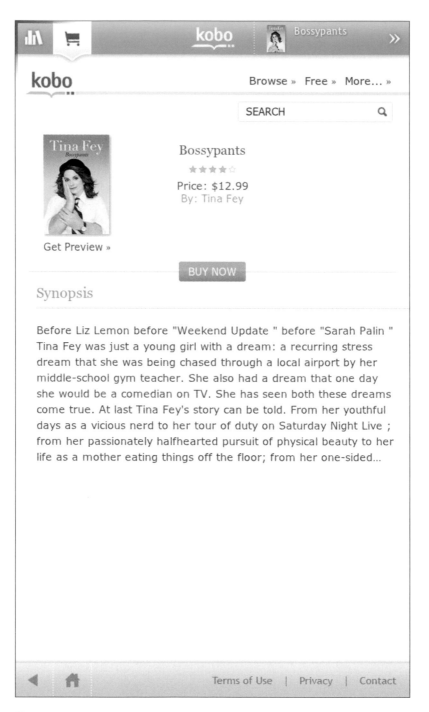

Figure 12-6: Click a book, read a summary, survey the price, and tap Buy Now. In seconds the file is on its way to your PlayBook.

Reading a Book (or a Play) on the PlayBook

The actual process of reading a book is about as simple as, well, reading a printed book.

1. **Open the Kobo Books Reader app.**

2. **Tap Library and find the title with which you want to meld your mind.**

3. **Tap the cover.**

   If you have already begun reading the book, the tablet will open up to the page you last perused.

   Once you're in the book, there are simple instructions (shown in Figure 12-7).

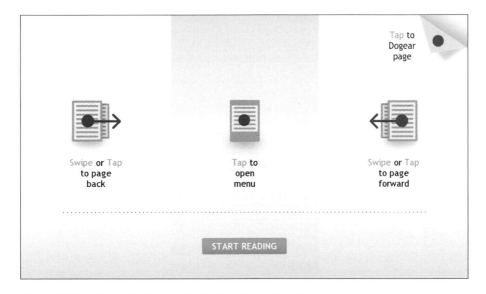

Tap to Dogear page

Swipe **or** Tap to page back

Tap **to** open menu

Swipe **or** Tap to page forward

START READING

Figure 12-7: Basic training for the simple Kobo Books Reader.

4. **Choose what you want to do.**

   The following sections explain what's possible and how to get there.

Advance a single page forward

Either swipe from right to left, as if you were flicking a page deeper into the book, or tap anywhere on the right third of the screen.

Return one page backward

Swipe from left to right, as if you were flicking a page toward the front of the book, or tap anywhere on the left third of the screen.

Place a dogear on the page

To insert the electronic equivalent of a folded corner on any page, tap in the upper right of the text. A small green fold will show up on the page; to remove the dogear, flick it back up to the right corner.

Open the reading menu

Swipe down from the top bezel of the screen (or tap in the center of the screen). The following options are presented:

- ✔ **Library.** Tapping the icon all the way to the left in the status bar at the top (a small shelf of books) will close the current book and take you to your library; the book is marked with a green ribbon and will be the first one on the shelf.

- ✔ **Contents.** Tap here to display the table of contents for the book you're reading. You'll see a checkmark alongside the chapter you were most recently reading. To jump to another chapter, merely tap the chapter name. (Not every book will include a clickable table of contents.)

- ✔ **Overview.** In case you forget why you started reading a particular book, or for some reason need to reacquaint yourself with some of the details, you can tap here to view a synopsis.

- ✔ **Dogears.** Tap here to see the dogears you have electronically and non-destructively placed in the digital book. Tap any of them to jump to that location.

- ✔ **Adjust appearance.** When a page of the book is open, you can tap the gear icon to see controls that let you adjust the font (size and style); see Figure 12-8. Regarding serif versus sans serif fonts: there is no right or wrong choice here — choose what you prefer.

  - The **Font Size** slider (touch the bar and move it left or right) adjusts between very, very small and very, very large type. Pick the one that feels just right.

  - The **Display** button turns on (or off) night mode, which turns down the brightness of the screen when the BlackBerry PlayBook detects low ambient lighting. You can also manually turn up or down the brightness level of the screen.

- The **Reading** button lets you decide whether you want to see one or two pages at a time (Single Page or Double Page, respectively), although in most books only Single Page is available if you choose to rotate the PlayBook and read it in portrait mode. Some books let you choose a page transition, including a gentle fade from page to page or a more abrupt slide; again, certain effects aren't available in both single and double page designs.

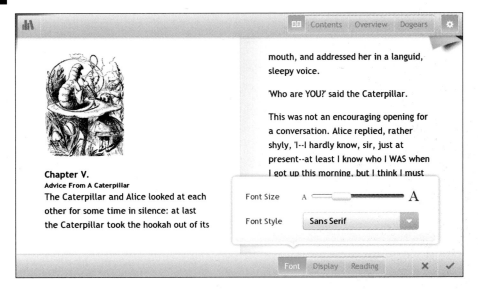

- **Return.** Click the open book icon to go back to the page you were reading before you got distracted by other options.

Figure 12-8: Adjustments for most books include the size and style for the typeface displayed on screen, a choice of single or double columns of text, and settings for screen brightness. The text here has been changed to Sans Serif.

Turning the BlackBerry PlayBook sideways while you're in the Kobo Books Reader app (and most other apps) will automatically change the presentation of the screen from landscape to portrait, or the other way around. In fact, you might want to give your eyes and your brain a bit of a break and switch from one view to another every chapter or so. In Figure 12-9, I rotated J. Alfred Prufrock so that I can absorb more of his amusing, intriguing, neurotic rant at a glance.

Prufrock And Other Observations

streets, After the novels, after the teacups, after the skirts that trail along the floor-- And this, and so much more?-- It is impossible to say just what I mean! But as if a magic lantern threw the nerves in patterns on a screen: Would it have been worth while If one, settling a pillow or throwing off a shawl, And turning toward the window, should say: "That is not it at all, That is not what I meant, at all."

* * * *

No! I am not Prince Hamlet, nor was meant to be; Am an attendant lord, one that will do To swell a progress, start a scene or two, Advise the prince; no doubt, an easy tool, Deferential, glad to be of use, Politic, cautious, and meticulous; Full of high sentence, but a bit obtuse; At times, indeed, almost ridiculous-- Almost, at times, the Fool.

I grow old ... I grow old ... I shall wear the bottoms of my trousers rolled.

Let Us Go Then, You And I, - 6 of 7

Figure 12-9: A single-column portrait mode page of T.S. Eliot's "Prufrock."

About serifs, or the lack thereof

Serifs are the extra little finishing touches used on most characters in that style. They're most evident in letters like T or B. The serifs are those little marks at the left and right side of the horizontal arm at the top of the T, or the extra bits at top and bottom of the vertical stem of the B. One theory for why old typefaces used serifs is that stone carvers — some of the first typesetters, if you think about it — needed them to finish off letters and keep the edges from crumbling. Which style is better? What's the best color for your next new car? It's mostly a matter of personal choice, although most people find that serif is a bit easier to read. Your choice.

The body text of the book you're reading, including this sentence, is set in Times New Roman, which is a classic serif typeface originally designed for the British newspaper *The Times* in 1931 and still widely used in book production.

The other major class of type is sans-serif, which uses the French word *sans,* meaning without. Sans-serif type is type without serifs, like the text you see in this paragraph.

Going Elsewhere for Books

The Kobo Books Reader is intended for use with titles that are downloaded from the Kobo site. That doesn't, however, mean that this is the only possible source for reading material for your BlackBerry PlayBook.

PDFs

To begin with, you can download copies of thousands of public domain (out-of-copyright) books that are stored as PDF files. When you get a book in PDF format, store it on your PlayBook in the Books folder. Then use Adobe Reader (one of the free apps that comes with the PlayBook) to open and read the book. In Figure 12-10 you can see the famous opening chapter from Herman Melville's *Moby Dick,* downloaded from a website called Planet PDF.

You may find it easier to search for and download PDF files using your personal or laptop computer and then use the USB cable to drag and drop the file over to the Books folder on your BlackBerry PlayBook.

Moby Dick   **Planet PDF**

Chapter 1

Loomings.

Call me Ishmael. Some years ago—never mind how long precisely—having little or no money in my purse, and nothing particular to interest me on shore, I thought I would sail about a little and see the watery part of the world. It is a way I have of driving off the spleen and regulating the circulation. Whenever I find myself

Figure 12-10: I downloaded this copy of *Moby Dick* from a site offering free PDF files, viewable on the PlayBook using Adobe Reader.

Using Digital Rights Management files

Other sources for books include public and private libraries, research institutes, and publishers that send their wares directly to the public. In many cases, files from these suppliers are given with Digital Rights Management (DRM) encoding attached.

DRM is used for several reasons:

- **To limit the transfer of a file.** A license for a DRM file may state that it can only be used on a single computer or tablet and can't be transferred to another person or device.

- **To set a time limit on use.** As public libraries begin to offer digital downloads, many publishers are requiring the use of DRM schemes to prevent redistribution of a file and to limit the amount of time a book may be "borrowed" by a user. Why put a time limit? For centuries, libraries have allowed users to check out a book and then asked for its return so that other readers can use it; a time limit on a digital file accomplishes the same thing, de-authorizing or erasing the file after a period of time.

- **To enforce copyright restrictions.** A DRM license may keep someone from copying or changing a file, one of the key elements of a copyright placed upon it.

TECHNICAL STUFF

Adding books using Adobe Digital Editions

Although it wasn't available as this book went to press, Adobe Systems has announced that it intends to add the BlackBerry PlayBook to its list of electronic devices that can be managed using its Adobe Digital Editions software. This program serves as a supervisor for Digital Rights Management material, and is a key element of many library loan programs for digital material. Once Adobe Digital Editions is available (look for it on the BlackBerry App World site or at the website of adobe.com), you will be able to download files from many libraries in EPUB (Electronic Publishing) file format, or as a protected version of a PDF file and then transfer them to your PlayBook using a USB cable connection.

Read Free and Die

As authors, first we nearly kill ourselves to imagine, research, and then write a book. If we're lucky, we make a bit of money from sales. And then we die. However: A vast library of great knowledge has moved beyond copyright protection into what is sometimes called the *public domain*. And some contemporary authors don't copyright their work, or allow free distribution.

These sites are worth visiting for great free reads:

- **Gutenberg.org:** Project Gutenberg offers some files in plain text (which you have to format and convert), and others are converted to PDF (which the BlackBerry PlayBook can read using Adobe Reader). EPUB files will be useable when Adobe Digital Editions is made compatible with the BlackBerry PlayBook.

- **ManyBooks.net:** This site has some of the same books you'll find on Project Gutenberg, along with some new books whose current authors are hoping for an audience.

- **FeedBooks.com:** With a specialty on nineteenth-century classics, this site offers EPUB downloads that will be compatible once Adobe Digital Editions is available for the PlayBook.

- **PlanetPDF.com:** This commercial site has many free classic books in PDF format.

- **http://books.google.com:** Google has classic and obscure books, some of which are in plain type, some are scans, and some are delivered as EPUBs.

Part IV
Keeping House

The 5th Wave   By Rich Tennant

AT THE MIT SMART APPLIANCE LAB

RICHTENNANT

"It's good at distinguishing between pleats and wrinkles, but it still goes nuts around the zipper."

In this part . . .

Where is it written in stone that my tablet has to look and act the same as yours? In fact, just the opposite is true. In Chapter 13, I show you a whole passel (or maybe two passels full) of things you can do to make your BlackBerry PlayBook match your needs and style. After then, it all comes down to maintenance. Chapter 14 shows you what to do to help your BlackBerry PlayBook live a long and productive life. If you want help with your car, there's probably an app for that somewhere else.

13

Customizing and Securitizing

*H*ave it their way. Have it your way. Have it a little bit of theirs and a little bit of yours. And while you're at it, have it as secure and safe as possible. That's where you are: the customization and securing of your BlackBerry PlayBook. The OS allows you a great deal of leeway when you're personalizing the look (and much of the response). And its connection to the BlackBerry Enterprise Server and other features of the BlackBerry smartphone network allow IT departments and individuals to control much of the tablet's security features in this insecure world. This chapter starts out with the sexy stuff: customization. Then it moves onto protection, the smart thing to do.

Looking Marvelous at Work and Play

For many people, it's all about appearance. But you're here because you're a serious, purposeful BlackBerry PlayBook user. However, you might also like your tablet to look really, really attractive.

For an overview of the ways you can customize your PlayBook, follow along:

1. **Open the browser.**

2. **Tap Favorites.**

   You'll need to be connected to a WiFi network.

3. **Choose the BlackBerry page.**

   You'll go directly to a Get Started welcome screen, like the one shown in Figure 13-1.

4. **Tap Personalize Your Tablet, and watch the short video that appears.**

Consider the ways you can give the PlayBook a makeover. It's easy to personalize the tablet in these three golden moments:

- ✔ **During the initial setup.** A number of the early decisions will affect the appearance and operation.

- ✔ **During ordinary use.** Almost every screen has an Options subscreen, which you can get to by swiping down from the top bezel. Tap it and make choices.

- ✔ **Upon visiting the setup screens or help screens.** From the home page, tap the gear icon to display Setup screens. Or go to the home page and select the help app. A helpful help app about personalizing your PlayBook is shown in Figure 13-2.

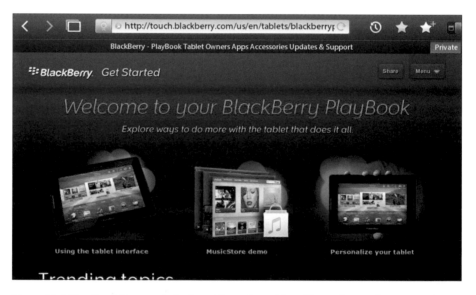

Figure 13-1: The BlackBerry website has videos about things like wallpaper, icon arranging, and other features.

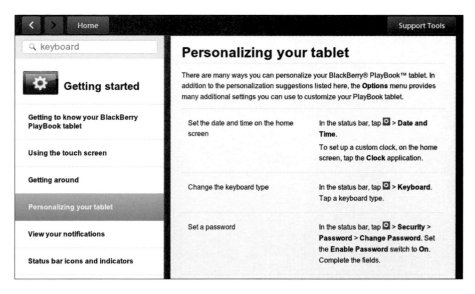

Figure 13-2: The help screens guide you through many personalization options. Get there by tapping the help app from the home screen.

Hanging wallpaper

Your home page is kind of like your rec room; it's a place where you hang out while you think about where you want to go next. Or perhaps, a place where you bring in other forms of entertainment and forget about where you are. Depending on your personal sensibilities and your tendency to distraction, you can choose to have a subtle, unobtrusive background (it's called *wallpaper*) on the home screen, or you can go for something flashy and wild. You can choose from a set of abstract drawings or landscape photos provided by RIM, or you can use one of your own pictures.

Here's how to set a picture as wallpaper:

1. **Open the pictures app.**
2. **Tap Pictures from the home page.**
3. **Choose one of the folders.**

   - **Wallpaper:** Not surprisingly, this is the home of 25 pieces of art supplied by RIM, as shown in Figure 13-3.

   - **Photos:** Holds any images you have transferred to the storage of the tablet from your personal or laptop computer.

- **Camera Pictures:** The home of any photos you have taken using the built-in cameras of the PlayBook.
- **All Pictures:** Shows you every image the tablet can find.

4. **Tap the image you want to use as wallpaper.**

5. **Swipe down from the top bezel to display the status bar, and then tap Set as Wallpaper.**

Figure 13-3: The set of images from RIM are generic and mostly unobtrusive.

When you return to the PlayBook's home page, the image appears in the background. If you want to change the wallpaper, there's no need to bring in a specialist with brushes and buckets; simply repeat the process and select a different image. In Chapter 15 I show you some special tips on how to customize your wallpaper even further.

Want to completely remove the wallpaper? Well, you can't. At least not in the operating system version first released with the BlackBerry PlayBook; I expect RIM to fix this deficiency in upcoming updates, but in the meantime I offer a special workaround in Chapter 15.

Arranging icons

It doesn't take long for a clean desktop to begin to look like the aftermath of an explosion in a cartoon candy store. The total of basic apps alone is about 40, and I imagine most users will double that with ordinary use.

Here's a quick but temporary way to organize your icons: turn the BlackBerry PlayBook 90 degrees so that you're looking at the home screen in portrait mode. In landscape mode, you'll see a maximum of 18 icons on screen; as a portrait the PlayBook can display 24.

Now, consider how to organize the icons to make them easier to find and use. To my way of thinking, the icons I use most often should be at the top of the list and those I use less often should go to the bottom; you may see the world differently, and that's fine.

Here's how to move around icons:

1. **Select the group to be customized.**

   The operating system comes with folders labeled All, Favorites, Media, Games, and BlackBerry Bridge.

2. **Open the folder.**

   If the group doesn't already occupy the lower two-thirds of the screen, swipe up to maximize them.

3. **Tap and hold on to an icon.**

   After about a second, all of the icons in the drawer will start pulsing — enlarging slightly and shrinking, almost as if they were breathing in and out.

4. **Touch an icon and drag it where you want it.**

   When you let go, the icon will drop into place and push other icons to the right, or to the next row down as necessary.

5. **When you're done, tap the small checkmark icon in the upper-left corner.**

   The icons will stop pulsing or jiggling or breathing and they will be locked into position.

Placing icons in a folder

Properly arranged folders are a beautiful thing — a work of organizational art. It also helps you find things in a hurry. The catch-all folder is the one with the appropriate name All.

When you place an icon in one of the other folders, it will appear there *and* be displayed in All.

Here's how to put an icon into a folder to make it easier to find:

1. **Tap and hold on an icon.**

   After about a second, all of the icons in the drawer will start pulsing.

2. **Touch any of the icons; drag it up and out of the main section of the home page, and bring it into one of the folders.**

   The folders are labeled Favorites, Media, or Games. When you let go, the icon will drop into place.

3. **When you're done, tap the small checkmark icon in the upper-left corner.**

   Now when you tap one of the folders, you'll find the icons you put there.

To delete an item from a folder, follow these steps:

1. **Tap and hold it.**

   The icons will pulse.

2. **Tap the small X below an icon you want to delete.**

   The icon is removed from the folder but still shows up in the All collection.

Choosing a keyboard

The BlackBerry PlayBook, as first delivered, can work with three slightly different keyboard layouts: QWERTY, QWERTZ, or AZERTY. I discuss the set of available keyboards in detail in Chapter 2.

I fully expect Research in Motion to add more keyboard choices as the BlackBerry PlayBook gains acceptance around the world. It is relatively easy for programmers to introduce new layouts; I expect to see Cyrillic and perhaps some Asian character sets among the first offerings.

The tablet, as sold in the United States and Canada, comes with the familiar QWERTY keyboard as default. To make a change, do the following:

1. **Tap the gear icon in the upper-right corner of the home screen.**

2. **Tap the Keyboard tab.**

3. **Tap the pull-down menu alongside Keyboard Type.**

   See Figure 13-4.

4. **Select from the available character sets.**

   While you're in the neighborhood, consider whether you want to turn off keypress popup, which gives you an onscreen validation of your typing (by momentarily enlarging the character you pressed). I think it's a very useful feature to have on, but you can turn it off.

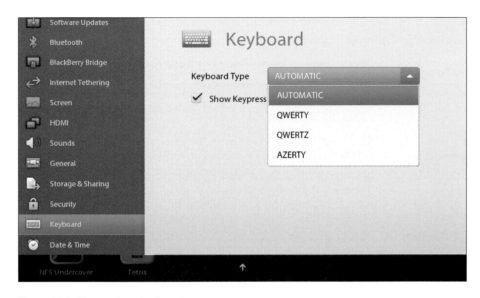

Figure 13-4: Choose from keyboards.

Locking Things Up Tight

One of the reasons for the success of the BlackBerry smartphone in business, government, and other enterprises is its security apparatus. The operating system for the phones themselves is pretty strong, and then there's RIM's own BlackBerry network, which handles most of the routing and management of e-mail and instant messaging for devices. Added to that is a suite of software utilities called the BlackBerry Enterprise Server. This allows an IT department to set rules for devices, control access to data, and otherwise watch out for unauthorized outgoing or incoming traffic or trouble.

I'm going to make an important distinction here between personal users and those who work for a company that has an information technology department that actively manages the deployment of a fleet of BlackBerry smartphones and PlayBook devices. If you work for a company or enterprise that manages devices, most (or all) of the security decisions are going to be made by the IT department. You can request special dispensation if, for example, your work requires you to have access to baseball scores or if you need to shop for shoes from the road; good luck with that argument.

For those of you who own and operate your own BlackBerry smartphones and BlackBerry PlayBook devices, you can make certain security adjustments.

Here are some of the steps I recommend you take, and the following section tell you how to do these things:

- ✔ **Set a password for access to your PlayBook.**
- ✔ **Change your password from time to time.**
- ✔ **Consider setting a password for your BlackBerry smartphone.**

Set a password for your PlayBook

Choose a password that's easy to remember but difficult to guess. And please don't write it down on a sticky note and attach it to the back of the tablet!

To add the requirement for a password, follow these steps:

1. **Tap the gear icon in the upper-right corner of the home screen.**
2. **Tap the Security tab on the left side of the screen.**

   You'll see the screen shown in Figure 13-5.

3. **Tap Password.**
4. **Move the slider for Enable Password to On.**

Figure 13-5: The shorter the time period, the more secure the setting.

5. **Enter a password, and then confirm it by entering it a second time.**

6. **Choose a Lock After time.**

To be safest, choose one or two minutes. That way someone will have to type the password anytime after the BlackBerry PlayBook hasn't been actively used for that period of time.

Change your password

If you're concerned that someone has your secret code, change the password. Some users do this every few months just as a matter of course.

To change the code, follow along:

1. **Swipe down from the top bezel.**

2. **Tap on the gear icon in the upper-right corner of the home screen.**

3. **Tap the Security tab (on the left side).**

4. **On the Password page, tap Change Password.**

5. **Enter the existing password.**

6. **Type the new password, followed by a confirmation.**

Set a password for your BlackBerry smartphone

Setting a password on your smartphone keeps unauthorized users from making phone calls or accessing your calendar, contacts, notes, and other apps. If you do set a password on your BlackBerry smartphone, you'll have to enter it every time you want to access information from the phone using the BlackBerry Bridge application from the tablet. That's annoying, but safe.

One trick I use often in choosing passwords is to use a phone number that I can remember, but one that isn't directly associated with me (for example, the number for a distant relative who has a different last name, or the pizza joint you order from regularly). You can also split up a number familiar to you and place an unrelated, obscure word in the middle: 276beachplum0825 is a pretty good code.

Safe WiFi and Bluetooth practices

Connecting a BlackBerry PlayBook to the Internet and to e-mail servers using a WiFi network is convenient and relatively quick, and it's usually inexpensive or free. Communication between a PlayBook and a BlackBerry smartphone for access to data stored on the phone is quick, easy, and always free.

What could be wrong with either? They might both be fine, or they might be compromised by someone snooping in on the conversation or attempting to steal important personal or business information.

The best practice when it comes to WiFi is to only use networks that you know, and to only know networks that are set up with the highest levels of security. That just might mean the following: don't use free and open networks in cafés, airports, hotels, libraries, or other places.

I make that recommendation knowing that it will be widely ignored because sometimes you will have no choice of networks. And, to be honest about it, I regularly use WiFi networks around the world without knowing the details of their ownership or management.

But one thing you *can* do is avoid sending sensitive information like credit card numbers or passwords over unsecured networks. If you absolutely must do so, change your passwords often; keep in regular contact with your credit card company and financial institutions; be on the lookout for fraudulent access to your accounts. In general, you're protected against loss if you contact financial companies within a short period of time after you discover a problem.

Bluetooth offers a bit of built-in protection because it's a low-power, short-range form of communication; it's unlikely someone could snoop on your systems from hundreds of feet away. However, you can do two things to tighten the latches on this sort of network:

- **Consider whether you want to make sure your BlackBerry PlayBook is discoverable at all times.** If you change Bluetooth settings to make the device not discoverable, no other device can access it.

- **Set a time limit.** That limit will close down discoverability after a specific, short period of time.

The problem with turning off discoverability, though, is that you'll need to go back in and turn it on any time you want to use BlackBerry Bridge or a Bluetooth accessory like an external keyboard or headset.

To make the PlayBook device's Bluetooth radio discoverable (or not), follow along:

1. **Tap the gear icon in the upper-right corner of the home screen.**

2. **Tap the Bluetooth tab on the left side of the screen.**

   You'll see the screen shown in Figure 13-6.

3. **Tap Discoverable.**

4. **Tap the ↓ down arrow and select an option:**

   - On

   - Off

   - 2 Minutes

Figure 13-6: Both ends of a Bluetooth communication session must be discoverable.

Controlling file-sharing security

The BlackBerry PlayBook will let you share certain files via USB cable as well as by WiFi wireless connection. In order for either to happen, you have to enable sharing; the safest setting is to turn both off when they aren't needed. The operating system issues a warning if you enable file sharing without a password; see Figure 13-7.

To turn sharing on or off, or to apply a password, do the following:

1. **Tap the gear icon in the upper-right corner of the home screen.**

2. **Tap the Storage & Sharing tab.**

   This particular tab, shown in Figure 13-8, has five sets of controls; you'll need to work your way down the page moving text up to get to the lower portion.

   Start by making a selection on the USB Connections control.

3. **Tap the ↓ down arrow and choose one of these:**

   • **Automatically Detect** (which should be able to distinguish between Windows and PC devices)

   • **Connect to Windows**

   • **Connect to Mac**

4. **In the File Sharing section, move the slider to On or Off.**

   When it is set to On, you're allowing the transfer of files over a USB cable anytime one is detected by the system.

5. **Make a choice in the WiFi Sharing section, moving the slider to On or Off.**

   Set to On, this permits transfer of files wirelessly. WiFi Sharing is on the lower portion of this page, seen in Figure 13-9.

6. **To make it so a password must be entered** *each time* **before files are transferred, move the slider for Password Protect to On. Then enter and confirm a password.**

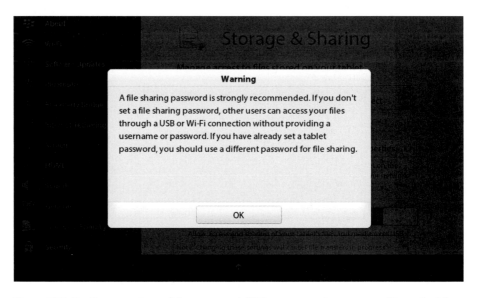

Figure 13-7: Don't say you haven't been warned; RIM recommends a password to protect the data files on your PlayBook and smartphone.

Figure 13-8: The first part of the Storage & Sharing tab sets the behavior of USB connections and controls file sharing.

Figure 13-9: The lower part of the Storage & Sharing tab controls WiFi sharing and whether a password is required before moving files.

Safety while surfing

The BlackBerry PlayBook's Internet browser has many of the latest security and privacy components that you see on personal or laptop computers. But you do need to consider which settings to use. The safest way to surf the Web is to enable private browsing. It's not perfect, but when this setting is enabled, your tablet won't maintain much (or any) information about places you've been and won't keep *cookies*. Cookies are deposited on your device as records of your visit.

When you use private browsing, you will *not* be completely invisible to places you visit, though; many sites can determine your general geographic location based on the WiFi router you use or (if you use BlackBerry Bridge to a BlackBerry smartphone, or if you have BlackBerry PlayBook with a built-in cellular radio) your location can be determined based on the cell tower in use. This sort of information may be of great interest to some advertisers who will attempt to send highly localized offers and come-ons to your BlackBerry smartphone and through it to the browser in your PlayBook. Some users also worry about Big Brother always knowing where they are; that's almost impossible to avoid in our modern world. Just smile for the cameras that track you nearly everywhere you go.

When you get to the Privacy & Security page, these options present themselves:

- ✔ **Keep History.** You can store your browsing history for a period of one to five days. Although it's nice to quickly return to sites you visited a few days ago, leaving this set on anything other than one day makes it possible for an unauthorized user (or your boss) to see where you've been browsing *if you haven't enabled private browsing*.

- ✔ **Block Pop-ups.** Amen to that. *Pop-ups* are those annoying boxes that appear within some browser pages; they're especially bothersome on the smaller screen of a tablet. The blocker isn't perfect; advertisers are constantly trying to find ways around roadblocks. To enable the block, move the slider to the On position.

- ✔ **Accept Cookies.** In a perfect world, you'd keep this setting in the Off position; however, many sites require that you accept cookies. You can, though, erase cookies and history; I show you how in a moment.

- ✔ **Enable Websockets** and **Enable Web Inspector.** These aren't security issues — at least not yet. *Websockets* allow for faster communication in certain circumstances; you can experiment with it as you like. Web Inspector allows you to peer inside a website and learn about its construction; most users will leave this switch off. You must enable a password in order to use Web Inspector.

To turn on private browsing, do this:

1. **From the home page, tap the browser and connect to the Internet.**

    You need an active WiFi or cellular connection. See Chapter 4.

2. **Swipe down from the top bezel to display the status panel.**

    This browser is different from the general display of the home page.

3. **Tap the gear icon in the upper-right corner of the browser status panel.**

4. **Tap the Privacy & Security panel on the left side of the screen.**

    You'll see the page shown in Figure 13-10.

5. **Move the Private Browsing slider to On or Off.**

    You can change a bunch of other settings on the Privacy & Security panel. In general, I recommend turning on all security features and limiting the amount of time that history is kept.

6. **Make choices:**

    * **Keep History**

    * **Block Pop-ups**

    * **Accept Cookies**

    * **Enable Websockets**

    * **Enable Web Inspector**

7. **On the lower part of the same Privacy & Security page, make choices:**

    * **Clear Cache:** Erase the temporary storage of certain material from the web. See Figure 13-11.

    * **Clear Cookies:** Erase cookies placed on the tablet.

    * **Clear Local Storage:** Delete data and other material stored on your tablet by a website.

    * **Clear All:** Take away all of this private information at once.

    For the utmost in privacy, I recommend tapping Clear All any time you're concerned about performance or security.

Ultra security

One of the big selling points for the BlackBerry PlayBook is its ability to display Flash scripts, the fancy animations and interactive elements that seem to bring a web page to life. (As of the writing of this book, the browser on Apple's iPad doesn't work with Flash.) The PlayBook also allows the more commonly compatible Javascript.

Figure 13-10: The upper portion of the Privacy & Security tab allows setting of a number of browser features.

Figure 13-11: The lower portion of the Privacy & Security tab allows you to clear information stored on your tablet by websites you visit.

Although problems with Flash and Javascript have been relatively rare, there is the possibility that evildoers can hijack some of that code to identify users and perhaps compromise the data on a computer. I'm not saying this is something that I stay up nights worrying about, but if you do have concerns, you can turn off either or both technologies.

To turn off Flash or Javascript:

1. **Load the browser.**
2. **From the home page, tap the browser and connect to the Internet.**

   You'll need an active WiFi or cellular connection. See Chapter 4.
3. **Swipe down from the top bezel to display the status panel.**

   The browser is different from the general display of the home page.
4. **Tap the gear icon in the upper-right corner of the browser status panel.**
5. **Tap the Content panel on the left side of the screen.**

   You'll see the page shown in Figure 13-12.

   You might want to set Load Images to Off if you have a very slow connection, or if you're roaming and paying exorbitant fees for Web access. You'll be able to see text, but images are blank and marked only with a filename.
6. **Move the Enable Flash slider to On or Off.**
7. **Move the Enable Javascript slider to On or Off.**

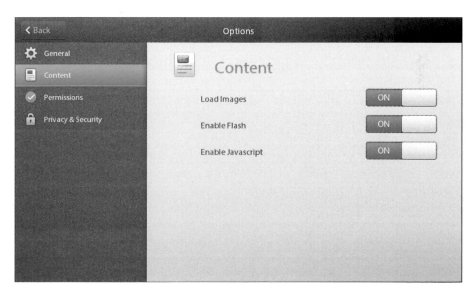

Figure 13-12: The Content panel lets you turn on advanced browser features such as Flash and Javascript.

Enabling a virtual private network

A *virtual private network (VPN)* is a fine addition to any communications system; it is not often used by individuals, but instead is commonly included as part of a corporate or enterprise information technology plan. A VPN can carry any kind of network traffic, including data, video, or voice. It uses authentication to deny access to unauthorized users, as well as encryption to make any pilfered data difficult or impossible to read or listen in on. It's way beyond the scope of this book to discuss how to set one up for yourself; but here's how to add a new VPN profile if your organization already has one in place:

1. **Swipe down from the top bezel.**

2. **Tap the gear icon in the upper-right corner.**

3. **From the panel options on the left, tap Security.**

4. **Tap VPN.**

5. **On the VPN screen, tap Add New.**

6. **Fill in the requested details as provided by your IT department.**

Using Security Certificates

Digital certificates, also called *security certificates,* are encrypted, locked documents that prove your identity as a user, or prove that a website or other Internet destination is the place it claims to be. You've been involved in this authentication process if you use a browser to visit your bank's website. Once again, this is an area where few individual users become personally involved; an IT department or a network security agency will instead configure websites and provide special instructions to users of computers or tablets like the BlackBerry PlayBook that seek to use them.

If you're instructed to import security certificates to your PlayBook, do the following. But before you start, make sure you get in touch with an IT pro and find out the class and the certificate store (or stores).

1. **Connect the PlayBook to your personal or laptop computer using the USB cable.**

2. **On your computer, locate the certificates you want to move to the tablet.**

3. **Drag and drop the certificates from the computer to the folder on your BlackBerry PlayBook called Certs.**

4. **On the PlayBook, swipe down from the top bezel of the tablet.**

5. **Tap the gear icon in the upper-right corner of the browser status panel.**

6. **Tap Security (in the panel options on the left side of the screen).**

7. **From the Security panel, tap Certificates, as shown in Figure 13-13.**

8. **Tap the Import button.**

9. **Based on instructions provided you by an IT professional, select the class and the certificate store or stores to be used.**

   This same screen also allows you to tap an existing certificate to view its details. You can delete a certificate by tapping the pen icon and then tapping the X next to the certificate.

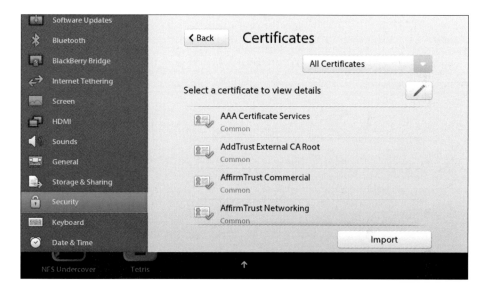

Figure 13-13: The Certificates panel is the place to import new digital certificates, view existing ones, and delete unneeded security documents.

14

Maintaining PlayBook

*T*he hardware is solid, its components are regarded as well chosen, and the operating system is stable and capable. The PlayBook has no moving parts, so you don't have to worry about hard disk drives or CD/DVD drives or fans. The only mechanical elements are the four little ports for cables and four buttons on the top edge.

What could possibly go wrong? In no particular order, here are the possible sources of trouble:

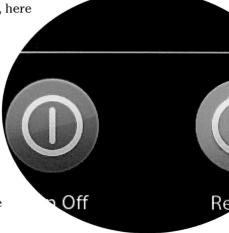

- ✔ The battery
- ✔ The touchscreen
- ✔ The ports and buttons
- ✔ The operating system and apps

Getting some Help

TIP

When something doesn't seem right, you can start the rescue process a myriad of ways:

- ✔ Consult the help screens that are built into the BlackBerry PlayBook; see Figure 14-1 for the entryway, which you can reach from the home screen. Of course, this won't work if your PlayBook is frozen (read: no longer responding to your taps and swipes).

✔ Consult the extensive help pages, forums, and knowledge base available from a personal or laptop computer by going onto the Web to blackberry.com.

✔ Consult a living expert. Don't overlook one of the nice features you get when you buy a BlackBerry PlayBook: 90 days of free telephone support. This isn't just for problems, crashes, and disasters: RIM's patient representatives can tell you where to find the power button or how to plug in the USB cable (although that's also covered in this book with flair and full color photographs).

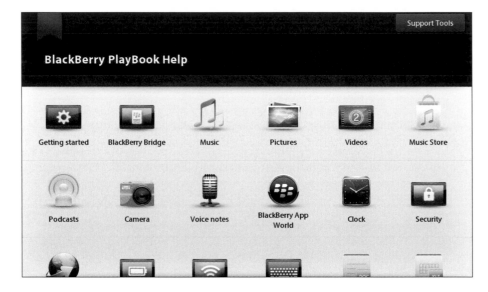

Figure 14-1: The help icons offer basic training and tips for many of the tools and apps.

Resuscitating a BlackBerry PlayBook

The following sections are equal to emergency CPR — something that you may never have to perform on your PlayBook. But just as with humans, it's a tool you should have ready at all times just in case. You should understand four skills:

✔ Doing a soft reset.

✔ Doing a hard reset.

✔ Clearing the browser.

✔ Doing a factory reset (which is serious business).

Both soft and hard resets are *non-destructive.* They don't delete any files, apps, or settings.

The soft reset

If you shut down and then restart your PlayBook, it powers off the operating system and closes any apps that are running. This just may solve an occasional problem.

You can do this sort of soft reset two ways.

Soft reset: Way 1

Follow these steps:

1. **Tap the Power Off app on the home screen.**
2. **You're offered a choice of turn off or restart; see Figure 14-2.**
3. **Tap Restart.**

Figure 14-2: If the system locks up, reset by pressing and holding the power button for ten seconds.

Soft reset: Way 2

Follow these steps:

1. **Press and hold the tiny power button for about ten seconds.**

   The power button is on the top edge of the PlayBook. After pressing for a bit, you're presented with the option to turn off or restart.

2. **Tap Restart.**

The hard reset

A hard reset is similar to a soft reset, except that it also clears the processor's temporary registers (electronic hiding places, if you will). This may clear the mind of your BlackBerry PlayBook if some of the installed software misbehaves seriously.

To do a hard reset, follow these steps:

1. **Press and hold the + and – volume keys *and* the power button for about ten seconds.**

   All three buttons are on the top edge of the tablet. After you press them for a time, the system will shut down.

2. **Wait a few seconds and then press and hold the power button.**

   The PlayBook restarts. There is a very subtle difference in the appearance of the Turn Off/Restart panel displayed in a hard reset (versus in a soft reset); see Figure 14-3 and see if you can spot it.

Figure 14-3: A hard reset appears the same as a soft reset, except that the former overlays whatever's running on the PlayBook when you give the command.

Clearing the browser

Research in Motion, Google, Microsoft, the United Nations, and your local gardening club are all equally powerless when it comes to managing web page authors. There are evildoers who try to plant viruses or to spy on users, there are businesses that attempt to put things on your tablet you don't want, and there are some simply incompetent programmers who allow pages to send things that can cause problems.

I discuss how to clear the browser cache and cookies — two possible ways to clean up from a web mess — in Chapter 13. Here's a quick recap on how to go clear:

1. **From the home page, tap the browser and connect to the Internet.**

   You need an active WiFi or cellular connection, as described in Chapter 4.

2. **Swipe down from the top bezel to display the status panel.**

   This status panel is different from the general display of the home page.

3. **Tap the gear icon in the upper-right corner of the browser status panel.**

4. **Tap the Privacy & Security panel on the left side of the screen.**

5. **On the lower part of the page, choose an option:**

   • **Clear Cache:** Erase the temporary storage of certain web material.

   • **Clear Cookies:** Erase cookies placed on the tablet.

   • **Clear Local Storage:** Delete data and other material stored on your tablet by a website.

   • **Clear All:** Take away all of this private information at once.

   You can try each of the cleanup options individually, but if you really want to perform a deep cleaning, choose Clear All.

Wiping everything clear: Factory reset

Stop, wait, and think: if you've done all there is to do (including calling RIM for their advice), you may have to wipe out your PlayBook's memory. Think of Hal singing "Daisy, Daisy, give me your answer do" in the film *2001* as the anthropomorphic computer's mind was deleted bit by bit.

A *wipe,* or a *factory reset,* will restore your BlackBerry PlayBook to how it was when you first got it: the operating system and the standard set of apps but nothing else. A factory reset deletes apps you have downloaded, any photos or videos you took by yourself or transferred from another device, and any configuration settings you made. You'll lose the registration of your PlayBook to a BlackBerry ID; you'll have to re-enter that ID in order to connect to the mothership for updates, support, and the download of apps.

If possible, use the BlackBerry Desktop Manager on your PC in connection with your BlackBerry PlayBook and make a full backup of the contents of your tablet in a folder on your personal or laptop computer. This will allow you to reinstall apps and data to the tablet after a factory reset. If you suspect that one of your apps is the source of the problem, install your apps selectively; test the PlayBook after each one is in place to see if the PlayBook still works properly.

You've been warned at least twice. And if you ever try to do this command from the screen of your BlackBerry PlayBook you'll be warned once again. Here's how to perform a factory reset:

1. **From the home page, swipe down from the top bezel**

   The status screen opens.

2. **Tap the gear icon in the upper-right corner.**

3. **Tap Security in the left panel.**

4. **On the Security screen, tap the Security Wipe section.**

   You'll see the cautionary screen displayed in Figure 14-4.

5. **If you're truly ready to proceed, tap in the entry box.**

   The onscreen keyboard comes up.

6. **Enter the super-secret password: blackberry.**

Figure 14-4: The Security Wipe is the nuclear option for the BlackBerry PlayBook. It will erase all data and reset the system back to its factory defaults; if possible, save your data to a file on a personal or laptop computer before doing a wipe.

The password to confirm a Security Wipe is the simple word **blackberry**. It's the same password on every BlackBerry PlayBook tablet. This is a great reason to place a general password on your PlayBook; otherwise anyone could pick up your tablet and wipe out its mind. Read Chapter 13 for password creation help.

7. **Stop. Think.**

8. **If you're ready, tap Wipe Data.**

Powering Up

Most BlackBerry PlayBook users are cordless for much of their time with the tablet because the PlayBook uses a high-tech rechargeable battery. The battery itself isn't something you should ever expect to see (unless your BlackBerry PlayBook suffers a catastrophic disaster or you absolutely insist on opening the sealed case and possibly voiding the warranty). It has no external door so you can get at it; a repairperson has to pry open the case, remove the motherboard inside, and pry out the battery which is *glued into place*. Get the picture?

The battery isn't intended to be replaced by mere mortals (read: the user, a.k.a: you).

The battery itself is a 3.7-volt 5400mA lithium-ion polymer device, rated at 19.95 watt-hours. What does all that mean? It's pretty much state-of-the-art for consumer devices, squeezing a lot of power into a tiny package a bit smaller than a stack of three credit cards. Of all those numbers in the specs for the BlackBerry PlayBook battery, the most important to you is 19.95. That's its watt-hour rating. One watt hour is the amount of electrical energy that a one-watt load would draw for one hour. You can extrapolate that the PlayBook draws, on average, perhaps three watts per hour, which is where its charged life of about four to eight hours is delivered.

Playing battery percents

According to RIM, you should be able to get somewhere between six and eight hours of continuous use from your PlayBook if you start with a fully charged battery. When they say continuous use, that could mean two hours of use on four days spread across a week, or it could mean Monday from 9 a.m. to 5 p.m. Some users will get more time from their charged battery, and others less. And the same user will find different results on different days. Why? Because different types of activities and various patterns of work draw power from the battery at differing rates.

In Figure 14-5, the battery icon in the status bar at upper right is fully green, which means it has close to a 100 percent charge. When the battery level drops to 9 percent, you get a warning message on the touchscreen like the one shown in Figure 14-6. Make sure you save any work to a file and think about finding an AC outlet soon.

When the battery reaches 0 percent charge you may still be able to work for a while, but eventually the PlayBook will call it quits and shut down all by itself; you'll need to connect it to an AC power source and give it a bit of a head start before you can use it again.

About the charger

Your BlackBerry PlayBook battery is rechargeable. RIM is kind enough to include a charger in the nifty box that comes with the tablet.

The PlayBook charger uses the same Micro-USB connector as the charger for BlackBerry smartphones, but the one for the tablet puts out more amperage; think of amperage as the force of water coming out the garden hose. The tablet charger, in fact, puts out 1.8A or 1800mA, while a regular BlackBerry smartphone charger pumps out less than half the amperage, 700mA.

Battery charge indicator

Figure 14-5: How much charge do you have left? Glance at the icon in the upper-right corner of the status bar.

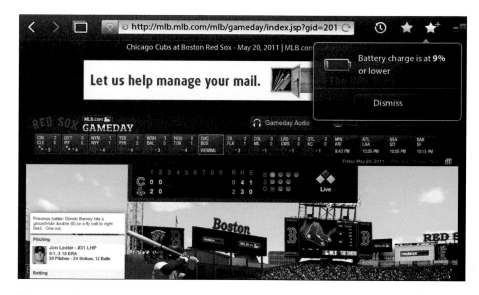

Figure 14-6: A warning shows up when you have just 9 percent capacity.

Here's what this means:

✔ Don't use a BlackBerry smartphone charger to top off the battery in your BlackBerry PlayBook; it doesn't have the horsepower.

✔ You can use the BlackBerry PlayBook charger to repower your BlackBerry smartphone; it should recharge the battery much faster than the original device.

You can charge your BlackBerry PlayBook with the power on or off; it will top off faster if you're not using the device while the electrons fill up the battery.

When the tablet was first released to the public it had a rather odd recharging scheme: if you plugged in the charger while the BlackBerry PlayBook was off, it just sat there like a piece of plastic and glass and did absolutely nothing at all. You had to turn it on to allow new juice to flow. That restriction went away a few months into the life of the PlayBook with one of the updates to the operating system. Now, if you attach the charger to a tablet that's off, the system figures out what's going on and turn itself on to accept the charge.

Lithium-ion batteries are meant to be kept within a specific range of charge at all times. The minimum charge level is why the PlayBook may work for a short period of time with what the system declares to be a 0 percent charge; there's obviously still some juice in the can, but when the microprocessor gets worried about the actual level, it will shut down the system. Recharging a battery should take between two and three hours. The charger can run on 110 volts, which is what we get from the wall socket in the United States, Canada, and many other places around the world. It will also accept 240 volts.

You don't need a converter to use it in places around the world that use the higher voltage but you *will* need to obtain an adapter plug that sits between the prongs of the charger and a European-style wall outlet.

If you connect your BlackBerry PlayBook to a personal or laptop computer using the USB cable, it will provide a small amount of power to the battery — enough in most cases to keep it from discharging — but not enough to repower a depleted battery.

Troubleshooting the charger

The BlackBerry PlayBook charger is a small sealed black box. You can only assume it is working when you plug it into your tablet. (It doesn't even have an LED light to tell you if it's working.)

Examine the charger and the full length of its cable, looking for any obvious signs of damage. A crimp or cut in the cable could render the charger useless and even possibly damage the PlayBook. Scorch marks near the AC plug are an indication of a possible electrical short or other problem. Don't attempt to repair a damaged charger; a replacement unit costs much less than a new tablet.

Make sure that the electric outlet you're using is live. Test it by plugging a portable radio or lamp or other device into the outlet and see if it receives power. Assuming that the outlet is live, you can do two things to assure yourself that the charger is sending power to the battery:

- ✔ When it's plugged into an AC source and then attached to a PlayBook, look at the tablet's home screen and tap the battery icon. If it shows a small lightning bolt across the battery, the charger is sending power. You can also look at the percentage of charge left in the battery; it should slowly climb toward 100 percent.

- ✔ Plug the BlackBerry PlayBook charger into a BlackBerry smartphone. RIM's phones have a small LED that flashes as the device is charging. (Memo to RIM: how about adding that to the PlayBook in future models?)

Getting the most from your battery

Usually, when you look at the things that use up battery in a computer, you consider things like the hard disk drive, CD/DVD motors, and fans. But the BlackBerry PlayBook has no moving parts. Instead, its biggest electrical power suckers are the touchscreen backlighting, the power consumed by the microprocessor and memory, and the various radio transmitters it uses (WiFi, Bluetooth, and cellular).

With good luck and good practices, the BlackBerry PlayBook battery should last for several years and a full charge for a day's work. What are good practices?

And I'm spent . . .

At least at the start, allow your PlayBook battery to become completely or nearly completely discharged before you recharge it. Do this four or five times in a row to teach the battery a bit about its capabilities. (I'm serious; engineers talk about something they call the *memory effect* in modern batteries. If a battery is regularly recharged when it is only half discharged, it begins to act as if half a charge is all it can handle.)

Light bright

Set the screen brightness no higher than you need it. The higher you set the brightness, the more battery power is consumed. From the Options page, choose Screen. Use the slider to make it darker.

Time out! Stand by

Make the Backlight Time-out and Standby Time-out options as short as what you can deal with. The system will hibernate when it detects no activity, but will quickly come back to where it was with a horizontal swipe. You can manually put the device into standby mode by briefly pressing the power button on the top edge of the tablet. To bring it back to life from this form of standby, swipe down from the top frame to the bottom frame. See Figure 14-7 for the adjustment panel.

Don't forget:

- ✓ Auto hibernation: Swipe side to side
- ✓ Manual hibernation: Swipe top to bottom

Figure 14-7: You can give a time out on the Screen panel.

Say 'bye to WiFi and Bluetooth — for now

Turn off WiFi when you don't need it. From the Options page, tap the WiFi icon and turn the switch to Off. Also turn off Bluetooth when you don't need it. From the Options page, tap the Bluetooth icon and turn the switch to Off.

Taking a pause for the cause

If it doesn't affect your working pattern, set the system to pause apps when you show the home screen or switch between apps. See Figure 14-8.

1. **From the Options page, tap the General tab.**

2. **Set the Application Behavior switch to Paused.**

Plug the drain

Although the tablet uses a small amount of power when it's in standby mode, you need to turn it off to completely stop the power drain. You can do this in one of two ways:

- ✔ Press and hold the Power button until it displays the Turn Off panel. Tap Turn Off. (Refer back to Figure 14-2.)
- ✔ Tap the Power Off app (on the home screen) and then tap Turn Off.

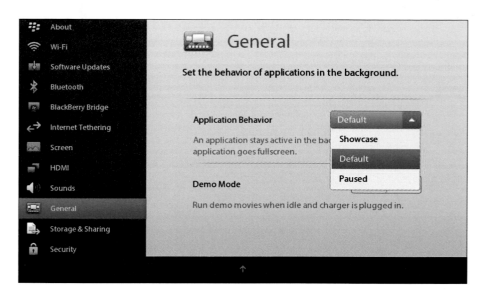

Figure 14-8: Save some battery power by pausing any application that's in the background.

Staying Up to Date at All Times

You can count on RIM to notify you any time there's an important update to your PlayBook's OS. But you can also check whether a *patch* (a repair) or an *update* (fixes and new features) has been made available by checking the Software Updates panel.

It is very important that you keep your PlayBook current via updates.

Here's how to check for updates:

1. **Plug your PlayBook into a wall outlet.**

   Don't rely on battery power during this operation! You should perform any software update while the PlayBook is plugged into a wall AC outlet (or after checking that its battery has 20 percent or more charge). If the update is interrupted because of lack of power, the operating system of the tablet could become corrupted and unusable.

2. **Make sure your PlayBook is linked by WiFi to the Internet.**

   Some models with a cellular data link may also permit updates using that method; make sure you understand the terms of your contract with your cellular provider to see if you'll be charged for using the system to download an update.

3. **From the home page, swipe down from the top bezel to display the status screen.**

4. **Tap the gear icon in the upper-right corner.**

5. **Tap Software Updates in the left panel.**

    On the screen you'll see the version number for the BlackBerry tablet OS.

6. **Tap the Check for Updates button.**

    If an update is available, you're prompted to download it. A full update might be 300MB or larger; depending on the speed of your WiFi connection and other conditions, it could take ten to 20 minutes to fully download the new OS. You're notified of the progress of the download as it occurs; see Figure 14-9 for a completed session.

7. **Press Restart (if you're asked to).**

    A restart is usually needed because the operating system underlies all features of the tablet. In Figure 14-10, the update is in place on the PlayBook, but isn't being used yet.

Figure 14-9: Updates are downloaded to your tablet; they must be installed in place of the previous OS.

Most of the changes aren't usually visible to users, but instead are aimed at improving the system's performance. But some updates bring new features such as Video Chat, which arrived a few weeks after the BlackBerry PlayBook was introduced to the market.

Figure 14-10: After the new OS is installed, restarting is the de rigeur.

Cleaning Up the Place

The BlackBerry PlayBook *doesn't* have an oil-resistance surface. It accumulates smudge marks quite easily, and I suspect that some people (not me) might even occasionally eat a candy bar or a bag of greasy French fries at their desk and then touch the screen. I'm not just talking about hygiene here; oil and other stuff that accumulates on the surface of the touchscreen can make it less responsive. It also doesn't look very good.

Use the cleaning cloth provided by RIM to keep the screen clear. *Don't* apply any cleaning chemicals to the surface; in a worst case scenario you can ever-so-slightly dampen a tissue or a soft cloth to remove some dirt but please do not go overboard: the BlackBerry PlayBook should *not* be placed in your dishwasher for cleaning.

It's also worthwhile to clean out the various openings in the case of the PlayBook: the USB and HDMI ports, the high-speed recharger pins, and the tiny headphone connector. The best thing to use is plain air; if you have a photographic squeeze blower you can use that. Or you can use a vacuum.

One cleaning method I do *not* recommend: bottled air sprayers. Most use a liquid propellant that can come out with the air if you hold the can at the wrong angle.

A home for your PlayBook

The tablet comes with a thin little sheath to protect it during shipping; that fabric cover will also serve as an extra protection against scratches while traveling. However, I do recommend buying a cushioned case for the PlayBook. The seven-inch screen is fairly common and you can use any design intended for a tablet of that size, including the PlayBook, the Sony Galaxy Tab, and the Dell Streak 7, among others. If you use a case, it will block the rear-facing camera; you'll have to remove the PlayBook from the protective housing if you want to use that feature. Some cases are considered convertibles in that they can hold the tablet upright on a desk when they're fully open.

Calling in the Pros

Computers of all sizes — including the tiny BlackBerry PlayBook — come with almost no printed manuals (for which the authors of *For Dummies* books are thankful) and the advice from the pros is this: If you can't fix it from the outside, don't even think about looking inside.

There are some problems that proper practices, above-average intelligence, and extremely good looks cannot fix. The fact is that there are no user-accessible parts within the tablet's slim case.

The fine print that comes with the BlackBerry PlayBook defines the terms of the limited warranty. Note the word *limited*. RIM agrees to repair or replace your unit if it fails or is less than fully useable "because of defects in materials and workmanship under normal use." If you take good care of the tablet and an internal part simply dies, RIM should be good for a replacement. If you left it on the roof of your car and then it flew onto the highway and was run over by a circus truck carrying two elephants and 26 clowns, you just might have to buy a new one. Oh and one more hint: the first thing a repair department looks for is any sign that a device has gotten wet.

Here's my advice on dealing with problems with your PlayBook: Try the tips and troubleshooting advice included in this book. Who knows? They might help. If not, try the following sources.

Dot-com

Using a personal or laptop computer, consult the BlackBerry knowledge base at blackberry.com. Select the section about the BlackBerry PlayBook and search for solutions from the company and from the user community.

What is a *user community?* Besides the help that RIM gives to BlackBerry PlayBook users, there is bulletin board where you can ask questions; provide answers or tips you have worked out on your own; and otherwise share compliments, suggest new features, and even air the occasional complaint. The PlayBook user community is open to any registered users: that is, anyone with a BlackBerry ID.

Getting support

Call the BlackBerry PlayBook support line (which varies according to where you live and from where you bought your PlayBook). Your tablet (when purchased through ordinary consumer outlets such as retail stores and online outlets) comes with 90 days of free telephone support; don't hesitate to use it. I called the number many times in the frantic first few weeks after the PlayBook was released and there was no question too dumb or too complex for the staff to tackle. In fact, I wouldn't hesitate calling the number *after* the 90 days have passed; the worst that could happen is that they would politely refer to the calendar, but they just might still help.

The support technicians (I spoke with representatives in Halifax, Dallas, and Singapore on various calls) may ask you to change settings on your tablet, or to go to the built-in troubleshooting system and produce a log of the devices configuration and events. They may ask you to e-mail that log to them so they can examine the electronic innards of the tablet from afar.

555-RIM

Call or contact RIM (or your cellular provider if you bought a tablet through them) for warranty repair service. The tablet comes with one year of coverage. You'll almost certainly have to ship the tablet to a depot; RIM will decide whether to repair the device or replace it with a new or refurbished unit.

What about the data on your tablet? If you've made backups of the data and apps to a personal or laptop computer (using the BlackBerry Desktop Manager software), you'll be able to reinstall that information on the repaired tablet or a replacement you receive. If you haven't made backups, you may be out of luck — unless RIM chooses to repair your tablet and send you back the same unit without wiping it clean.

What about any personal or financial data stored on your tablet? If the tablet is only partly out of commission (the WiFi or Bluetooth is flaky, for example), you may be able to turn on the device and run a wipe, something I discuss earlier in the section, "Wiping Everything Clean: Factory Reset." Or you could try connecting the BlackBerry PlayBook to a personal or laptop computer and then examining the folders on the tablet for any personal information; make a backup to your computer using BlackBerry Desktop Manager and then delete the files from the tablet's folders.

Many premium credit cards include a warranty extension program for products purchased using their plastic. Check with your credit card company to see if you're entitled to this benefit. The extension — usually an additional year — mirrors the terms of the original warranty, so you'll be covered for manufacturing defects but not for a tumble off the kitchen counter into the water-filled sink.

Part V
The Part of Tens

The 5th Wave   By Rich Tennant

"Has the old media been delivered yet?"

In this part . . .

The Perfect 10 is the goal of many an athlete. The Ten Most Wanted is probably not something on which you've set your eye. And then there is the nearly universally recognized and admired Part of Tens. It's in the contract, and it's in this book, and I think it's pretty useful: In Chapter 15, I show you ten terrific troubleshooting and diagnostic tools for the BlackBerry PlayBook. The good news is that they're quite easy to use; the even better news is that you may well never need to use them at all. Chapter 16 has some hidden pearls dug out of the official support documents of Research in Motion, and a few come from a very unofficial but irreplaceably important source: PlayBook users.

Top Ten Troubleshooting Tips

*T*rouble? Oh, we got trouble. Right here in your city. With a capital "T" that rhymes with "P" and that stands for PlayBook. With apologies to Meredith Willson and his great work *The Music Man,* we are gathered here in this chapter to consider ways to hunt down, isolate, and (if we're lucky) fix problems that may arise with the BlackBerry tablet. I'm not saying that the PlayBook is prone to problems (speaking of rhyming with "P"), but things do happen.

Minding the Whys and Wherefores

One of the first things you should know how to do is to obtain the whys and wherefores of your machine. To know the basics, consult the About screens (About: General, About: Hardware, About: OS, and About: Network). Here's a refresher on how to get to them:

1. **Tap the gear icon in the upper-right corner of the home screen.**

2. **Tap the About tab on the left side of the screen.**

   You'll see your own version of the report. Mine appears in Figure 15-1.

3. **Tap the arrow in the upper-right corner to choose an option:**

   - **General**
   - **Hardware**
   - **OS**
   - **Network**

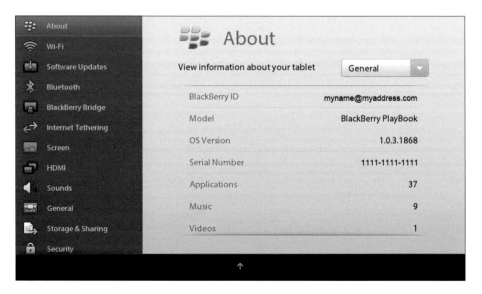

Figure 15-1: The About page tells things you need to know. Full disclosure here: I edited my BlackBerry ID and serial number. A guy or gal just can't be too careful these days.

From About: Network details may be of interest to a technician attempting to diagnose a problem with your WiFi connection. The following sections tell you the most important details you can get from the other About pages.

From About: General

These details are on the General page:

- **BlackBerry ID.** The username that's associated with the PlayBook and registered at Research in Motion. This is essential for all updates, support, and online troubleshooting.

- **Model.** Not the phone number for the latest fashion superstar, but the name of the device you're using. The first wave of tablets were all called BlackBerry PlayBook; subsequent units may add numbers or letters after the model name to indicate later versions or cellular radio models.

- **OS Version.** Very important information here, telling you (and anyone who's ready to assist you) whether you have the latest edition of the operating system.

- **Serial Number.** Each tablet has its own number, and together with the BlackBerry ID they link a machine and its user.

From About: Hardware

These details are on the Hardware page:

- **PIN.** The assigned ID for your BlackBerry PlayBook that's used for things like BlackBerry Messenger and other services. Just as with the serial number, no two devices are meant to share the same PIN.

- **Total Storage.** The first wave of BlackBerry PlayBook devices offered 16, 32, or 64GB of internal flash memory storage.

Computer manufacturers sometimes play a bit loose and fast with the math when it comes to memory. Some numbers are rounded up and some portions of memory are reserved for things like indexes to the data stored within. For that reason, you'll see things like "14.7GB of total storage" on a device that you know for certain was marketed as having 16GB of memory. I would only be worried if the reported number is way off (say, a 64GB model that shows total storage of 24GB).

- **Free Storage.** The amount of unused space in storage.

- **Total Memory.** All of the first round of models of the BlackBerry PlayBook came with 1GB of internal memory dedicated solely to the needs of the microprocessor, operating system, and apps. Later models may offer more.

- **Free Memory.** The amount of unused space in that block of internal memory. If the amount of available memory becomes very low, the tablet may slow down or even crash; consider closing down unneeded apps.

From About: OS

These details are on the OS page:

- **Build ID.** You already know the OS version in use, but the build ID can tell a RIM technician just a bit more about the system. For example, some cellular phone providers may customize a few screens (or enable or disable some functions). Why? Because they're the cellphone company.

- **Flash Player Version.** The particular edition of Adobe Flash available for use by the web browser is likely to be updated over time with new versions of the BlackBerry Tablet OS.

- **AIR Version.** Another Adobe tool, this allows developers to use Flash, Javascript, and other nifty tools to build applications that run independent of the web browser. Again, the version information here may be of interest to a technician.

Generating General Logs

The BlackBerry PlayBook is almost a sentient being; I'm not going to go so far as to say that it knows it exists, but it clearly knows what's going on within and without itself any time it's powered on. If you don't believe me, just check the logs. Nearly every element of the operating system and most system apps generate a continuous stream of information about settings and events. Most of this data is never examined and the tablet throws out the records (oldest first) over time.

If you have a problem with any part of the BlackBerry PlayBook, the logs are somewhere you should look for solution. Contact BlackBerry support to begin the process and get an incident number. The data may not make sense to you, but it can be sent automatically from your tablet to BlackBerry customer support if it has a functioning e-mail link, or you can copy the logs over to a personal or laptop computer and send them to RIM that way.

Getting and sending logs from the PlayBook

Here's how to create a log and send it by e-mail to customer support. Make sure you get an incident number from BlackBerry customer support before starting this process.

1. **From the home screen, click the help app.**
2. **Tap the app you wish to investigate.**

   For example, in Figure 15-2 I asked for help with the browser.

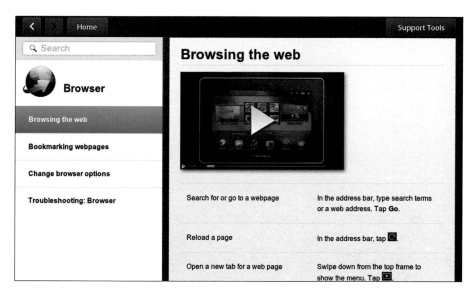

Figure 15-2: Each of the screens in the help app includes a Support Tools option in the upper-right corner.

3. **Tap Support Tools.**

   The Report Log Submission Form will appear; see Figure 15-3.
4. **Tap the Incident Number box.**

   The onscreen keyboard appears.
5. **Type the number given to you by BlackBerry customer support.**
6. **Enter your e-mail address.**
7. **Tap Create Report to generate a log.**
8. **Tap Send to transmit the log by e-mail from your BlackBerry PlayBook.**

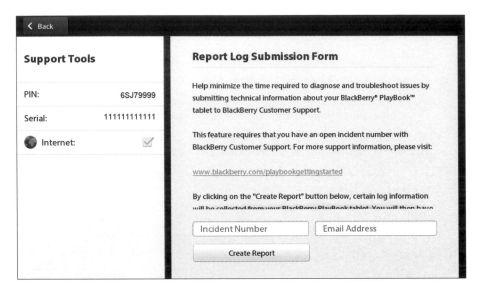

Figure 15-3: Enter the incident number and create a report.

Getting and sending logs from another device

Make sure you get an incident number from BlackBerry customer support before starting this process.

1. **From the home screen, click the help app.**

2. **Tap the app you want to investigate.**

3. **Tap Support Tools.**

   The Report Log Submission Form will appear.

4. **Tap the Incident Number box.**

   The onscreen keyboard appears.

5. **Tap Create Report.**

   You'll see a notice like the one in Figure 15-4.

6. **Attach your BlackBerry PlayBook to a personal or laptop computer using the USB cable.**

   The device must be recognized by your computer.

7. **From the computer, go to the Documents folder on the PlayBook, and then go down one level deeper to the Logs folder.**

8. **Locate the file automatically assigned the current date and time, with a filename extension of .pb.**

   For example, 22052011.pb.

9. **Copy it to your computer.**

10. **From the e-mail program on your computer, create a message to the address provided to you by BlackBerry technical support services.**

    You're given an incident number. Enter it on the screen so a technician can associate the log report with your BlackBerry PlayBook for analysis.

11. **Attach the log to the message!**

12. **Tap Send.**

    If you're sending the message from your computer instead of your PlayBook, tap Cancel and then transfer the log file to the computer using the USB cable.

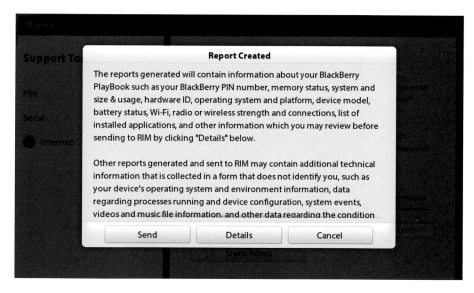

Figure 15-4: When a report is created, you can read it by tapping the Details button.

Perusing the Browser

What should you do if your browser won't browse? The first thing to do is figure out who is at fault: you, the BlackBerry PlayBook, your Internet connection, or the web page itself. If the PlayBook isn't connected to the Internet, it isn't going to be able to display web pages.

In Chapter 5, I discuss how to use the browser and the available settings. You may want to review that section before proceeding.

Okay, you're back? Let's start with the finger closest to the tablet: yours. Here are the questions to ask.

Check your web connection

This could be by WiFi, by Bluetooth to a BlackBerry smartphone using Bridge, by Bluetooth to any smartphone using Internet tethering, or on a cellular model directly to a cellular data stream. If you get a network error like the one shown in Figure 15-5, that means the tablet can't find its way onto the Internet.

Check the status screen in the upper portion of the home page and, depending on how you're connected, see if the blue Bluetooth icon is illuminated, the green WiFi bars are lit, or (on a model with cellular communication) if the cell connection icon is on. If the communication system you want to use isn't turned on, enable it.

Figure 15-5: This error is generated by the PlayBook browser itself.

Test the link

If you can connect to the Internet but you can't get to a particular web page, test the link by going to a simple page like google.com. If that page works but the one you want to visit doesn't, then there are two likely problems:

✔ The web page you want is unavailable. A "Page Not Found" message (sometimes with the code 404) means that you've gotten all the way to a website but not to the specific page you requested. The page may have been removed, the link may be broken, or it may never have existed. In any case, it's not your fault.

Figure 15-6 shows an error message generated by an Internet provider telling me that the website I tried to get to couldn't be found. Why does it show the name Comcast? Because my PlayBook is connecting to the Internet by WiFi through a router in my office that uses a cable modem provided by that company. Your results may be different.

✔ You've made settings (like refusing cookies or turning off Flash or Javascript) that the website is unhappy about. If you can't get through to a website you know exists, and it's important enough to change your settings, try going to the browser's Options screen and enabling any privacy and security settings you've turned off. Make note of any changes you make to privacy settings so that you can reenable them later if you change your mind.

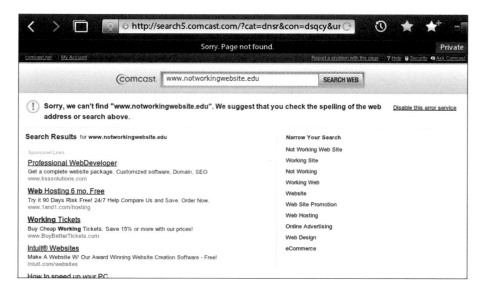

Figure 15-6: When a particular page can't be found, you usually get an error message from your Internet service provider.

Check the media format

If you reach the website you want, but can't play the song or video you see there the media format may be incompatible with the BlackBerry PlayBook, or the underlying link may be broken. Visit the site from a personal or laptop computer and see if it works there. See Chapters 10 and 11 for details about multimedia file formats that work on the BlackBerry Playbook; the list is extensive but doesn't include every possible format.

Crossing the BlackBerry Bridge

As I discuss in Chapter 3, the BlackBerry Bridge allows users to gain wireless access to material stored on their BlackBerry smartphone. It also allows Internet use via a BlackBerry smartphone data stream. In general, after you have the BlackBerry Bridge up and running (something I discuss in Chapter 3), the system will work without problem.

If the Bridge isn't working, the first things to check are these:

✓ Is the Bluetooth radio on the BlackBerry PlayBook turned on? See Figure 15-7.

Figure 15-7: Both ends of a Bluetooth connection need to have their radios on, be discoverable, and be paired. See Chapter 3.

- Is the Bluetooth radio on your BlackBerry smartphone on? See if your BlackBerry smartphone shows a message requesting your approval to initiate a Bluetooth communication session. Highlight Yes and click to tell it to begin the conversation.

- Have you made any changes to configuration for either device? Both ends of a Bluetooth connection need to be discoverable before they can communicate.

- Are the two devices within about 40 feet of each other, without any major metal objects (your fridge counts) between them that might block the signal?

- Is your smartphone already connected to another tablet? Only one connection at a time, please; open the BlackBerry Bridge app on the smartphone and disconnect the other tablet before trying again to connect to the one you want to use.

Verifying a Video Chat

Conducting a video chat is among the niftier tricks of the BlackBerry PlayBook; two individuals — or two rooms full of people — can talk into the screen and see each others' faces. It all takes place across the Internet, of course, and specifically it requires a WiFi connection. Read Chapter 8 for more about Video Chat.

If you're having trouble starting or continuing a video chat, try these approaches:

- Make sure you have a working connection to a WiFi network.

- Make sure it can get to the Internet; one quick way to test that is to launch the browser and see if it will display a web page.

- Find another WiFi network with a stronger signal. (And of course, the same applies for the other end of the connection; the link can be broken at either end.)

Just as with a BlackBerry Messenger call, using Video Chat requires two other things:

- It only works between two BlackBerry PlayBook devices.

- It must verify the BlackBerry ID used by each participant. See Figure 15-8.

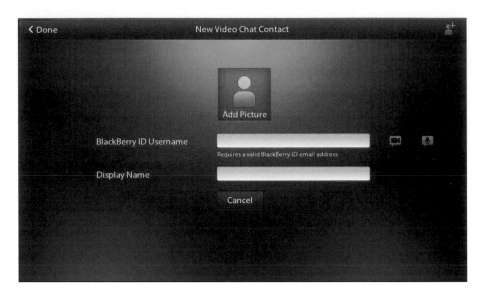

Figure 15-8: Video Chat can connect a pair of BlackBerry PlayBook tablets over the Internet via strong and stable WiFi.

Working Out WiFi Problems

Two types of problems tend to disturb the peaceful pursuit of WiFi communication: problems with establishing an initial connection, and problems maintaining a link when conditions change. If you're old enough to remember hand-held radios, or if you use a radio in your car as you travel, this analogy might make sense: establishing the initial connection is a bit like finding the right station, and maintaining the link is like fine-tuning.

Troubleshooting

Try these approaches:

- ✔ Ask the essential question: Is the BlackBerry PlayBook's WiFi radio turned on? It won't work if it's switched off. See Chapter 4 for a review session if necessary.
- ✔ See if you have a strong signal. You can judge this visually by looking at the green WIFI Icon In the status bar of the home page. If all four arcs are lit, you have a strong signal; fewer than four means a weaker link. Move the BlackBerry PlayBook closer to the WiFi router or just elsewhere on your desk to see if the reception improves.

✔ Tap the WiFi icon to see the name of the network to which your tablet is connected. If there's no connection, open the WiFi panel and choose from Available Networks, Open Networks, or (as shown in Figure 15-9) Saved Networks. Get thee to Chapter 4 for a refresher if needed.

Figure 15-9: The WiFi panel is the quick route to reconnecting to previously saved networks or to set up a new relationship.

If you're trying to connect to a new secured network, you'll need a username and password. Open systems may allow you to sign on directly from the browser once you have selected them; you may need to type login information on the page.

You also can try these advanced WiFi troubleshooting tips:

✔ On some secured networks, the date and time on your tablet *must* be synchronized with the network's. This may be a component of identity verification, or the use of a security certificate that has an expiration date.

✔ Some WiFi networks may be hidden; if you know the network name, try connecting to it manually.

✔ If you're trying to connect to a WiFi Protected Setup (WPS) device, you or the system administrator will have to press a button on the router to send its profile to your tablet; verify that there isn't another device attempting to connect at the same time.

    ✔ Talk with your IT department or a network administrator if you're trying to connect to a secured WiFi system that requires a root certificate or an authentication certificate on your tablet.

If you run into problems when connecting PlayBook to WiFi for the first time, some detailed pieces of information can help BlackBerry technical support diagnose your issue. Additionally, typical networking tools to troubleshoot most forms of network connectivity issues are also available. I expand on these tools (and where you can find them) in the following sections.

WiFi diagnostics

Because of the importance of WiFi to the BlackBerry PlayBook, the operating system includes a very detailed set of diagnostic and testing tools. Here you can read more than you ever thought you might want to know about WiFi (or to be able to provide information to a support technician).

To get to the diagnostics, do the following:

1. **Tap the gear icon in the upper-right corner of the home screen.**

2. **Tap the WiFi tab on the left side of the screen.**

    You'll see the WiFi panel shown earlier in Figure 15-10.

3. **Tap the WiFi bars that have the embedded question mark.**

    This opens the first of a number of troubleshooting pages.

4. **Tap the Diagnostic Information arrow and choose an option.**

    I discuss the most important options here:

      • **WiFi Information.** Information here includes the current connection status. Assuming an active link, you'll see the name of the SSID (the identifier used by the router), information about its communication and security methods, and the Signal Level being received, expressed in dBm; received signals are negative numbers, and the closer they are to 0 dBm the stronger they are. See Figure 15-10 for an example.

      • **Internet Connection.** The report tells you details of the hardware at the router.

      • **Logs.** This geeky treasure trove of information is something a technician might use. The logs can be copied to a file and then sent by e-mail for review. For an example, see Figure 15-11.

Figure 15-10: The WiFi Information diagnostic IDs the current connection and gives other important bits of information.

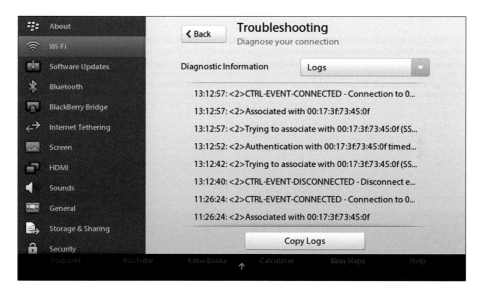

Figure 15-11: Diagnostic logs of part of a day spent connected to the Internet through a WiFi router.

- **Ping.** This isn't a video game. This tool sends short messages to a test site and then calculates the time it takes for a response. Shorter is better than longer. You can compare the ping results across differing WiFi networks or locations; the information can be affected by network congestion and other conditions.

- **Traceroute.** This tool allows you to enter an IP address or a web domain name and then see how many hops it takes to reach the address. You have no control over the route, but it does tell you whether a particular domain requires a great deal of digital gymnastics to reach.

Breaking Down Bluetooth Blues

Bluetooth is meant for short-range communication, used as the transport mechanism for the BlackBerry Bridge and Internet tethering. Peripherals like external keyboards, headsets, and other devices also use Bluetooth.

After a device connects to your PlayBook, the record should be maintained by the tablet (allowing for automatic reconnection). You may have to authorize the link by tapping a permission button when a device comes into range. Both ends of the link need to have their Bluetooth radio turned on, and they must both be discoverable.

Certain Bluetooth devices require a profile that may include a passkey; the code is usually set by the manufacturer. If you can't find any passkey information, try this super-secret code that no one else knows about: 0000.

Unblocking the BlackBerry Desktop

The BlackBerry Desktop software is essential for communication between a BlackBerry PlayBook and a personal or laptop computer. It creates backup copies of data and apps and for the synchronization of calendar, contact, and e-mail information. Some users may also synchronize music, video, and picture collections. But your best efforts at protecting the security of the data on your computer may cause you problems: if you have a personal firewall in place, the firewall may consider the PlayBook an unauthorized intruder when it's connected by USB cable. The BlackBerry PlayBook presents itself as a network adaptor to the host computer with an IP range of 169.254.X.X. The solution here is to configure your firewall so that this IP range is white-listed and ports 80 and 443 are open for its use. If this all sounds too technical, that's because it is.

This is the sort of situation where a quick call to BlackBerry customer support should result in the appropriate quick solution. You might also consider contacting the support desk for your firewall, but I'd ask RIM first.

Untangling Internet Tethering

Although it sounds like you're tying down your BlackBerry PlayBook, the act of tethering actually opens it up to use of (in theory) any smartphone's cellular data stream for access to the Internet. That's a good thing, but it may not be a workable (or affordable) solution for all users.

Here's the inside skinny:

 ✒ Some cellular providers may block their network from this sort of second-hand browsing. Others may apply extra charges — which can be substantial — for such use. Their rationale is that a tablet like the BlackBerry PlayBook consumes a great deal more bandwidth than the screen of a small smartphone. Bottom line, though, is that they want to find ways to get more money out of the pockets of their customers.

Before you attempt Internet tethering, I strongly recommend you contact your cellular provider and discuss the data plan in place for your smartphone.

✒ Internet tethering, when you're roaming in a foreign country, can be extremely expensive and usually isn't covered in any way by a domestic "unlimited" data plan. I know this from personal experience: I ran a short experiment using tethering, connecting to the Internet from a laptop to my BlackBerry smartphone for about an hour. The bill from my carrier was more than $350; we're still arguing about it six months later. If you choose to go ahead and use Internet tethering, you need to know which of several Bluetooth profiles the phone uses. The information should be available in product documentation or in online specifications.

✒ The Bluetooth DUN (dial-up networking) policy must be enabled. If you're working with an IT department, they may have to allow this; otherwise, contact your cellular provider and hope for their help.

Viewing HD in All Its Glory

As spectacular as the high-definition touchscreen of the BlackBerry PlayBook is when you hold it in your hands, it's absolutely stunning when connected to an HD television or projector. That said, the process is a little bit squirrely.

I'm not 100 percent certain that the operating system tweaks for use of the HDMI output were complete as of the time this book went to press; I also know that some HD televisions and some cables aren't perfectly compatible with the tablet.

If you have problems with the display on an HDMI monitor, try any or all of the following:

- Check that the HDMI mode settings on the PlayBook are correct; see Figure 15-12.

- If the image is distorted (too big, too small, the corners are cut off, or the entire image is shifted to one side), adjust the Aspect Ratio settings on the tablet.

- Make sure the HDMI cable is connected directly to the HD television, and not through a receiver or cable box.

- If problems persist, try using a different HDMI port on the HD television; most sets offer several connections. Some may be on the sides and others on the back of the monitor.

- Try using a different HDMI cable. Some cables, regardless of how much you paid for them, are made with inferior materials.

Figure 15-12: The HDMI control panel lets you adjust the signal sent from the tablet.

16

Top Ten Hints

*E*veryone seems to have a top ten list of some sort or another. (Remember Moses and those first significant tablets? Top ten there, too.) This chapter presents a decidedly subjective list of ten hints and tips that will help you get the most out of your BlackBerry PlayBook. Some of these hints come from the support team at Research in Motion, some come from the user community, and a few I stumbled across all by my own across weeks of non-stop work with the PlayBook.

And yes, we're already planning for the next edition of *BlackBerry PlayBook For Dummies*. I'd love to hear from you about any secret or obscure-but-wonderful tip or trick you've uncovered; send me a note at **PlaybookForDummies@sandlerbooks.com** and if I use your suggestion I'll send you an autographed copy of the next version of this book.

Resetting a BlackBerry ID Password

The BlackBerry ID is an essential part of the BlackBerry PlayBook and BlackBerry smartphone experience. You'll need it for things like updates and upgrades to the operating system, using services like BlackBerry

Messenger, and video chats. It's also an element of your contact with support and warranty services and BlackBerry App World. The good news is that you can use any e-mail address as your BlackBerry ID. The not-so-good news is that you'll also need a password in certain circumstances (not for updates; the tablet keeps all the information it needs to do that automatically).

If you forget your BlackBerry ID, you can find it out by going to the About page. Refer back to Figure 15-1 in Chapter 15.

But not to worry: you can reset your password *from a personal or laptop computer.* Here's how:

1. **Use a browser in the BlackBerry PlayBook or a personal or laptop computer and go to** http://blackberryid.blackberry.com/bbid/ recoverpassword.

   You'll see the appropriately named BlackBerry ID Password Reset page; see Figure 16-1.

2. **Enter your username (your BlackBerry ID) in the first box.**

3. **Enter the slightly scrambled verification code in the second box.**

   The CAPTCHA system helps prevent computerized attempts at cracking password codes; presumably humans are better at reading those oddly shaped characters. If you have trouble with one set, tap Refresh the Image to get a new group.

4. **Click Submit.**

   If you've done it correctly, a confirmation message tells you that reset instructions have been sent to the BlackBerry ID e-mail address. For security reasons, the reset instructions *don't* go to your BlackBerry smartphone or to your BlackBerry PlayBook. The idea is to prevent an unauthorized user from picking up either device and gaining control of it.

5. **On a personal or laptop computer, log in to the e-mail account you specified and find the message.**

   You can log in also on any other e-mail–capable device other than your BlackBerry PlayBook or BlackBerry smartphone. The message comes from bbidpw-donotreply@blackberry.com. If you can't find it, check the spam folder.

6. **Click the link in the message.**

   A web browser should load on the device; if it doesn't, tap the link and copy; then open a browser and paste it there.

7. **When the password reset page loads, enter a new password for your BlackBerry ID.**

8. **Now confirm.**

Figure 16-1: The BlackBerry ID Password Reset page, as seen on a PlayBook; for security you have to finish from another device.

Capturing a Screen

Want to make a high-definition copy of the image on your screen for posterity? (Or for bragging rights, or perhaps to send to BlackBerry Support to show them an unusual situation?) How about grabbing work you've done in a drawing app or a web page?

Simply display the image on the screen and press (at the same time) the volume + and – buttons at the top edge of the tablet. The image you took will appear in the Camera Pictures folder on the BlackBerry PlayBook, as seen in Figure 16-2. You can keep it there, send it by e-mail, or drag it over to a computer by USB cable or other connection. The image is saved as a compressed JPG file, and images are sequentially numbered; you can rename the file after you move it to a computer. It can also be edited in a digital editing program on a computer.

Figure 16-2: Screen captures are in the Camera Pictures folder; this screen capture shows 18 grabs I made while collecting the images you see in this book.

Creating Your Own Wallpaper

In Chapter 13 I show how you can select one of your own images to serve as your home page background, but the image might get cropped or squeezed or otherwise changed. That's because the OS is designed to handle both landscape (wider than tall) and portrait (taller than wide) views.

If you want to make your own image appear properly on the home page, edit it on your computer so that it's centered in a 1024 × 1024 box; for most pictures that means expanding the canvas that surrounds an image. Make the canvas black for the best effect.

What if you'd like to either remove all wallpaper, or prefer a minimalist black screen behind your home page? In the original version of the operating system for the PlayBook, there was no official way to do this. However, not to worry: I figured out a workaround. I find the results simple, yet elegant: the equivalent of the little black dress for a BlackBerry PlayBook. See Figure 16-3 for a glimpse of my homemade modification.

1. **From the home page, tap the camera icon.**

2. **Take a picture of a black surface (or take a picture in a completely dark room).**

3. **Go to the Camera Pictures folder and select the black screen.**

4. **Swipe down from the top bezel and tap Select as Wallpaper.**

Figure 16-3: Elegant and not distracting: a black wallpaper for the home screen.

Adding a Browser Shortcut

Is there a web page that's so important to your lifestyle and business that you need it one finger tap away from the home page? Things like the Boston Red Sox season stats, your life's savings in an investment account, or an online shopping site with fabulous prices on electronic items you didn't even know you absolutely needed? From the home page you can add a shortcut to a site on the Internet. You don't need to open the browser, select a favorite, or (can you imagine?) tap away at the virtual keyboard.

Creating a desktop browser shortcut is as simple as this:

1. **Open the browser.**

2. **Go to the site for which you want almost-instant access.**

   You'll have to be connected to the Internet by WiFi, Bluetooth, or cellular link, of course.

3. **With the page displayed, tap the Add to Bookmarks icon.**

4. **Tap Add to Home Screen.**

See Figure 16-4. The shortcut will appear on the home screen.

You can move it to a place of honor, or hide it in the secondary group of apps by pressing and holding it until all of the icons jiggle onscreen; touch and hold the icon and move it to a new location on screen. Tap the checkmark to stop the jiggling and lock icons where they are. You can delete shortcuts by following the same initial steps: press and hold on an icon and then tap the garbage can that appears. Tap the checkmark to stop the jiggling.

Figure 16-4: To add a shortcut to the home page, browse to a website and tap the add to bookmarks icon.

Removing an App

Nothing lasts forever, including what was once an ineluctable fascination with a new app. You have two ways to remove an app from your BlackBerry PlayBook. The first keeps an electronic safety net in case you change your mind, while the second is more permanent.

Current versions of the operating system for the BlackBerry PlayBook don't allow you to manually delete system apps, including the browser, music, pictures, videos, and other software provided by RIM.

Here's how to remove an app but retain a backup plan:

1. **Launch BlackBerry App World.**

   You'll need to have an active connection to the Internet.

2. **Tap My World at the top of the screen.**

   You'll see a list of all currently installed applications; see Figure 16-5. Swipe up from the bottom if the app you want to remove is not visible on the first screen.

3. **Tap the Delete button next to the application you want to remove.**

4. **Confirm the deletion.**

   Apps you delete this way from My World can be reinstalled later. Just reload BlackBerry App World and tap My World; then tap the Uninstalled button; find a deleted app and then tap Reinstall.

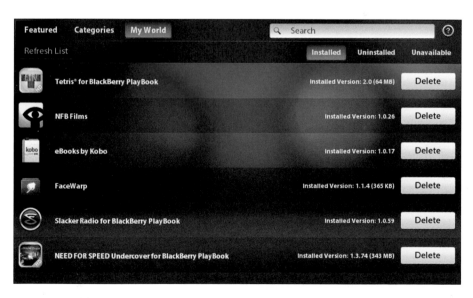

Figure 16-5: You can delete apps you got from BlackBerry App World by visiting that site and tapping My World.

Here's how to manually remove an app:

1. **Display apps on your home screen.**
2. **Tap the All button.**
3. **Press and hold your finger on any icon to enter edit mode.**
4. **Tap the trash can below the app you want to delete.**

   See Figure 16-6.

5. **Confirm the deletion.**

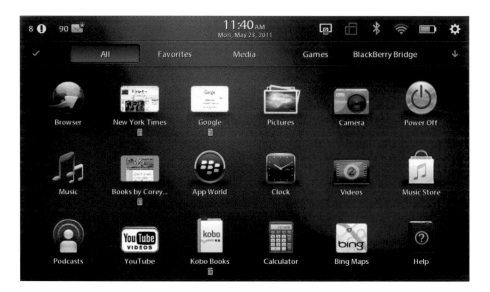

Figure 16-6: You can manually delete an app.

Bringing Backup

The BlackBerry Desktop Software, installed on a personal or laptop computer, is a powerful assistant to any PlayBook user. You can back up data and apps on your tablet and later restore some (or all) of that information to the tablet.

To restore data to your BlackBerry PlayBook, follow these steps:

1. **Connect the tablet to the computer that has both BlackBerry Desktop Software and your backup files in place.**

The BlackBerry Desktop Software should automatically detect the presence of an attached and powered-on BlackBerry PlayBook. If it does not, open the software by loading it in the personal or laptop computer's operating system.

2. **Click Device, then click Restore.**

3. **Select a backup file that contains the data you want to restore.**

   If you've made more than one backup, choose the one with the appropriate date.

4. **Do one of the following steps:**

   • To restore all your device data, click All Device Data and Settings.

   • To select particular files or apps, click Select Device Data and Settings. Select the check beside the data type that you want to restore.

A warning appears, saying that data on the BlackBerry PlayBook will be replaced with the contents of the backup file.

5. **If you're ready to proceed, click Yes.**

6. **If the backup file is encrypted, enter the password you used.**

7. **Click Restore.**

Sleeping and Waking Without Pain

I expect they did it with the best of intentions — to avoid unintended powering or unpowering of the tablet — but one of the few oft-uttered complaints about the BlackBerry PlayBook involves the tiny and somewhat difficult-to-use power button on the top edge. You've really got to stick the edge of your fingernail into it to get it to realize you mean business.

But:

✔ You don't need to press the button — ever — to turn the BlackBerry PlayBook off. Instead, tap the Power Off app that appears on the home screen. It electronically shuts down the device.

✔ When the tablet's in sleep mode, it draws very little power; you can let it sleep while it's recharging. (Remember: the tablet *can't* be recharged while it's turned off.)

✔ If the tablet goes to sleep, give it a substantial swipe on the touchscreen from the top to bottom, bottom to top, or one side to the other. Don't be too timid with the swipe: it should cross most of the screen in one direction or the other.

Prioritizing Your WiFi Networks

As through this world you wander, you'll see many WiFi networks you may choose to use. The BlackBerry PlayBook will keep track of those with which you have had successful communication, and sooner or later that list may become unwieldy. Besides being hard to manage, you may have a preference for one network over another because of signal strength or security.

Here's how to prioritize your saved WiFi networks. That way the PlayBook first tries the one you prefer and then works its way down the list if necessary:

1. **Tap the gear icon in the upper-right corner of the home screen.**

2. **Tap the WiFi tab on the left side of the screen.**

   You'll see the WiFi panel shown in Figure 16-7.

3. **Tap the down arrow next to Select a Network.**

4. **Tap Saved Networks.**

   The list appears.

5. **Touch and hold on the network you prefer and drag it to the top of the list.**

   You can do this as many times as you want with other networks so that you end up with their names in the order you prefer.

Figure 16-7: Drag a network up or down on the list to establish your priorities.

Cropping a Photo without an App

It isn't the same as importing a digital image file into an image editing program — not even close — but if you want to make a quick but imperfect crop of an image taken with the BlackBerry PlayBook camera (or one you imported onto the tablet), try this:

1. **Display the image on the full screen within the pictures app.**

2. **Touch the screen and pinch out to enlarge the image as much as you'd like.**

   Move it left, right, up, or down to show as much of it as you want on the screen.

3. **Take a screen capture of the image by pressing the volume buttons (+ and –) at the same time.**

   The buttons are on the top edge of the tablet.

You're digitally enlarging an image, which usually results in some resolution loss. But in some situations, this is the quickest way to highlight a portion of an image to send to someone. In Figure 16-8, I've cropped in tightly on a photo of a *For Dummies* author on an expedition in far northern Canada, apparently searching for BlackBerry tips and hints on the tundra.

Figure 16-8: You can make a quick and imperfect crop by enlarging an image on the touch-screen and then taking a screen capture.

Shortcutting Domain Names

There's a thoughtful .com key on the onscreen keyboard; it appears when you're typing a web address in the browser. But what if you want to go to somewhere that ends with one with .net, .org, .edu, .gov, .biz, or .ca? Piece of (hidden) cake. Just press and hold the .com key for a second. Tap any of the options that appear; in Figure 16-9 I'm inserting an .edu to go to my alma mater's website. And, of course, the fine folk at Research in Motion never seem to forget their roots.

Figure 16-9: Press and hold the .com character to see other common domain name extensions.

Appendix

Icons

. . . .

*A*s befits a touchy, feely device like the BlackBerry PlayBook, much of the communication between we mortals and the machine (what engineers called the Human Interface) involves a great deal of tapping and sliding on icons (little pictures or symbols).We're quite used to icons in our lives; we can recognize a stop sign from a great distance just because of its color and shape. And fast food companies spend millions developing, testing, and deploying symbols that will catch your eye as you travel. On the BlackBerry PlayBook, many of the icons are quite obvious: a trashcan as a place to delete a file or an envelope as home for messages. But some icons don't immediately jump out at you and announce their name and purpose. In this chapter I gather some of the more common icons you'll encounter when you're using the PlayBook.

Home Screen Icons

Icon	Name	Description
	Notifications	View all notifications
	Airplane	Turn off airplane mode
	Notification	View a new notification
	Flag	View a flag for follow-up
	Presentation	Turn off presentation mode

(continued)

Icon	Name	Description
	Video Chat	Access Video Chat application
	Calendar	Access Calendar application
	BBM	Access BlackBerry Messenger application
	Development	Turn off development mode
	Update	Download a software update
	Bridge	Turn off the BlackBerry Bridge application
	Alarm	Set the alarm
	Lock	Lock the screen orientation
	Bluetooth	Turn on or off Bluetooth
	Wi-Fi	Turn on or off Wi-Fi
	Battery	Check battery power level
	Option	Access settings
	Maximize/Minimize	View more or fewer applications

Browser Icons

Icon	Name	Description
	Next/Previous	Go to previous or next web page
	Tab	Open a new tab
	Clear	Clear the address bar
	Reload	Reload web page
	History	View browsing history
	Bookmark	View bookmarks
	Add Bookmark	Bookmark a web page
	Navigation	Show or hide navigation bar
	Views	Switch views
	Edit page	Edit a web page

Keyboard Icons

Icon	Name	Description
	Capitalize	Capitalize a letter
	Hide keyboard	Hide the keyboard
	Symbols	View symbols
	Secondary	View secondary symbols
	Language	Change keyboard language

Camera Icons

Icon	Name	Description
	Mode	View camera scene mode
	Geotag	Turn on or off geotag
	Video/Still	Switch between video and still camera
	Shutter	Take a picture
	Front/Rear	Switch between front and rear camera

Video Chat Icons

Icon	Name	Description
	Video Chat	Begin video chat
	Video/Audio Chat	Switch between video and audio chat
	Chat History	View chat history
	Preview	Preview video
	Contact	Add contact
	Select Contact	Select contact for video chat

Word To Go Icons

Icon	Name	Description
	Font	Change font
	Center	Move text to center
	Align Left	Make text flush left

(continued)

Icon	*Name*	*Description*
	Align Right	Make text flush right
B	Bold	Make text boldface
I	Italicize	Make text italic
U	Underline	Make text underlined
ABC 1 2 3	Count	Count words in a document
¶	Paragraph	Apply paragraph formatting

Index

Apple & Macs

iPad For Dummies
978-0-470-58027-1

iPhone For Dummies,
4th Edition
978-0-470-87870-5

MacBook For Dummies, 3rd
Edition
978-0-470-76918-8

Mac OS X Snow Leopard For
Dummies
978-0-470-43543-4

Business

Bookkeeping For Dummies
978-0-7645-9848-7

Job Interviews
For Dummies,
3rd Edition
978-0-470-17748-8

Resumes For Dummies,
5th Edition
978-0-470-08037-5

Starting an
Online Business
For Dummies,
6th Edition
978-0-470-60210-2

Stock Investing
For Dummies,
3rd Edition
978-0-470-40114-9

Successful
Time Management
For Dummies
978-0-470-29034-7

Computer Hardware

BlackBerry
For Dummies,
4th Edition
978-0-470-60700-8

Computers For Seniors
For Dummies,
2nd Edition
978-0-470-53483-0

PCs For Dummies, Windows
7 Edition
978-0-470-46542-4

Laptops For Dummies,
4th Edition
978-0-470-57829-2

Cooking & Entertaining

Cooking Basics
For Dummies,
3rd Edition
978-0-7645-7206-7

Wine For Dummies,
4th Edition
978-0-470-04579-4

Diet & Nutrition

Dieting For Dummies,
2nd Edition
978-0-7645-4149-0

Nutrition For Dummies,
4th Edition
978-0-471-79868-2

Weight Training
For Dummies,
3rd Edition
978-0-471-76845-6

Digital Photography

Digital SLR Cameras &
Photography For Dummies,
3rd Edition
978-0-470-46606-3

Photoshop Elements 8
For Dummies
978-0-470-52967-6

Gardening

Gardening Basics
For Dummies
978-0-470-03749-2

Organic Gardening
For Dummies,
2nd Edition
978-0-470-43067-5

Green/Sustainable

Raising Chickens
For Dummies
978-0-470-46544-8

Green Cleaning
For Dummies
978-0-470-39106-8

Health

Diabetes For Dummies,
3rd Edition
978-0-470-27086-8

Food Allergies
For Dummies
978-0-470-09584-3

Living Gluten-Free
For Dummies,
2nd Edition
978-0-470-58589-4

Hobbies/General

Chess For Dummies,
2nd Edition
978-0-7645-8404-6

Drawing
Cartoons & Comics
For Dummies
978-0-470-42683-8

Knitting For Dummies,
2nd Edition
978-0-470-28747-7

Organizing
For Dummies
978-0-7645-5300-4

Su Doku For Dummies
978-0-470-01892-7

Home Improvement

Home Maintenance
For Dummies,
2nd Edition
978-0-470-43063-7

Home Theater
For Dummies,
3rd Edition
978-0-470-41189-6

Living the
Country Lifestyle
All-in-One
For Dummies
978-0-470-43061-3

Solar Power Your Home
For Dummies,
2nd Edition
978-0-470-59678-4

Internet

Blogging For Dummies,
3rd Edition
978-0-470-61996-4

eBay For Dummies,
6th Edition
978-0-470-49741-8

Facebook For Dummies, 3rd
Edition
978-0-470-87804-0

Web Marketing
For Dummies,
2nd Edition
978-0-470-37181-7

WordPress
For Dummies,
3rd Edition
978-0-470-59274-8

Language & Foreign Language

French For Dummies
978-0-7645-5193-2

Italian Phrases
For Dummies
978-0-7645-7203-6

Spanish For Dummies,
2nd Edition
978-0-470-87855-2

Spanish For Dummies,
Audio Set
978-0-470-09585-0

Math & Science

Algebra I For Dummies,
2nd Edition
978-0-470-55964-2

Biology For Dummies,
2nd Edition
978-0-470-59875-7

Calculus For Dummies
978-0-7645-2498-1

Chemistry For Dummies
978-0-7645-5430-8

Microsoft Office

Excel 2010 For Dummies
978-0-470-48953-6

Office 2010 All-in-One
For Dummies
978-0-470-49748-7

Office 2010 For Dummies,
Book + DVD Bundle
978-0-470-62698-6

Word 2010 For Dummies
978-0-470-48772-3

Music

Guitar For Dummies,
2nd Edition
978-0-7645-9904-0

iPod & iTunes
For Dummies,
8th Edition
978-0-470-87871-2

Piano Exercises
For Dummies
978-0-470-38765-8

Parenting & Education

Parenting For Dummies,
2nd Edition
978-0-7645-5418-6

Type 1 Diabetes
For Dummies
978-0-470-17811-9

Pets

Cats For Dummies,
2nd Edition
978-0-7645-5275-5

Dog Training For Dummies,
3rd Edition
978-0-470-60029-0

Puppies For Dummies,
2nd Edition
978-0-470-03717-1

Religion & Inspiration

The Bible For Dummies
978-0-7645-5296-0

Catholicism For Dummies
978-0-7645-5391-2

Women in the Bible
For Dummies
978-0-7645-8475-6

Self-Help & Relationship

Anger Management
For Dummies
978-0-470-03715-7

Overcoming Anxiety
For Dummies,
2nd Edition
978-0-470-57441-6

Sports

Baseball
For Dummies,
3rd Edition
978-0-7645-7537-2

Basketball
For Dummies,
2nd Edition
978-0-7645-5248-9

Golf For Dummies,
3rd Edition
978-0-471-76871-5

Web Development

Web Design
All-in-One
For Dummies
978-0-470-41796-6

Web Sites
Do-It-Yourself
For Dummies,
2nd Edition
978-0-470-56520-9

Windows 7

Windows 7
For Dummies
978-0-470-49743-2

Windows 7
For Dummies,
Book + DVD Bundle
978-0-470-52398-8

Windows 7 All-in-One
For Dummies
978-0-470-48763-1

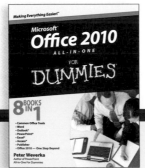

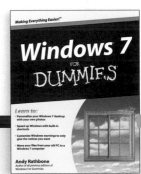

Available wherever books are sold. For more information or to order direct: U.S. customers visit www.dummies.com or call 1-877-762-2974. U.K. customers visit www.wileyeurope.com or call (0) 1243 843291. Canadian customers visit www.wiley.ca or call 1-800-567-4797.